AF334753

Death of an Ordinary Life
Aaron Mitchell

INNERCIRCLE PUBLISHING

Death of an Ordinary Life
Copyright © 2008 Aaron Mitchell

Edition 1

ISBN: 1-882918-11-8

Edited by: Angela McKenzie
Page Design by: Chad Lilly
Cover Design and Creation by: Chad Lilly
Original Cover Photo by: Aaron Mitchell

Are You Aware?
www.innercirclepublishing.com

Contents

Contents

Prologue

The following story is a fictional tale mixed with true or similar events that have happened in my life; all of my teachers have expressed to me the importance of sharing the skills that I've learned from them. These skills are not mine to posses or hold secret. My teachers learned it from their teachers, and the teachers before them and so on. Each generation passes down these skills with respect and reverence to those they feel guided by. I have been guided to share these skills in this way.

My way is not new, as elders have passed down lessons to children in their tribes using true and fictional stories, thus empowering the lessons - this is the old tribal way of teaching.

It is with great gratitude and honor to be able to share these skills and experiences with you. All I ask is that you treat the things you learn from this book with the utmost respect and reverence. The teachers that ensured these skills' survival went through a lifetime of dedication, impeccability, and selflessness.

Welcome to the adventure.

- Aaron Mitchell

Chapter 1
How Did I Get Here?

Glancing out of the thin crack at the base of a tepee, my mind surged with wonder, "How did I get here?" A chilling breeze slides through and etches the angles of my face. With every panicked breath, I am made aware of the numbness of my nose. However, the discomfort of my nose is a petty thought in my mind shadowed by a towering giant of fear mixed with excitement and anticipation for tomorrow's events.

But this is no ordinary fear that one might have at a job interview with a scrutinizing boss glaring down with pursed lips and squinting eyes. This is the kind of fear that one gets when they sense death lurking around the corner, knowing that turning back is not a viable option because it would mean returning to an ordinary life so boring that it makes death seem alluring. This is the fear that sits within my soul; what I have been so desperately running away from by occupying my mind and body with meaningless tasks of nothingness, which is what nearly every human being on this planet has done and continues to do. Prior to this moment I had not realized how tenaciously people busy their lives, me included, to keep them from truly looking at themselves. Everyday I go through a routine: wake up, commute, work, go to school, commute back home, pay bills, eat dinner, watch TV, and go to bed. Every moment is filled with a meaningless task to take my mind away from the pending issues that matter. Now, after years of ignoring the large elephant that sits in the room of my life, I've decided to face it. To be completely honest, I have never been this scared in my entire life. I am so nervous that I now know why actors tend to vomit before a show.

This fear begins to build and develop from infancy. Its powers grow stronger and stronger with every inching day that passes our lives, all the while we pretend not to notice. I was no different than anyone else. "The king of worry and fear," I thought. From the moment my mind started to develop until the present day; worry and fear had been driving my life like an omnipotent god.

As a twenty-two-year-old college student, I had accumulated the fear of a fifty-five-year-old man worrying that his life had no meaning. Lying in the tepee, staring up towards the center of the roof where the confluence of poles joined together, I traveled back through my history, back to the age of four when I could recall my earliest memory of fear and worry. I was afraid that I would never be able to survive in this large complex world; my remedy was to make as many friends as possible to help me along the way. While this was my solution, my worst fears came true. I did not make that many friends through school, I was somewhat of a recluse. There was so much that I did not know about the world, I was sure that I would not have enough time to learn all the things I needed to know to survive when the moment came when my parents would no longer be there. An example of this came when, as a child, my mother bandaged up one of my many cuts; I realized that I needed to hurry up and learn how to take care of myself in case of a medical emergency. If I did not learn this quickly there would come a day when I would be injured and I have to know how to stop the bleeding, otherwise I would surely die from bleeding to death. As you can see, this is an awful lot to be worried about at the age of four.

At the age of six, I learned about the great and wonderful solar system. I began to imagine that if I was able to step back until the universe shrunk down to the size of a comprehensible tennis ball - where would that tennis ball be? The thought that our universe has no place startled me to the very core of my young mind. Scientists may speculate that there is more space beyond the mind's finite capacity for comprehension; but in my mind, I felt that there had to be an end to the universe. This thought would penetrate my mind daily with such frequency that after a short time I would fall ill and have the compulsion to heave the treacherous thought from my mind. I hated not having the answer to the simple question of, "Where are we?"

As I got older, my fears began to change. I went through traumatic events of being teased and taunted by schoolmates, getting beaten up by the twice-my-size-bully, or being made fun of by my so-called "best friend", who called me Spock (from Star Trek) in front of everyone, because one ear is slightly pointed.

Kids are cruel; it felt to me as if love had abandoned the souls of every classmate in high school. When kids are young they seek out their identity by adhering to a group like the jocks, the cheerleaders, the users, the geeks, the sluts, the art freaks, the cowboys, the gang-bangers, the honor roll nerds, or the loners. I barely fit into the latter, leaving me with no security blanket of having a true group of friends to back me up. I had mild acquaintances but no real friends. People could not place me in one particular group, and I did not feel like I could pretend to be something I was not in order to have the security of belonging to a like-minded group. As a matter of fact, I did not even feel like I was even from the same planet as everyone else. Naturally, this opened me up to virtually insufferable torment by fellow schoolmates, even the people I worked with at my after school job, cleaning up the butcher and baker shop in a dead-end, super-duper grocery store. Primarily, I had a quiet and shy personality and this made many people very uncomfortable around me because they were afraid of what I might be thinking. Fearing I was criticizing and judging them, I was on the contrary criticizing and judging myself, based on my own fears.

Combine all these repressed issues from growing up in public schools of painfully mellow-dramatic suburbia with typical "colossal" problems at home, add the bizarre feeling of being a visitor from another planet, and you get a person with tremendous fear and confusion wrapped into the space of one body when it could barely fit into the space of ten. Ironically, this fear became my platform of stability in life. But it was so fragile that the slightest breeze would send my life crashing down into complete oblivion.

Now I lie here trying to sleep in a tepee deep in the Rocky Mountains on the outskirts of Harrison, Idaho. My head is throbbing, my cheeks are flushed pink from the earlier sweat lodge ceremony, my body is still sweating in an attempt to release the heat, and my bladder feels like a stretched water balloon. A sweat lodge ceremony is ancient Native American ceremony performed for healing, preparation for something, or for just praying. Basalt rocks are heated in a fire then brought into a dark lodge so small that you cannot stand up in. Water is thrown on the rocks and the ceremony begins and, let's just say, you sweat a lot. I will explain more about this ceremony later.

I throw the brain-tanned hides aside, stumble

around the tepee in an attempt to not wake Tilauth, and crawl out of the tepee flap into the cold. Hobbling over to the small dug out latrine in the bushes, I relieve myself as the silver moonlight slices through the trees, casting peculiar shadows that seem to move in the corners of my eyes and startle my senses; I look but there is nothing. The shadows seem to move in silence and my head spins with tension.

As I creep back into the tepee and quickly slide under the covers to regain the warmth I have lost, I think back to the moment that brought me to this place. First, navigating my mind back to the sunny day when I first saw Tilauth. I began to ponder the bizarre events.

If I want to get to the root of the where it all began, I have to go back several years. I was working in a doctors' office in the "strip mall capital of the world" - Lynnwood, Washington. I had the titillating job of billing insurance companies for the doctors' services. This was as an exciting job as counting hairs on doll heads in a manufacturing plant.

Bathed in the glow of fluorescent lights, I would call up the claim adjusters with the doctor's past due accounts spread out before me. Medical insurance adjusters have the personality of a brick and a microscopic fuse that itches to ignite. After pressing what seems to be a thousand buttons on the phone to finally speak to one of these wonderful human beings, who are just as lively as the recordings I had listened to on hold for ten minutes, I would ask them why they have not paid for a patient's bill. After a few clicking noises I could hear over the phone as they accessed their database (which seemed to conveniently freeze) they would vomit some excuse in my ear. Inside, I would wonder why the hell this employee, who apparently hates their job with a passion, care whether or not they saved this multi-million dollar insurance company even a dime.

After three hours of enlightening phone conversations with adjusters and persistent glances at the clock every ten minutes, my co-workers and I would charge down to Rory's Pub and Grill to down a couple of pitchers of beer and cram some greasy goodness down our throats. During these lunches, conversations would usually entail complaining about other co-workers or fantasizing about our dream jobs.

With a nice numbness in my mouth, and a buzz in my head, I would head to the restroom to brush my teeth and ponder about the first signs of alcoholism. This fleeting thought dissolved with the enjoyment of going back to work with a feeling of alcoholic bliss. My boss was clueless because of the extraordinary amounts of weed he smoked through college, which was a habit that he has never fully been freed. The endless day was followed with night classes at the community college in an attempt to earn more money doing almost the exact same type of work. With the aspirations of becoming a certified public accountant, I figured I could make enough money to allow myself time to do the things I really enjoyed; like acting, photography, writing, traveling, hiking, camping, or whatever my heart's desire at any given moment. Accounting was never my passion, it was just something I was good at and it happened to pay very well.

Days went by with the excitement of a yawn and I could feel my soul slowly deteriorating. I was a good kid, or so I thought. I achieved straight A's in my classes, collected more money for the doctor than he has ever collected during the entire span of his practice, went to church, and I stayed out of trouble, for the most part.

As my life began to head down a path of security and absolute boredom, I could sense a deep longing within. I remembered the strange feeling I would get when I was younger. The feeling of being from another planet surfaced again, and I could feel the old fire I felt before; I knew that I needed to find my purpose in life. I needed to know who I was. I needed to feel like there was something more to life than growing up, getting a good job, getting married, having kids, retiring, and then eventually having a heart attack, and ultimately dying. Ahh...the American dream at its best.

So I turned to the only thing I could think of that would help me find the answers I so desperately desired. It felt like an urgency of life or death. If I did not find answers, I would surely die of an ordinary life with alcohol my only joy. I turned to the non-denominational Christian church my family went to. I started going to church weekly and attending Bible studies, frantically hoping for an answer, sign, or ideally, a big, fat arrow pointing the way. The Bible study revealed to me ancient stories of people that conversed with God, who told them what to do and what not to do. Worship, praise, and love God daily, ask for forgiveness for your sins, and attempt to not do them again. The church sermons consisted of reiterating why Christianity is right and all other religions are wrong, including other Christian denominations using scripture to prove these findings. I left with no more answers to my questions than when I started.

So began my own search into Christianity since the weekly Bible study and Sunday sermons produced more suggestions on what not to do, rather than on what direction I should head and how to go about it. As I studied the Bible and other books about Christ, I learned that He was above all, a man with a purpose. But nothing was revealed as to how Christ found or came to know His purpose and subsequently, I found no resolution on how to find my own purpose in life.

The duty of any God-fearing Christian is to help bring people to Christ largely lacked any appeal to me. I was not so sure Christianity had all the answers (finding personal direction being one example) and my heart felt hollow at the thought of heeding this duty. But what did light a fire in my heart was Christ's ability to heal, raise the dead, love unconditionally, and help people whenever, and wherever. Not only did Christ do these things Himself, but he commanded the people of the world to do these things also. This was something that started to broach on the subject I was yearning for. I did not want an ordinary life that went through all the typical roles and then you die.

I found the place in the Bible where Christ commands people to heal, perform miracles, raise the dead, love unconditionally, and help people whenever, and wherever. But that was it. Nothing was revealed as to how Christ did it or how one might go about learning how to do these things. If anything the Bible revealed that one should have faith; however, having faith and building faith are two different things, and I was unable to find the directions on how to build faith. This area of the Bible was entirely too vague for me. I needed something more tangible, something that made sense, or something that at least gave me a first step.

In my research of the Bible, I did find one possible answer to my question. That answer was through faith in God. So with all my might and with every fiber of my body I tried to grasp and embody faith. This felt like the old saying of trying to squeeze water from a rock. Needless to say, I got nowhere fast.

There was one thing that stood out in my mind from all my research - the story of Christ going out into the desert for sixty days without food to overcome Satan's temptations. All my searching's left my stomach tied up in knots, but this made my gut unravel; however, I still felt at a loss. Questions arose within me; I would not be able to survive in a desert for sixty days, let alone take sixty days off from work to starve to death. Ultimately, the Bible was not revealing its secrets to me.

I continued my ordinary life, hoping for an opportunity that might increase my faith or help me find purpose in my life of commonplace. But nothing brought me any closer to the answers I was looking for. I dreaded the idea that this was all that life had to offer. I would rather poke a pencil in my eye than accept this blandness of this life.

My life continued in this way for a long time and suicide seemed to be a more appealing option than the dullness of my ordinary life. I continued to trespass on this planet performing the ordinary motions that everyone else seemed so content with. That was until when I met Tilauth – or at least I thought I had.

Chapter 2
Beach Dreams

One weekend in October during the few remaining warm days of fall, I sat on the sands of the Puget Sound with my back against a rock, and studied for my mid-term exams at the local Community College. The beach was virtually vacant, aside from the occasional dog walker. Tiny waves lapped the sand as I poured over my books, memorizing useless details of the macro economic workings of the world commerce. I felt the uneasy pang in my stomach that I was becoming accustomed to as I forced myself to push on with my studies.

A breeze whispered in my ears on its way in from the Sound, and the smell of the saltwater filled my lungs. With soft eyes, I watched the sunlight glare down on snow-capped peaks of the Olympic Mountains and shimmer across the great expanse of the Sound. The coolness from the grey sand seeped through my jeans and caused my legs to stiffen. I decided to take a break from my consuming studies and rest my eyes. I stretched my back and legs and laid down beside the rock onto the sand to let the waves lull me into a slumber.

Arduous accounting formulas drifted through my thoughts before it finally forgot the world and slept for what could have been an eternity, as time becomes irrelevant during sleep. Suddenly, I awoke to the sound of a eerily calm voice that seemed to contradict itself with the poignant words of "Neal, wake up! You're dying!" This was followed by a loud clap of someone's hands that seemed to be an inch from my ear. I sat up so quickly that my head spun, and I blinked in attempt to focus my eyes. I frantically looked around and saw sand, rocks, my notebook, alder trees, water, mountains, blue sky, and the sunlight. No one was nearby; in fact, the whole beach was vacant with the exception of a man standing about a hundred yards away. When I squinted I saw him looking thoughtfully towards the Olympic Mountains, but he was too far away to have said the startling words that I'd heard. The clap was so close that I could feel the puff of air against my ear as the hands came together. Since this man was the only other person on the beach, I could only assume that he was the author of the words and the clap, and this thought unnerved me to no end.

I watched this man whom seemed to posses a strange calmness. Sure, anyone who is out strolling on a beach would seem calm but there was something about him that seemed extraordinary. He wasn't like most people you see on the beach or anywhere with a nature backdrop. Most people seem to clumsily move about in the natural world as if they were walking on an uneven surface for the first time. This man looked different in the sense that he was made to be in a natural setting. He stood there as if there was no separation between him and his surroundings. He almost seemed to blend into his environment, leaving him invisible.

His hands were clasped comfortably behind his back as he stared out over the water with a deepness that made time stand still. I looked at him and noticed that he wore loosely fitting jeans, comfortable shoes, and a simple jacket. The breeze off the water moved through pieces of his long white hair that slipped free from his pony tail. He was a very handsome man that held himself with confidence. He had high prominent cheekbones and a large, yet not overwhelming nose. His skin seemed tanned but from where I sat, it was hard to tell. His body was still like a statue and his gaze unfaltering. He watched something far off in the distance that held his undivided attention. My curiosity heightened as his gaze seemed to grow with intensity. As I turned to see what he was looking at, an orca whale breached the water displaying an impressive amount of grace. My eyes widened at this beautiful sight, and I felt a churning sensation in my stomach. I returned my attention to the man, only to find that he had disappeared. I scanned the beach but there was no sight of him. I turned to scan the other half of the beach and saw nothing. I looked out in the water from where he stood in case he was crazy enough to go swimming, but saw nothing. I looked inland from where he stood thinking he had slipped past the alder trees and I just could not see him anymore.

I quickly grabbed my notes and jogged down the beach to where he had been. I looked back into the trees and saw no one. Confused, I searched in all directions to find the elusive figure, but to no avail.

With the man gone and night approaching, I decided to head back to my Jeep. I felt the acid surge through my stomach as I recalled the words I awoke to, "Neal, wake up. You are dying." The words grabbed a hold of my fear and left me with nothing but angst. Perhaps it was all just a dream. But dismissing this as dream did not make the feelings of worry go away. Something kept pulling my attention back to the man I saw earlier. I could not shake my mind free of him and found myself searching for him as I walked back to my car; perhaps he was sitting in his car letting it warm up. Everywhere I looked I found no one.

I drove home, ate some dinner, went for a run, showered, watched a little mindless TV, and went to bed. That night I dreamt of the man that stood on the beach. He stood just as he stood when I saw him at dusk. His eyes looked into the golden sunlight and I felt and understood the peace that he felt. Then his eyes lowered and looked at the sand to his left. His eyes slowly drifted along the grey speckled sand until they rose and met mine. I wanted to look away but I couldn't. His eyes looked at me like the way he looked at the sun. They seemed to penetrate right through me as if he were looking into the confines of my soul. Then I heard his voice but his lips did not move. With a calm tone and an accent I could not place he said, "You are dying - so let go." His words penetrated so deeply that my heart leapt out my chest and I awoke to my body falling into bed.

Wide awake, my heart pounding, the words resounded in me like an echo in a cave. Then there was the feeling of falling into my bed; had I been floating over my bed? This idea unnerved me but I had no explanation. I had to have been floating at least two feet above my bed. The sensation was so real that I couldn't ignore it.

Needless to say, I didn't sleep at all that night. The next few weeks passed like forgotten memories. I went to the beach a couple of more times but never saw the man again. I began to wonder about my health since the man said I was dying but I felt no aches or pains. In fact I felt physically pretty good. Mentally and spiritually my heart felt absent, like an empty hole.

My boss and doctor gave me my regular check up and said I'd live forever if I stayed this healthy. My knees ached a little bit from all the hiking I do in the mountains but the doctor said that wasn't anything to worry about. He diagnosed me with a minor patellar tendonitis and put me on anti-inflammatories. Days and weeks passed like drifting clouds until I met the elusive man again. This time, I ran into him where I least expected it.

Chapter 3
Hiking Into Oblivion

By late June, I had completely forgotten about the man on the beach and the haunting words he had spoken. The dream of floating above my bed had happened only once, and since then I slept without disruption for nearly a year.

I headed up Highway 2, turned down towards Index, and continued deep into the Cascade Mountains far from civilization. My Jeep bumped down the road crunching the gravel under my tires as I swerved to avoid the pot holes. My destination - an alpine hiking trail. The act of hiking by myself had become a weekend ritual. Hiking was like taking a mini-vacation from my monotonous life. I felt at home in the forest listening to its songs. The giant Douglas firs, Alaskan cedars, hemlocks, Red-Tailed hawks, Fiddle Head ferns, and the occasional Black-Tailed deer reminded me of a life that seemed normal and without force, unlike the world I was living in; the material world of cars, buildings, jobs, bosses, vacant stares, and coveted money that seemed to reiterate my feelings of not belonging to this world. Or perhaps I did belong to this world, but to a different era.

I rounded the bend and pulled up to a small parking lot at the end of the road. I stepped into the fresh mountain air and stretched my bones. All I could hear was the wind rushing up the mountainside and rustling through the hemlocks and mountain spray. The sun shone down upon me and my Jeep pinged as it cooled from its steep ascent. I tightened down my hiking boots and began the steep climb up the ridge.

I glanced at the ground as I put one foot in front of another and saw only deer tracks; but none that were human. "Good," I thought to myself, "I've got the whole mountain to myself." The winds whipped through the firs and the chipmunks squawked as I passed by. After about three hours of hiking I arrived at my final destination, an old fire lookout shack perched precariously on the peak. The shudders were open, so I thought I would take a look inside. I threw my leg over one of the cables that strapped the shack down during windy storms and made my way towards the door. It was locked so I looked into the windows and saw a cot, a meager kitchen, a chair, clean wood floors, and some empty shelves. The old fire lookout appeared to be unoccupied. I glanced around and realized that the fire season had not yet begun.

I turned to appreciate the panoramic view of the Cascades. The mountains looked as if they were dripping rocks into the sky as their bases clung to the Earth. I captured the view, snapping a few photos with a click and a whir. Sitting on one of the rocks, I let my mind drift into thoughtlessness. The view began to inspire me to do something less ordinary with my life. The big question was – what? Deep inside, I could feel that there was something important that I was supposed to do; a call I should heed. I needed to find out what that something was, but the answer eluded me and my mind cramped in frustration. I said a silent prayer of thanks for the view, and I began to cry for an answer to my predicament. The tears flowed down my cheeks as the frustration billowed up inside of me and released itself in a quiet sob. "Is life supposed to be this empty? Is the world supposed to be full of human beings filled with vacancy? Are my expectations of life and the world too high?" My questions went on and on layering upon one another and my heart sank into the idea that there could be nothing more.

Picking up my water bottle, I began my slow, somber descent down the trail. My head hung low as I watched my feet shuffle in repetition. Then my eye caught a strange depression in the mud. I knelt down to get a closer look and found the track of a human. This track was definitely not mine. It had no tread but it was not barefoot. The tracks were smooth, and lead off the path down a steep and overgrown deer trail.

The tracks intrigued me and concerned me at the same time. "Why hadn't I noticed the tracks before when I came up?" I thought to myself. "Was somebody following me during my ascent? Did they go down this deer trail?" I continued to question as I felt the hairs stand up on the back of my neck, and I got the feeling that I was being watched. I looked around and saw no one, and tried to shake off the feeling. It could not be a hunter since it was not hunting season.

I pulled a watch from my pocket and saw that I still had at least five hours before sunset. My mind reeled with curiosity and I quickly gave in. Adventure was what I needed from my ordinary world, so I started down the deer trail checking for the tracks again and again. I kept glancing further down the trail to see if I was coming up on the author of the tracks. I saw no one, and continued my slow descent, twisting my body over and under branches. The occasional bird would fly out from one of the bushes chirping madly. "I suppose they don't get too many humans passing by," I thought.

Finally, the trail began to level off in to an area of Douglas firs and old growth cedars. The deer trail broke off in several different directions and I scanned the ground for the tracks. Looking back in time, I now realize my tracking skills were very limited. The forest debris under the large trees was too thick to identify any tracks with my limited skills. My eyes scanned the area for any sign that suggested where this person may have gone. I saw nothing, and took a deep breath and sighed. Just then I realized that I had seen two eyes looking at me from deep in the trees, but I couldn't remember where from. The hairs rose on my neck, and I scanned again and saw nothing out of the ordinary. The image of eyes staring right at me was burned in my mind. My stomach twisted in knots with a feeling of fear. Panic-stricken, I decided to climb back up the deer trail to the hiking trail and quickly make my way back to the Jeep; my sense of adventure had its limits. I've heard of hermits living deep in these woods. Their solitary lives drives them to do heinous acts, and I wasn't about to become another heinous act.

Half way up the deer trail, a rock gave way from under my right foot. With a loud pop, I felt my ankle twist unnaturally and I fell forward. Sitting on the mountain side, I clasped my ankle and clenched my teeth tightly as I examined my foot. My ankle started to throb with pain as I tried to slowly move it. The pain shot up my leg like a bolt of lightening. Looking up the nearly vertical trail, I felt like I was staring at Mt. Everest. "How the hell am I supposed get up there with one foot?" I questioned in anger. My eyelids squeezed together as my ankle washed my whole body in a wave of pain.

I had no choice, I could either wait here in hopes that someone would come looking for me in a day or two or I could try to crawl up this trail. The idea of sitting on a mountain side waiting for days for help to come seemed absurd to me. I would have to endure the freezing nights without water, food, or shelter. I would die for sure from hypothermia, if I did not die from thirst. The last thing I would want to be known for is the guy that died from a sprained ankle. So I gritted my teeth and began to crawl on my hands and knees to the top. My ankle bumped into shrubs, seizing my body in pain. Once the pain subsided, I continued crawling, feeling like the beginning of one of those survival stories I have watched on TV. I was not about to cut off my ankle with a dull knife – at least not yet.

What rested directly in front of my face was a large fallen tree. I glanced down to both ends of the tree to see if I could crawl around it, but the brush was too thick and the land too steep. I was going to have to climb over it which meant standing up. I hesitated, in hopes of thinking of another way, but my mind drew a blank. Grunting in pain, I struggled to stand on the steep grade with one foot. It was not long before I lost my balance and was forced to put some weight on my right foot. It felt as if I stuck my toe into an electric socket as pain shot up my leg, hip, and into my low back, causing my leg to buckle underneath me. In the blink of an eye, I was toppling head over heels backwards down the mountain side. My back slammed into the ground, knocking the wind out of me as I watched my legs sail over my head. My feet circled back to the ground again and my ankle fired another shot of pain. My body spun in the air again and again like a rag doll slamming into the Earth with every bounce. I heard another crack and my left forearm felt strange which was then followed by intense pain as I helplessly gave into my increasing speed down the mountainside. The words entered my head, "Is this my death?" And I suddenly remembered the old man on the beach months ago and the haunting words that I heard. All this rushed through my mind as if I were falling in slow motion. I watched my body vulnerably take a beating as I smacked into rocks, soil, and bushes.

It was as if my mind left my body and I was sitting on a couch watching the horrific events unfold, unable to change the channel. Then in one of my spins I caught a glimpse of an upside down tree trunk and all went black with loud frightening pop.

Chapter 4
Intermittent Dreams of Reality

Flashes streaked across my mind. The sight of trees, bushes, rocks, and a river blurred by me in a haze of confusion. Sounds of bones and flesh cracking and sloshing echoed in my head like a slasher movie. An old wrinkled face with a rattle shaking over my head, sweet smells of smoke filled my lungs, and I heard songs sung in distant languages I never heard before. Shades of orange, red, and yellow washed across my body like a warm river of peace. Stillness filled my mind and everything went still like the surface of a lake in the morning.

My eyes slowly began to peel open and focus on a green bundle of herbs hanging over my forehead. I lifted my head a little stopping short to experience a throbbing pounding in my brain, leaving my eyes to wince with each thud.

The small bundle appeared to be a batch of cedar leaves dangling above me. I looked down at my body, covered in a blanket of animal fur and tried to sit up using my left arm as a brace. A sharp pain snapped up to my brain like a whip and I collapsed. A small fire was burning low with red embers against a primitive stone wall in the corner. The smoke swiveled upward to a small hole in the roof. The walls and roof were made out of rough cut wood with two open aired windows. One shutter was cracked open that allowed some light in; revealing a make shift table out of wood and some furs lying on the floor. I could feel a very slight breeze coming from the window combating with the heat from the dying fire.

I tried to move my legs but my ankle pierced with pain and the other leg just felt sore but I could at least move it. I took inventory of my pain; right ankle was either broken or sprained, left leg and right arm were covered in scratches and bruises but mobile, left forearm was undoubtedly broken and I felt an extremely tender cut near the break, my face was scratched and a large bump the size of my knee sat dead center in the back upper part of my skull.

I tilted my head up and saw a small wooden bowl of water beside me. With my right arm I reached over slowly and took a sip with a trembling hand. I lay my head back down with the swinging cedar over my head and passed out.

I awoke again later to the crackle and snap of wood burning in a fire. I slowly turned my aching head to see an old man with long white hair staring into the fire. He sat there still as a stone and I recognized him instantly from the beach. Without turning his head he calmly said, "Yes - you are still dying Neal." Confused, and bewildered by this comment, "How do you know my name?" I adamantly questioned.

"I can see it," he said as he turned and smiled at me.

"Why do you say I'm dying? Am I dying? How do you know if I'm dying? I've seen you before. How did you get here from- how did I get here?" I fired off the questions that begged to be answered but hurt my head to ask.

"Quiet down now. All answers will reveal themselves in good time. You rest so you can heal. You took quite a fall. You're lucky you're not dead now."

I laid my head down on the pillow again and quickly drifted off to sleep. My mind began to swirl with colors as I slipped deep into a dream. I dreamt I was walking down a cave where there seemed to be a soft glow of light flickering from around the bend. I kept walking towards the flickering light making my way around the bend. My body felt empty and lacked life. I stepped around the bend to see the most beautiful woman squatting there completely naked over a bed of furs. Her hand was resting softly against her face as her long raven black hair fell loosely around her cheeks. Her eyes gazed at me softly, and I felt a surge of life begin to fill me. A small lantern flickered against the wall casting a dance of shadows everywhere. Her other hand extended out to me, and she smiled softly as I walked towards her without a word. Her hand met mine and I felt a surge of energy rush through my body. I knelt down and she smiled at me filling me with a sense of intense longing, deep in my heart. My hand gently touched her soft cheek and she knelt forward and kissed me tenderly. I felt a love for her that I had known from a long time ago but I couldn't explain from where or when. Consumed in passion our bodies mixed together like water. I couldn't decipher if I was her or if she was me. This went on for what seemed like hours.

Then we somehow separated and I saw her smiling face again. I somehow knew that I was supposed to leave but I didn't want to and neither did she. But we moved apart knowing deep down inside we would see each other again. I walked out of the cave and accidentally stepped out too far and found myself falling down a cliff side.

Chapter 5
Tilauth

I awoke quickly with a scream to find the old man with a wet cloth dabbing my forehead. He left the cold cloth on my forehead and he began to laugh whole-heartedly as he stood up and walked to a small stool by the fire. "I've seen a lot of strange ways people have healed themselves, but you by far take the most provocative way."

Confused by his comments I chose to ignore him until I remembered my dream and it all started to come together. He saw an embarrassed look cross my face and he replied, "Oh, don't worry – I wasn't watching like some pervert. I was watching your healing energy grow, when I only caught a glimpse of its source."

I listened to him speak with this strange accent not saying a word as to why he knew about my dream. I looked him up and down. He wore buckskin pants with a pair of moccasins laced up his calf. The moccasins had to be the tracks I saw before I fell. He was shirtless, except for the tinkling sound that came from a necklace made from claws, bones, and beads that dangled from his neck. He reached down and pulled a fur robe around him and sat down by the crackling fire.

"Who are you?" I decided to ask letting one question

break the silence. Tilauth sat quietly for a moment not answering my question. This I would find to be very typical of Tilauth to always think thoroughly before speaking. "It is not polite to ask someone that question, from where I come from," he said as he quizzically glanced over in my direction, studying my face. "But you are not familiar with our customs, so I will tell you. My name is One Who Runs on Water. But my friends know me as Tilauth (Pronouncing it Tâ-lay-uth) because it's simpler to say. I come from the Siouxian nation – I'm Osage."

I felt a little taken back for not knowing his customs, so I decided to think carefully before I spoke not wanting to offend him. "My name is Neal, but then again, I guess you already know that." His facial expression remained unchanged as he gazed at the fire. A long silence passed and all that was heard was the crackle of the fire. "Thank you for helping me out back there," I said. Tilauth nodded slightly in a gesture almost unnoticed. "How long have I been here?"

"I believe this is day eight for you." I reeled back in astonishment, "You mean I've been here for over a week?"

"Yes."

"Well there must be search crews out looking for me," I asked.

"There have been, but I haven't seen any today. I think they may have called off the search," he said without expression.

"Well, why didn't you tell them where I was?" Tilauth studied me for a moment letting my question hang in the air, "I'm a solitary man and I like to keep my anonymity. I would appreciate it if you would honor that for me."

I settled down into my bed and thought about the situation. My family would be most definitely grieving now if they called off the search today. I couldn't argue with this man since he did in fact save my life.

Respecting his solitude is the least I could do to repay him.

It would be difficult to explain to my family and the authorities how I survived all week with my injuries. "You mean you don't want me to tell anyone that I've ever met you?" I asked.

"Yes, you must promise me that you will tell no one."

"I promise." I said seeing the seriousness in his eyes.

I searched my mind for a simple story that would sound believable. This was no doubt, going to be a struggle. "I will not mention to the authorities of your existence if they ask." It then crossed my mind that he may be wanted by the law and living like a hermit to avoid going to jail.

"No." Tilauth said as his gaze remained fixed upon the fire.

"No, what?" I said wondering if I was thinking out loud.

"No, I am not wanted by the law." Taken back, I realized he must have heard my thoughts. Feeling a little unnerved, "How did you know I was wondering that?"

"It's all written in our minds. I just listen, is all."

"But I didn't say it out loud?" I said, "or had I", I thought.

"Your question requires that you have more energy than you have right now, to understand. Save your energy and allow yourself to heal up so you can go home to your family. Drink the water there and get some rest. I'm going to head out and get you some food to eat."

I felt my stomach growl at the mere thought of food. I looked down at my belly and saw a concaved depression that I hadn't ever had before. "Some sort of food would be nice", I thought as Tilauth stepped out of the cabin without a word.

Chapter 6
Old Wisdom

The next ten days passed slowly, as my bones mended and my wounds began to heal. I saw Tilauth briefly here and there but our conversations were brief, he spent most of his time outdoors. When I slept he would often enter my dreams and I would feel my wounds close up and heal with flashes of heat and colors of red and orange. The fire would crackle through the night and I began to get up and walk around the cabin during the day. Often Tilauth didn't even come back at night. I'd wonder where he would go or stay during the night. I was beginning to wonder if the man ever rested.

One day I got up and walked around the cabin slowly with my limp. My muscles ached and burned but it felt good to stretch them out a bit. I peeked out the open-aired window into a thick forest of cedars, huckleberry bushes, firs, and ferns. I couldn't see very far into the forest but the cool moist air felt good in my lungs. "Why don't you come out?" Tilauth's voice came from the outside. His voice startled me. I looked down to see that I had no clothes on. "Your pants and shirt are sitting on the shelf to your left. Despite the blood stains and a few minor holes they're in pretty good shape." Tilauth said from the outside.

I pulled on my pants and shirt to notice that they had been washed but the blood stains remained. "I must have bled quite a bit", I thought.

I slowly limped my way out the door to see Tilauth sitting on a stump round and he gestured to a rock for me to sit. "It feels good to stand a little bit." I said.

"You are healing quickly. This is good" Tilauth said with a smile of approval. I nodded as a gesture of thanks and agreement.

I looked around the forest and took in the scene. A chorus of birds and insects came in from all directions. A chipmunk scampered up the large cedar that dwarfed the cabin like a pebble on the road. I watched it circle around the trunk like a peppermint stick. I breathed in the fresh air as we sat there in silence.

My foot began to throb so I sat on the rock Tilauth motioned to before. "I think you will be able to leave in the next couple of days." he said observing me closely. He had this strange way of looking at me. It was as if he wasn't looking at me but through me. I felt like he checked up on my wounds without even touching me and then he would examine the very essence of who I am. I would feel a little uneasy but his gaze seemed so soft and compassionate that I didn't mind. "How am I supposed to get out of here when I don't even know where here is?" I said assessing my quandary.

"I'll walk you out." Tilauth assured me.

"I suppose my car has been towed away."

"They towed that away when they called off the search."

"I need to get home before my folks spend all kinds of money on a funeral arrangement. It's weird to think that people think I'm dead." My mind ran down the possibility of a new path. "I could just start over. I hate my job and I'm going to college for some meaningless career. But I love my family dearly even though they criticize my every move. I couldn't just pack up and leave them to think I'm dead." Tilauth assessed me as I thought out loud but said nothing. I wondered if he might have some opinion in what I was talking about. "Why did you say that I was dying the other day?" I said changing the subject. He turned and looked out to the forest as if he were listening to some imaginary person there. He was silent for awhile before he finally began to answer my question. "Because you are." he said simply.

"Yes, but how do you know" I fired back?

"I know because I can see it."

"What do you see?" I asked feeling a little confused.

He paused, seeming to debate whether or not he was going to explain himself. Finally, he responded with an answer that I could have never expected, "I see that your body is fighting with your mind and your mind is fighting with your body. These two pieces of you have been so preoccupied with not being heard that they have entirely forgotten your spirit." He paused to give me chance to digest what he was saying. "During the process of when a child is conceived to the moment of birth, the child's spirit goes through a death. The spirit becomes aware of the body and the mind - and the body and the mind forget who and what the spirit is. Your body is more than just a physical being. It is a housing of your emotions and your desires also known as your soul. Your mind is the base of logic and reason. It is the analytical, detailed-oriented, black and white of who you are. Your mind is without emotion. In your case, the body and the mind are forgetting who each other are because they are at such odds. Neither one of them are listening to each other. Each has created its own world while the spirit looks upon them with patience and compassion. Your spirit is waiting for your body and your mind to find and heal one another. From there they can discover who and what you really are."

"Which is...?" I interjected.

"That will be up to you to find." he said sternly. "But as your body, mind, and spirit continue to grow further apart you will continue down your path of dying or rather forgetting. It won't be until the moment you die that your body and mind will fall away and the energies can return to the spirit where the spirit goes through a born again process. You may have heard of this process before. When someone has a near death experience they often will have the life flash before there eyes in a matter of moments and then they head towards a light. The replaying of the life is the way the spirit rewinds or retracts its energy and the light is the true self at the end of the tunnel." I nodded slightly to assure Tilauth that I've heard of these near death experiences. "So to the spirit; the death of the physical body and mind is like a birth and the birth of the physical body and mind is like a death. You've already have gone through that death of your spirit when you were born and now you continue to further the process of forgetting by displacing your body and your mind. This is why I say 'you are dying'."

My mind felt like it was trying to run through a thick forest of complexity. Even though there was nothing complex about what Tilauth was saying, I just hadn't looked at life and death that way. The whole concept was new to me.

"Come on in and we'll have some soup." Tilauth said as he stood up and walked into the cabin. I got up slowly and limped into the cabin. Tilauth's soups were like nothing I'd ever had before. He cut up wild plants that grew in the area and had all kinds of unique spices and herbs I'd never tasted before. Not only was it different, but it was surprisingly excellent. We sat down at the table and ate our soup quietly enjoying our fill. I didn't have to eat much before I was full. My stomach shrunk quite a bit while Tilauth had me on a diet of fluids, but I did have an appetite.

"Tilauth, I was noticing that my wounds were

healing up extraordinarily fast and my forearm almost feels like new. Broken bones…I thought…usually take months before they heal not weeks." I said waiting for a reply. He smiled and said, "You're a good healer."

"I can't believe that I'm the only one doing the healing…so…well…are you healing me in some way?" I asked hesitantly.

"Absolutely not!"

"You had nothing to do with me healing so quickly?"

"I did not heal you. I just helped you heal by becoming a valley that the river flows through. What flows through the river and yourself healed you, not me," he said very sternly.

"What do you mean you were a valley and the river healed me?"

"You sure do ask a lot of questions," Tilauth smirked at me.

"I'm sorry…I guess…well I need to have some sort of explanation."

"I can't explain everything to you. You have to figure some things out on your own." A silence filled the room as we sat in front of our empty bowls. Tilauth got up and picked up the wooden bowls and began washing them in a bucket. He looked really old but he moved with such agility and limberness. He squatted by the bucket like there wasn't an ache or pain in his body. I on the other hand, felt the way he looked.

"Neal, you mentioned that you need to have an explanation. The fact of the matter is you don't need anything. You already have everything and every answer to every question. You have just blinded yourself of who you are. If you knew who you were you would realize that you need nothing and you already have the answer to everything. The blindness comes from the illusory walls you built between your body, mind, and spirit. Tear down the imaginary walls you've created and you will have all the answers and all your needs will be met." His words had a way of complicating things in a simple way.

"I'm not sure if I understand what you mean about the walls that I've somehow built up?" Tilauth sighed as if he needed to back track to kindergarten to explain himself to me.

"Your mind ignores your body, your body ignores your mind, and they both ignore your spirit. They do this because you have let your fears and worries separate these pieces of you. You put your fear in the driver's seat and it controls your life. Some people let love and compassion drive while you let fear drive. Fear is supposed to be something to be aware of, not something that controls your life" he said looking up from the bowls he was cleaning. This left my mind to chew on things for a bit.

Tilauth stood up shaking the water off the bowls with a few grand whips of the hand. He set them down on the shelf and stretched his back. "I'm going to head out for an evening stroll. You rest up. You've got a long walk the day after tomorrow." He went out the door to leave me with my thoughts. I began to rummage over in my mind what fears I may have. I racked my head for a long time but I couldn't really think of any one fear that controlled my life. Sure I was a little afraid at night in the woods, but who wouldn't be? What if something is hunting me and I can't see them? That seems like a valid fear. And that's not something that is steering my life around. I'm a little afraid of heights too, but that's not in control of my life either. My head talked in circles like race cars on a race track - spinning myself into a slumber as I raced off to sleep.

That night I dreamt of a very large structured man pummeling a fragile young boy. Up on a mountain top I saw a man in a long robe that glowed with colors of indigo, blue, yellow, and white. He looked down the mountain upon the large man and fragile boy with compassion for both. He didn't seem disturbed by the site but rather compassionate and patient. I awoke in the middle of the night to find Tilauth sleeping on the floor. "Are you hungry, Neal" He said startling me.

"Uh, yeah... I guess I am. But you sleep, I'll eat something in the morning." I was kind of surprised at how hungry I felt.

"You know, you've slept through an entire day." Tilauth said, not moving in his blankets. "You should eat something to keep your healing energy up. I'm still planning on heading out tomorrow morning," he said without moving.

It's always disorienting when you sleep or take naps during the day. I tried to wrap my head around the idea of sleeping through a night and a day that felt like a matter of moments. But I did feel wide awake and ravenously hungry. "Well, I guess I could use something to eat," I said, accepting my situation.

Tilauth dished me up some more soup. I shoveled it down quickly. This time it had chunks of meat in it and my belly stretched tight like a little volley ball. Tilauth went back to sleep as I finished my soup, then I crawled back in bed feeling like a sluggish sloth. I just laid there but couldn't sleep. I was beginning to like Tilauth. He was so thoughtful and mysterious. He rarely spoke but when he did he would completely rewire my mind. I wasn't looking forward to leaving tomorrow – I would miss my new friend.

Chapter 7
Bears of the Past

Morning came slowly and I didn't get much sleep after my late night meal. My body felt good and rested for the most part. Tilauth and I got up with the sun rise – filled our bellies – packed some supplies, all of which Tilauth carried – and we headed out with out a spoken word. Well...Tilauth spent a few moments saying his morning prayers by himself.

It felt good to get out in the fresh air and move around a little more. I had gone for little walks around the forest here and there but I never went too far. My sprained foot wasn't feeling too bad, I could put most of my weight on it without too much pain. Tilauth took the lead wearing his buckskin pants, a simple shirt, and moccasins. He had a small cloth bag that wrapped diagonally around his chest and hung on his back. He walked lightly swerving around small plants to avoid breaking or smashing them. I'd never seen someone walk the way he walked. It seemed so graceful and effortless, but he moved with such speed – unlike my gimping clumsiness. Tilauth would stop often and patiently wait for me to catch up.

"You know you won't get as tired if you look up and soften your eyes when you walk," he said to me as I limped towards him with my chest heaving. "You soften your eyes by looking at the entire view all at once. Not only will you be able to walk farther, but you will be able to see more. Your mind will be embraced in the moment at hand and you'll enjoy it more." I nodded as I tried to catch my breath, "I'll give that a try."

We walked for several miles before he let me stop and rest. I hated myself for not being as fit as Tilauth, who seemed to be in his eighties or so and leaving me in the dust. "Don't be so hard on yourself Neal. Your body is still healing so it's using a lot of energy to repair itself. So you're not going to be moving at your best." I nodded, while wondering in my head how he knows what I think about all the time.

"Tilauth, I've got a question for you and I want you to let me know if it is rude of me to ask."

"Don't worry about that. There is no way you could know my culture. It has taken me awhile to adjust to the modern culture of today and I'm just not used to it is all. But go ahead and ask your question."

"You seem to know a lot about things that most people I've met do not. Like for example; what you told me yesterday about the mind, body, and spirit, the way you walk, talk, the way you live, and the way you read my mind as if my thoughts were written on my forehead. I guess my question is... what are you?" "That didn't sound right," I thought. "I mean, what do you call someone like yourself?" I said, which didn't sound any better. Tilauth looked at me with his brow furrowed and was probably wondering, 'What kind of question is that?' "Well...I'm what you might call a human being. What are you," he said, as a smile spread across his face and he began to chuckle. Feeling a little silly about my wording and realizing I'm not explaining myself very well, "I know you're a human being..."

"Actually, I've met quite a few people lately that I wouldn't call human beings, because there is nothing humane with the way they're being." I smiled recognizing his play on words. "I guess that would be true. There aren't too many humane people left in the world. But I guess what I was asking was, are you like some sort of medicine man or holy man or something?" Tilauth sat back and looked up the mountainside as if listening to something I couldn't hear. This seemed to be a regular thing with Tilauth. His words always seemed to be well thought out, as if he were examining where they might lead. "I don't like to give myself the title of anything because it often gives others the opportunity to make predeterminations about me. This leads to expectations and I can guarantee you I will almost always be and do what you least expect. Expectations only lead to disappointment and frustration. But to answer your question, yes I do follow the ways of a Shaman. But a Shaman is a wide open title. To be more specific, I am a healer, warrior, and a seer. But of course, this is not all I am." I sat there a moment listening to him and to the chorus of mid-day birds and watching the large cotton clouds pass over head. "This explains some things to me – thank you."

"Sure," he nodded in politeness.

I watched a small beetle trudge his way through the needles on the forest floor. "You know, about a month ago or so, I could have sworn that I saw you on the beach about forty miles from here. Was that you that I saw?" Tilauth tilted his head as if he were trying to remember, "It could have been. We should keep moving. I know a good stream where we can refill on water." he said, quickly changing the subject.

Tilauth stood up and started walking down the trail again and I took up the rear. The sun was actually getting pretty warm today and beads of sweat began to run down my face like little race cars taking off. My foot was beginning to swell a little bit and throb. I tightened my laces to prevent it from swelling too much. The terrain was a little thick with brush and I had to bend over and sometimes crawl to get through. This made the going slow for me, but not Tilauth, he bent like a Gumby doll. This was quite the amazing quality for a man of his age.

"Now this question is rude in my culture but you seem to be in really great shape which is why I'm asking, but how old are you?" I asked as I straddled a log sliding over it. "I don't find the question rude, but I really don't know exactly how old I am. I think that comes with old age. Let's just say that I'm older than you think and leave it at that." as he swerved down the trail. "Fair enough," I said accepting his answer.

"I've got a question for you now." Tilauth said as he slid on his belly under some thick brush.

"By all means, ask away," I said.

"Have you figured out what the fears are in your life, that are forcing your spirit down the road of its death."

"Uh…I don't think so. I'm afraid of heights – but that doesn't really steer my life around," I said, now sliding on my belly.

"Being afraid of heights is a good thing," Tilauth said as he stood up exiting the thick brush.

"Why is that?"

"Because when you're near a cliff, you might fall." he said laughing hard at himself. "Very funny," I said, trying to hide my smile.

"You know you should laugh more," Tilauth said as he reached his hand to help me up. "Thank you." brushing myself off.

"If you laugh a little more you can break down your illusory fears a little more. Laughing in the face of fear takes away its power."

We continued to walk more upright with the large firs way overhead. "Instead of focusing on those common fears that most people have, I want you to look at what has stopped you from living out your heart's desires. It is these fears that are an illusion. These are the fears that stall the relationship between your body, mind, and your spirit."

"I guess I'm having difficulty understanding. Give me an example of what you mean."

"Well, how about you give me an example of something that you don't do that your heart wants to do," he replied.

"That's easy. I wish I didn't work at my stupid job, studying the boring subject of accounting, and do the ordinary things that everybody does."

"Ok, so why don't you stop doing the things that you seem to hate and do the things that your heart wants to do?"

"If I don't study accounting I will have no future and I would be poor and have no money," I replied, not seeing any fear but rather logic.

"So might you say that your fears are being poor and being afraid of not having a stable future," he said quickly.

"I suppose you're right," feeling a little astonished.

"The idea is to face these unfounded fears. Unless you have been poor, then you may realize that it isn't so bad and there is nothing to be afraid about. And unless you have been to your future and know what is in store for you than you can be or not be afraid of it. These fears are illusions when you stop, listen to them, learn from them, and move on. Fears offer great lessons in life and should be embraced with gratitude as wonderful opportunities. When you face these fears you will begin to heal and live your life with more heartfelt purpose."

"Well yes but, what if I don't have enough money to do the things my heart wants to do?" I said, certain I found a hole in his theory.

"The statement of 'what if' is worrying about the future. Whenever you say 'what if' you are bringing your fear to the future to what might happen. You can have a billion 'what if's' and none of them could happen or all of them could happen. But what is certain, is you will live your life avoiding the 'what if's' and that is putting fear in control instead of allowing your passions to steer your life."

My mind tackled the idea of being afraid of the future for long time as we walked in silence. I began to think about all the 'what if's' I had placed in my life. I had them piled on top of each other creating a web of confusing fears. All of them tied into the simple statement of, I'm afraid of the future and what might happen. Here was just another example of Tilauth rewiring my brain and painting things so simply. I felt like saying 'Duh, why didn't I think of that.'

We continued to walk as Tilauth allowed me the silence to think about my fears. The trail began to meander next to a stream. I hobbled over large rocks and fallen trees and my ankle began to ache to no end. In front of us I could hear a loud roaring sound rumbling through the trees. There must be a large river up ahead, I imagined.

We pushed on down the valley until the roar was unmistakable. The trees turned into cedars with moss draping down from their dropping branches and I could smell the moisture in the air. The ground turned to soft beds of Sphagnum moss with the Fiddle Head ferns unwinding upward reaching out to slap the sky. The ground was bouncy feeling as I limped along. I gazed at the ground to see that it was covered with life in every square inch. Nothing was bare with soil.

"Lets sit and eat for a bit," said Tilauth as he pulled off his bag and sat down on a spongy blanket of moss. I found a nice patch and limped over and bent down slowly as my muscles allowed me to.

"Has it helped by keeping your eyes soft and not looking at the ground while you walk?" he asked as he watched me slowly sit down.

"Actually it has. It feels like I've got more endurance, but my ankle is killing me. It's throbbing and it's starting to swell up pretty bad," I said grabbing my ankle, touching it lightly. "It's sore to the touch."

"Take your shoe off and lay down on your back," Tilauth said. He came over and rolled a small log under my foot to elevate it. "I want you to close your eyes and breathe deeply and gently." So I closed my eyes and paid attention to my breath, welcoming the rest. "Breathe slower – you breathe too fast," he said as he placed my hand on my stomach. I slowed my breath and felt my muscles melt into the ground like butter. "Good...now just relax your whole body and focus on your breathing. Listen to your breath go slowly in and slowly out." I lay there listening to my slow breath feeling myself relax more than I've ever known before. "You're going to notice some strange sensations going on in your body, just relax and allow them to happen." At that very moment I began to feel a deep push in my right lower abdomen. The feeling was not his hands pushing on my abdomen but rather like something was being moved in my gut that I couldn't explain how or why. The pressure moved upward stalling at the base of my ribcage. A hot spot began to develop there like someone put a warm rock inside of me. Then there was a flash of yellow light that streaked across my eyes and it felt like my whole body shifted into a different world. Suddenly I was lying on this stone table that was covered in furs. The trees moved like they were under water and flower petals slowly floated down from the sky like confetti. Tilauth stood somewhere down at my feet but I couldn't see him I could only sense him. Then a beam of white light came down from the sky and the ground began to light up and glow a brilliant white. I watched the light come down from the sky slowly and enter into Tilauth's head whom I could see clearly now. The white light gathered in his chest and swirled around concentrating it into the size of a softball. Then I saw swirls of yellow mix in with the white. Tilauth pointed to the trees with his index finger and slowly brought it down to the bottom of my foot. The ball of light slid down the inside of his arm and stopped at the tip of his finger. Then his finger barely touched my foot and I felt the pressure in my ankle drain away like someone pulled the cork. The light spread out through my leg and the pain subsided like a gentle hug.

I stared at my glowing ankle illuminating colors of white and yellow. All of it glowed except for one spot that seemed dark brown. Tilauth noticed the brown spot too and he reached into my ankle with his right hand and he pulled it out with a sharp ripping feeling. My foot then relaxed and felt free of all pain. I watched Tilauth put his right hand on the Earth for a second then put his left hand on my left foot and his right hand on my right foot. His arms were crossed and the left leg began to glow like the right. Both legs relaxed and I felt a pop in my low back and a relief went throughout my whole body.

All of a sudden I couldn't see Tilauth anymore and I felt a different pressure in my abdomen pushing down toward my right hip. Then in a flash of green and blue I slowly opened my physical eyes. I slowly moved my ankle around feeling like it was brand new. Amazed and relieved, I turned my head to see Tilauth pulling some dried meat out of his bag along with some veggies he collected along our walk. "Did you just heal my ankle?" I asked in bewilderment.

"No, I'm just like a hollow bone. As you saw the light came from somewhere else," he said as he broke up some of the fresh veggies and threw them into his wooden bowl. "Wow that was a miracle," I said completely astonished – moving my ankle around! He began one of his deep laughs that came from deep in his belly. "What's so funny?" I said taken back by his reaction.

He finally stopped laughing and said, "You are still far away from your spirit. If your three parts were put together properly, you would think it not miraculous but rather normal. Not that you shouldn't be appreciative for such things. You should be very grateful, not to me, but to the Creator. One should see the miracles of the Creator everywhere, everyday. But you are blind and they are unusual to you."

I stood up and walked over to Tilauth to help him with the food. He put together this great lunch that would compete with the highest quality restaurants in Seattle. We ate our fill in silence. Tilauth would always eat his food slowly, savoring every bite, while I gorged it down and was a little too full before I stopped. He seemed to know when he'd had enough food. He always ate what seemed like so little but he didn't look malnourished. His arms were strong, and his body seemed sturdy, like an eighteen-year-old. I could tell I was doing something wrong, because I looked like the malnourished skin-and-bones kid even though I ate like a pig.

I thought a little bit about what Tilauth said about me being blind because my parts are all mixed up. So I decided to focus on identifying my fears while we rested. I began to surprise myself over and over again. Everything that I didn't do in my life that I really wanted to do was always hindered by a fear I was unknowingly harboring. My fears were usually camouflaged by a series of excuses and 'what if's'. I began to realize that it would take days on end to unravel the infinite myriad of excuses and fears I had compiled in my life like a complex cushion.

We silently got up and began down the trail without a word. Tilauth must have known that I was deep in thought and didn't want to disturb me. The fact of the matter was Tilauth does disturb me. He has disturbed me more in my life than anyone I've ever known. His intuitive nature was rattling my very core and it was turning my life upside down. In a matter of a week or so, Tilauth had completely reorganized my view on my life and the world around me. And deep down I'm beginning to get the feeling that Tilauth is capable of doing much more. I can feel him holding out and only giving me pieces here and there, never giving me too much.

But this is what I've been looking for, for so long. I want to learn how to walk through life without the ordinary boring problems of the typical life. After experiencing the healing work Tilauth has done on my ankle, I'm realizing that not only is such healing possible, but I really want to learn. I feel like miracles only exist in some sort of fantasy book or some long ago religious leader or guru. Tilauth has the knowledge and the skills that I want to learn. I know I'm not going to find this in some college or trade school. The kind of teacher that I'm looking for doesn't really seem to exist anymore. But here is one walking directly in front of me.

I watched Tilauth as he effortlessly moved across the landscape with ease while I struggled over rocks and crashed through bushes. A slight sprinkle began to patter on the leaves, creating a random rhythm to the beat of my footsteps. Misty patches of fog began to immerge like ghosts throughout the river valley that whispered around our shoulders as we cut through them like aliens that didn't belong there.

"Have you lived out here all your life?" I asked sliding around a large river boulder. Tilauth didn't speak for awhile; he seemed to be really thinking about how he was going to answer his question. This was something I was starting to get used to. He was obviously very careful with his words. "No, I've only been here for the past two years. Before living here I was a wanderer, and I wandered like the wind popping up here and there wherever my heart steers me. Before that I lived in the Mississippi basin area with our people." My head searched around his words again, "Wait a second, you said our people. Don't you mean your people?"

"Well we are all actually a part of the same race; the human race; however, you and I come from the same tribe." I could feel my brow begin to tighten in my confusion while Tilauth glanced over his shoulder to witness my confusion. "But I'm not...Native American," I said thoroughly confused.

"No, you're not full-blooded Osage. But you have the Osage blood that runs through your veins nonetheless. That makes you a part of our people." My mind reeled at the thought of being an Osage Native American. "Wait a second, how would you know whether or not I'm Osage or not?" I questioned. "For all you know I could be half Russian and half Greek!" This made Tilauth stop walking and laugh until tears fell down his cheeks. "We are all part of the great circle of life but you are definitely not Greek or Russian."

"Well then, how would you know my ancestry?" I exclaimed.

"Because some of our people marked their children, and their children's children, and so on and so forth. Your great, great, great grandkids will be marked and to the trained eye they will be able to see that mark. This was done by a shaman in your ancestry centuries ago. This shaman knew the likely future and was called to mark his ancestral line. This means that certain children in the future of this shaman's ancestry will have unique talents or a special calling that will require a mark so seers can identify the person," Tilauth explained.

"Ok, let me see if I'm getting this straight. What you're saying is, I've been marked by a shaman in my ancestry a long time ago. And you can see this mark?" Tilauth nodded. "So what does this mark look like then?" I asked.

"It's an imprint that reveals itself though your

energy. Or sometimes it reveals itself in an actual mark on the physical body, like the one you have on your right thigh," he said without flinching. I instantly remembered the birth mark on my thigh. I always thought nothing of it and never imagined that it actually had a meaning. In fact I found it to be an embarrassment growing up as a child; now I wasn't sure how I felt about it.

"Not only can these marks be passed down through a physical ancestral line, but they can also carry through on a spiritual ancestral line. Meaning; when a spirit's physical body of the shaman's blood line dies, the spirit may return in a different blood line altogether, and they will or can be marked also," Tilauth said, further continuing his explanation.

"Wait a second..." now shifting gears, "you mean to tell me that a spirit can come back?" I declared. "That's reincarnation. The Christian bible makes it clear that reincarnation is untrue. Once you die your spirit cannot come back and give it another go around. Once you're dead you're dead. Your spirit is then at the mercy of God who will judge you and send you to Heaven or Hell, simple as that." Tilauth stopped walking and turned around to look at me. His eyes stared directly into my eyes and it felt as if he were entering me like a train slipping into the black tunnel of my pupils. His face was gentle and he held a comforting smile that put my confusion at ease. I felt something deep within me shift sharply as if a rock was shoved through my insides and then stopped just as abruptly as it began.

Tilauth smiled softly and said, "I'm not going to tell you what you should or should not believe in, I'll let you decide that for yourself. The last thing this world needs is someone telling someone else what they should or should not believe," and he ended the subject with that.

Tilauth turned and we continued down the river

valley as the river grew larger and wider. White rapids splashed over large boulders creating a thunderous roar that dissipated in the surrounding trees. Mist filled the air and created a deep sense of inner peace. As I walked I noticed that my body felt different. My senses seemed more acute, yet my head felt like a giant sponge the size of the Earth. My mind registered everything that my senses picked up and then some. It was as if my head was working at the top of its game yet it felt up in the clouds somewhere. My mind felt like it was picking up the entire emotional state of the whole world and beyond. I looked at the rushing water in the river and I could feel that water as if the water were a separate entity. I would glimpse at a large alder tree as I walked by and I could feel the deep connection to the earth and history of its life would flash inside my mind. I saw a very cold winter with extremely heavy snows where it barely survived as a sapling, I saw period of a long draught that lasted years, and then I saw the heavy rains and healthy sunshine where it grew leaps and bounds. I passed by rocks, plants, squirrels, bugs, and I saw deep inside them again and again as if they where me and I was them.

Then in a blink of an eye everything changed, as if I walked through a sheet of water. The forest was now filled with rhododendrons and giant sequoias that loomed to unimaginable heights. The air smelled like wet soil after a long overdue rain. I looked forward to see that Tilauth had disappeared. My heart was pounding hard and fast throbbing like a drum. My head spun around by a force within me that felt like I had no control over. Behind me on the trail a large lumbering black bear barreled through the bushes sending a series of leaves shaking flinging droplets of water everywhere. My chest heaved up and down as we stood eye to eye about twenty five yards apart. The large bear stood up on its hind legs hefting its heavy body upright as a loud grumble billowed out shaking my body to my bones. The same unstoppable force spun me around and I took off running rising and falling with the bumps and dips in the trail. I could hear the bounding thuds of the bear's feet behind me but I dare not turn around to prevent me from slowing. The slightest mistake would surely mean my death.

As I sprinted through the forest, plants and trees passed by me like a blur of green and brown streaks. I also noticed that my ankle, nor the rest of my body for that matter, didn't hurt; in fact they felt better than ever. My body moved lightening fast with an ease and agility that I've never felt before. My skin was a golden brown and my limbs were smaller. I also noticed that I was shirtless and wore nothing but a breechcloth as my thighs swished forward with amazing speed. It was then that I caught a glimpse of the same birth mark on my right thigh, but it was not my body, at least not a body that I knew that was now running from this large beast.

Then in an instant; a flash of knowing flooded my brain. This was my body a long time ago, and this is my spirit that holds this body. I'm running from this bear because I swatted it on the rump while it slept. I did this because I wanted to prove to my grandfather that I was courageous and ready to be trained as a warrior. My grandfather was a highly respected elder, seer, and a warrior in my tribe. He told me that I was still too young and not ready to be trained in the ways of the warrior. He told me that I was afraid still and my first challenge would be having the courage to face my fears.

These statements frustrated me to no end. I desperately wanted to be a great warrior and seer like my grandfather. There was nothing else in the world that I wanted more. All the meaningless tasks and chores throughout the day were belittling me everyday as I watched other young men go through their training. My father said that grandfather was going to be tougher on me because I was his own blood. He said that I was going to learn everything the hard way so that I would carry with me the wisdom that will surpass everyone else's. So many weeks passed by and my frustration grew with every passing day. All the other young boys my age had begun their training while I was left behind still doing the things of a child.

I didn't realize it at the time but my grandfather was teaching me an invaluable lesson. My training had already begun but I didn't realize it. He wanted to create within me a stronger passion to learn the ways of the warrior, more then the rest of the young boys. This way I would pursue the teachings when it came time with ferocious determination to surpass everyone else. But I didn't understand this lesson until it was too late.

My grandfather held a great story of courage that was whispered around the tribe like a myth. Once I asked my grandfather if this story was true, and he laughed out loud and then gave me a look and the slightest of nods without saying a word. I would jump with excitement and ask him to tell me the story for himself. He would always brush it off and say, "Get back to your chores, you don't want to hear that story anyways." Always being the respectful grandson I didn't press the subject anymore. But if my grandfather didn't tell me some of the other boys were happy to indulge my curiosity. The story always varied slightly between tellers so I was never certain which one was the truth. But they all had certain elements in common.

My grandfather as a young boy proved his courage by swatting a sleeping bear and then out running it. He ran for miles and miles before the bear got tired and gave up. When he came back to the camp where the other boys had assumed that he had most likely been killed by the bear, they praised his courage and endurance. The story spread through the tribe quickly and the elders questioned the truthfulness of the story. So the elders sent out one of their best trackers to confirm the events. The tracker came back confirming the whole story and the elders then looked at my grandfather as more of an adult than a child. He was then training in the sacred ways of a warrior and a seer.

With that story in mind, I set out to prove my courage and readiness to my grandfather. I found the old bear and almost couldn't go through with it. The fear inside me was like an atomic bomb of fire that was burning up my insides. I rolled my little body around the tree trembling so loudly that I was sure I was going to wake the old bear with my fear. I closed my eyes and swatted him as hard as I could feeling my hand swish through his long hair and smack his padded flesh. The air filled my lungs with the smell of a wet animal and I began to run unconsciously. My legs felt slow at first and hesitant but they quickly picked up speed when I heard a rumbling growl behind me.

This was the knowing that filled my mind as I now sprinted for my life. Everything within me wanted to be a warrior but now all I could feel was the need to survive this moment. I ran so fast and I could here the wind whipping around my ears whispering 'faster...faster...'

Up ahead I notice a fallen tree. I couldn't decide whether or not to go under or over it. But before I knew it I was already there and had no time to decide. With an amazing leap I bounded into the air like a blurred rabbit. In my peripheral vision I caught a horrific glimpse of where I was about to land. In that same instant I slammed down onto another fallen tree and I heard my leg snap between the tree and a large branch. I tried to get up hoping that it was the tree branch that snapped and not my leg but my leg didn't work right and a pain shot up through my body. I briefly glanced at my leg to witness a red stream spewed out like a shower spraying all over myself and the trees. In a split second I heard and felt the thumps in the ground of a 'ta dunt' - 'ta dunt' - ' ta dunt,' like a horse galloping towards me. But to my disappointment with the crackle of claws on bark I saw the mammoth beast growling above me as his front paws pull his body over the log and on top of me. His front paw came down upon my chest and I felt the air rush out like a popped balloon, crushing my rib cage. My last glimpse was of the bear's eye as his jaws clamped down around my neck crushing my windpipe.

I screamed, feeling the blood in my throat slowly gurgle away and I opened my eyes to see Tilauth holding me like a child on the ground next to the river we had been walking down. I suddenly realized I was still screaming and I stopped abruptly with the fear of death still in my eyes. I scampered wildly to my feet and looked around me for the bear. I grasped my throat, chest, and then my leg to realize that everything was fine. "Calm down Neal, you're fine. Nothing's going to hurt." My eyes began to slowly blur with tears as I stared at Tilauth. My knees buckled and I fell to the ground in the realization of what had happened to me.

Tilauth came to my side and placed a comforting hand on my shoulder. "Now you know what the truth is." he said in a gentle voice. My eyes slowly rose to meet his and I realized that the truth was inside me. To deny this truth meant to deny who I was and who I am now.

My mind bounced around like a pinball. I felt as if I had suddenly put a crucial piece of the puzzle of my life together and unexpectedly I could now start to see the whole picture. All my life I was afraid of challenges that could change my life drastically. I never had the courage to do anything that threatened my life in

the slightest. This fear or lack of courage sat so deep
within me that I led an ordinary life afraid to follow
my dreams. Reliving the experience of my death, from
the bear attack was terrifying yet enlightening.

Chapter 8
The Unsaid

"We'll make camp here and start up again early tomorrow," Tilauth said as he dragged a long hefty branch and rested one end in the notch of a tree. I sat down on a log and rested. My head was still spinning with thoughts, and all the while Tilauth acted as if nothing was out of the ordinary. He went about an unusual task of collecting many sticks that I assumed were going to be for a fire. He started snapping the sticks in half to the length he wanted, lining them perpendicular up along the larger branch resting in the notch of the tree. This seemed like an oddly shaped fire that he was making. He created this long 'A' framed tepee that ran maybe one to two feet off the ground. This was followed by hefting armfuls of leaves, pine needles, sword fern, and other miscellaneous debris and throwing it over the 'A' framed tepee. What was left was a large mound of forest debris with a long and slender hole under it all.

Tilauth smacked his hands together, swiped the dirt off and smiled at me. "This is my bed for tonight," he grinned, tilting his head like a dog questioning a sound it heard. "Will you be making a place to sleep for yourself?" Tilauth questioned me.

"Well uh…. I suppose I will." I said, realizing that I was going have to figure something out.

"Good, because it's going to get cold tonight. You're going to want to make sure you use a lot of debris, I don't want you crawling into my bed tonight," he said with a chuckle. He turned and walked along the river with his pack still strapped to his back. I watched him for a bit as he hopped from one large boulder to the next like some kind of dance. He was obviously very content and free in the forest. I envied his simple lifestyle. What stress could this old man possibly have in life? I thought about my life filled with anxiety and strain. My stomach started to get sick at just the thought of returning to my ordinary life far away from this beautiful river and these enormous trees. I shook my head as if to shake the bad thought out of my ears and began to look for a place to make my bed.

I found a large branch and rested one end between two large boulders. I then started breaking sticks and placing them along the branch just the way Tilauth did. I gathered large amounts of debris from the forest floor and threw them over my little 'A' frame. I grabbed lots of debris from further and further away from my bed. Finally I finished and I compared it to Tilauth's bed. My hut appeared to have much more debris than Tilauth's bed. Satisfied, I looked down the river to see if I could see Tilauth anywhere, but he was nowhere in sight. Feeling a little bored, I decided to go look for him.

I jumped from boulder to boulder without feeling an ounce of pain in my ankle. The river roared as it gushed through the valley showering mist everywhere. The air was crisp and cool and the sky had already begun to darken. I rounded the bend and notice a small stream of smoke trickling upward from the top of a very large rock. Atop the rock sat Tilauth with his arms outstretched towards the sky. It looked as if a small bowl sat in front of him where the smoke rose up slowly. I watched him carefully, feeling uneasy, as if I may be watching something very private. I noticed that his gestures were purposeful and seemed to be moving something I could not see. It was as if he were speaking to an imaginary old friend that he knew for years but I couldn't see anyone standing near him. That's when I noticed the tears streaming down his cheeks. I suddenly felt an urge that I was witnessing something private and personal. I quickly turned around and rounded the bend towards our camp. I sat down by our little huts decided to busy myself.

I grabbed some rocks and put them in a circle to create a fire pit. After that I walked into the forest in search for fire wood. The forest was thick but most of the wood was pretty wet. I gathered all the dry wood that I could find and piled it back in camp. When I returned I saw Tilauth digging a shallow hole in the ground in the center of my rocks. I hesitated before approaching but then walked near the fire pit and placed the wood in a pile.

"I couldn't find very much dry firewood. It's all pretty damp," I said breaking the silence.

"Your bed looks good," he said looking me directly in the eye. A strange surge of guilt coursed through me and I looked away towards the pile of wood. Tilauth watched me for a moment, "You may actually get too hot tonight with all that debris but you'll be fine." A silence filled the air except for the roar of the river gushing down the valley. "You act as if you've never seen someone pray before Neal," he said cutting to the heart of things. My eyes met his and I realized that there is very little hiding when it comes to being around Tilauth.

"Uh...well I guess I had never seen anyone ever pray with that much passion before – And I suppose I felt like I was intruding on something personal." Tilauth smiled putting me at ease.

"Prayers are sometimes personal, yes, but you shouldn't feel guilty for accidentally seeing someone pray." Tilauth gave me his usual stare as if looking right through me. "Someday, you will understand the truth about prayer."

He stood up and motioned for me to follow him as we walked into the forest. Tilauth showed me the places in the forest of where to look for dry fire wood. We gathered up a small amount of wood and stacked it near the pit. He reached behind a boulder and pulled out a couple of trout. "Praying wasn't all I was doing," he said as he hung the fish with a large grin. He laughed a whole-hearted belly laugh and built a fire in a matter of seconds. I had never seen someone light a fire that fast before. He took a stick and spun it in a notched board he had in his pack. In a matter of moments the fire was crackling and the trout sizzled over the pit. We both ate a fish and our bellies stretched in content.

After eating we both laid there in silence listening to the roar of the river. The sky darkened and the fire glow shone a flickering of shadows and light that danced on the trees around us like ghosts. I noticed Tilauth staring off into oblivion. He seemed to be listening to something I can't hear or see. I felt like asking him what it was that he was hearing but decided against it. We sat in silence for what seemed like an eternity as I stared into the flames. No words were spoken except for the ramblings of my thoughts.

The stars began to gleam through the branches of the giant fir trees and I let out a quiet sigh. There is no where in the world I'd rather be than right here, right now. It was a strange feeling for me. I am actually fully satisfied with this place. All my life I have wished to be somewhere else doing something else. Now I want nothing else and I'm perfectly happy. I could live here along the river like a hermit getting my food from the land and building a nice shelter. Tilauth and I could meet every once in awhile and have dinner like old neighbors.

Then my thoughts jumped to tomorrow. Tomorrow

I would go back to the same classes the same work and the same old everything. I was looking forward to seeing my family and friends but I was not looking forward to seeing my old life again. My heart sank inside me like a dead weight and I felt like crying. I fought back the tears because I didn't want to draw attention to myself. His eyes remained fixed upon the flickering flames that leaped up to lick the night air. I breathed slowly to calm my inner turmoil trying to think of something to talk about. A lump grew in my throat and I decided it was better not to talk at all. So I continued to wallow in the silence that encompassed us. Well all except for the constant rumble of the river.

I wanted to know what Tilauth knew. Tilauth had something inside of him that I couldn't quite put my finger on. I know that he has something but he keeps it to himself. He seems to tell me a little bit here and there and that little bit will turn my whole life upside down and slap it silly. In all actuality I'm glad that he doesn't tell me everything, I think that I might spontaneously explode into a million pieces if he did. Just then I heard a quiet chuckle come from his way and I saw him still staring at the fire smiling. "What's so funny," I asked? His eyes rose from the flames to meet mine, "Nothing, I was just thinking about something," and he looked back at the fire again. He obviously wasn't going to share with me his inside joke. His eyes gleamed as they reflected the light from the fire. His grey hair was pulled back tight into a braid, arms crossed, and his legs extended straight out in front of him crossing at the ankles as he leaned his back up against a boulder. He mystified me. I could usually figure someone out from the first time I meet them however, Tilauth was different. It was as if he purposefully did the opposite of what I expected just to keep me guessing.

"Tilauth, I understand that you've been wandering

around without a home but don't you have any family,"
I asked. He sighed and looked up towards the trees
in thought. It's almost as if the words to answer my
question were up in the trees somewhere but he looked
through the trees instead of at them. His silence made
me wonder if I was asking a sensitive question and I
wished I could retract it. "I have family..." he paused
leaving the statement up in the air for a moment. "They
understand why I'm here and not there with them. I
see them when we want to get together and talk," he
said smiling at me suggesting that he wasn't going to
tell me anymore. "You should try out your new bed.
Get some rest; we've got some more walking ahead of
us tomorrow," he said as he stood up stretching his
arms and smacking his gums loudly. He smiled at me
and walked to his little hut.

I smudged out the fire so that there were only some
faint embers glowing and threw a splash of water on
it from the river. I walked over to my makeshift home
and examined it for a moment. "This was going to be
an experience", I thought. I slid in feet first, carefully
trying not to destroy my little hut. Once I was in I
pulled more leaves from a pile I left outside, down
around my body. I pulled the last remaining leaves in
to create a pillow. I then pulled in a makeshift door
that Tilauth showed me how to make out of sticks and
debris. At first it felt like a zillion insects must have
been crawling all over me. I shut the thought out of
my mind and focused on relaxing. Surprisingly it was
very comfy and warm; it almost felt warmer than in
my bed at home. I realized that my imagination was
getting the better of me because I didn't feel any bugs
crawling on me now. I quickly fell into a deep sleep in
my strange new bed.

Chapter 9
Goodbye Hello

I awoke the next morning to something large, forcefully touching my head then my shoulder. I opened my eyes and saw nothing but darkness. My dreams were so vivid I had forgotten where I was. The rustling of the debris, the strange feeling of being cocooned, and something that was poking me sent a panic through my body and I thrashed around springing to my feet. Debris and sticks went flying everywhere, and I tripped over the large branch that supported the whole hut. I scrambled to my feet, arms flailing in some sort of meager defense. I heard a laugh grow larger and louder, and I spun around to the noise to see Tilauth doubled over laughing to the point tears ran down his face. He held a stick that he was using to poke me with through the debris hut.

The adrenaline was still coursing through my veins as I brushed the leaves and debris from my clothes. Tilauth sat on the ground still laughing and wiping away his tears. "Har, har, har." I said mimicking him. He finally stopped laughing enough to catch his breath and utter a few words.

"You sure are a jumpy one this morning." He started to laugh all over again. I walked right by him towards the woods to relieve myself. I could hear his laughter echoing through the trees, bouncing off a small rocky cliff just beyond them. I returned, and he had finally managed to calm down from his giggling fit. He pointed towards a rock where he had a pile of berries, dried meat, and greens gathered for breakfast. "I got you something to eat this morning."

"Thank you. I'm happy to have provided you with some entertainment this morning," I said, feeling a little annoyed.

"Don't be too hard on yourself. I used to be jumpy and high strung like you once," Tilauth said as he threw some berries into his mouth. I looked over to his bed and noticed that it wasn't there – in fact I had a hard time figuring out where it used to be. He walked over and began throwing the debris around from my hut. Things went flying everywhere like he was a tornado, leaves, sticks, needles, and branches. The old fire pit was a mound of fresh dirt and rocks that lined it were scattered everywhere. I looked at our campsite as a whole and realized that it for the most part looked the same as when we arrived the night before. "Wow, you can't even tell that we were here!" I exclaimed. "And after a good rain even the most experienced tracker will have difficulty identifying that someone had camped here," Tilauth added.

I looked at him as he briefly examined the site checking for anything that he may have missed. "Are you sure you're not wanted by the law or was wanted by the law at some point in time?" I asked.

"No, I'm not wanted by the law. It is something I've learned from my grandfather and he learned it from his grandfather and so on and so forth. Not only am I a shaman, but I'm also what you may call a warrior. Only I'm not the kind of warrior that you might expect. A warrior is someone who can move across the land with such speed and efficiency that they are unnoticed and untraceable. They can not only survive but they can thrive in the most inhospitable areas of the Earth. They are at most a shadow in the corner of your eye. A warrior uses this ability to walk their path with a stronger purpose." Tilauth said, watching me carefully. "A warrior as defined by today's standards is someone who kills to defend their way of life. This has little to do with the warrior of the Osage people. A warrior of the Osage people will fight in such a way to not fight anymore. This is done by the impeccability of the warrior following their heart." Tilauth paused as he studied the wind. "I'm sorry; I'm heading down a tangent. I can see where this conversation could go on and on, and I would only end up confusing you more and more. But 'no,' to answer your question, I'm not wanted by the law – it is in my culture to respect the land and not only leave it the same way as when we arrived but to actually help it."

"Don't worry about your tangents – I actually find what you have to say very fascinating. There is something about what you say that seems to make sense – a lot more sense than what I learn in school anyways," I admitted. "In fact I agree – humans should treat the land which is a gift from God, with respect. Instead we make a mess out of things and then complain when we have to sleep in the mess we made," I blurted out. Tilauth grinned at me calmly, "We should get started – we're not far from the highway."

We started our traverse down the rocky river valley heading south from what I could tell. The slate grey skies of Western Washington loomed above like a blanket that kept the warmth out. Today felt a little colder than yesterday and my breath swirled a puff of mist in the air as I heaved onward. My mind went over what I was going to tell everyone when I got out. It was going to be difficult to explain, how I survived. My arm felt fully healed and my ankle felt like a million bucks. I couldn't even find where most of my bruises and cuts were. Almost a full month has passed since my initial trip to the woods. Everyone is going to want some sort of explanation and I'm the worst liar known to man. When I lie it is unmistakably obvious so I decided to tell as much of the truth as possible. I will tell them that I mended my wounds together myself, built a small shelter, got water from the creek, ate a few wild plants, caught some fish from the river, and when I healed up enough to walk out, I slowly made my way back to civilization. Anyone who knows me will undoubtedly find this an unlikely feat for me but maybe they will excuse it as a miraculous story of a man's will to live.

We carried on down the valley of towering trees listening to the roar of the river when I heard a clank and squeak noise that didn't fit. I turned up the ridge towards the noise and noticed a white junker Chevy Suburban rattling up a dirt road. "Hey there's the road up…" I yelled to Tilauth but couldn't find him. He was just in front of me a second ago as I spun around calling, "Tilauth?!? Where'd you go?" But he was no where in sight. "I almost half expected it," I thought as I looked deeper into the trees to see if maybe he was lingering around in there. I saw nothing. Tilauth mysteriously disappeared in my life as mysteriously as he appeared.

I stood there for awhile looking around me with the feeling that he was watching me. I finally gave up looking for him and decided that he wasn't much for goodbyes, so I yelled it, "See you later Tilauth." My voice was drowned out by the roar of the river. "Thank you my friend." I yelled but the last syllable fell quiet as a lump unexpectantly emerged in my throat. My eyes started to water as I wanted to tell Tilauth so desperately how much I appreciated what he did for me. I quickly wiped a tear from my eye as I turned around to the road. I felt embarrassed from my emotions and tried to hide them by walking purposefully up the ridge towards the road. I couldn't shake the feeling that he was watching me as I trudged up the steep embankment.

When I reached the gravel road the clunker Suburban had long gone. I headed down the road listening to the crackle of the gravel beneath my feet in rhythm with my steps. All the trees and plants were covered in a thin layer of dust from the cars whipping down the dirt road. The forest seemed different here. It felt as if the animals had abandoned this area. "Who could blame them," I thought, I wouldn't want to hang out around this road either.

I walked for what felt like miles before hearing the rumble of a car. Then a luxury SUV rounded the bend from behind me. I held out my thumb while they whipped by me leaving me coughing in a cloud of dust. They didn't even slow down in the slightest and I barely caught a glimpse of a man and woman in front with a child in back. The parents didn't even look at me while the child glued himself to the side window and spun around to see me coughing in the dust. I pulled the collar of my T-shirt up over my mouth so that I could breathe.

As the dust gradually settled leaving a thin white layer all over my body, I noticed my clothes. They were torn and blood stained and my hair must be sticking up like some wild bush man. "In this day and age people don't pick up hitch hikers, especially if they've got blood stains on their clothes," I thought. I continued down the road trying to guess how long it might be before I got to the small town of Index. It takes a long time in a car, so I can't imagine what it would be like on foot. I trudged on and the road finally turned to pavement. This was a welcome change. At least I could have cars whip past me without leaving me to swim through their clouds of dirt.

The pavement was nice at first until the soles of my feet began to ache. I walked in the dirt along the narrow winding road as more cars whipped past me making sure to not make eye contact with me. I felt like a ghost and began to wonder if I was a ghost.

What if I really had died up on the mountain and all that could see me was the gifted child with some sort of sixth sense in the back seat. I waved emphatically at cars as if I were having an emergency, which I thought would explain the blood on my clothes, but people just whizzed by leaving me to suck down their petrol fumes.

Then I heard a loud noise echoing through the forest. It was the unmistakable sound of an exhaust pipe full of holes. I heard the annoying noise growing nearer and nearer for five minutes before I actually saw the vehicle that sang the horrific noise. A raised 1980 Toyota pick up truck covered in mud from roof to tread, came leaning around the corner. I reluctantly waved them down in hopes for a ride. They came to a squeaking stop as the passenger rolled down his window and the dirt grinded down the window. "Hey man, don't roll down the window you'll scratch it," the driver yelled at the passenger. "Sorry man," the passenger said.

"Your stupid truck is a piece a shit anyways, what do you care if the window gets a scratch on it?" I heard a girl's voice come from the center.

The passenger cracked open the door and several Natural Ice cans clanked to the pavement. "Oops." the passenger said in a half-drunken laugh. He opened the door a little more and hopped out to pick up the cans. He bent over and bumped his head on the foot rail. I stood behind him watching as he comically tried to stand and slumped into the door "Ow, who put that..., thing there," he said rubbing his forehead. "Son of bitch – that hurt," he said as he turned to face me. He looked me up and down along with the girl in the center while the driver leaned forward to see me. The two guys wore baseball caps muddied jeans and tucked in T-shirts. The girl sat in the center with her fake blond hair giving me a look of concern only it was more of a concern for herself and not a concern for me.

"Holy shit man, you look like you had some fun last night. Damn!" he said as he swiveled around to look at the driver. "Where you headed buddy?" the driver spoke up. "Uh…, well I'm headed to Lynnwood." I told him not sure if I wanted a ride. "Christ's sakes, you're a long way from fuckin' Lynnwood." the passenger blurted as he tried to focus on me. "Hop in the back – we can take you to Start Up," the driver said.

I climbed up the back wheel as the passenger jumped into the cab again. It felt good to get off my feet and sit down. The truck sped off with a loud roar of the exhaust and the large mud tires spit out one of the beer cans with a tink, tink. I huddled in a ball up against the back of the cab as the wind whipped around my shoulders like ice. The ride back was a chilly one on a frigid June day. "Or was it July already?" I thought. I had no idea what day it was. All I knew was that it has been about a month since I left. Or at least that's the way it felt. It was tough to tell since I slept through so much of it.

The trees whipped by me in a blur of green and brown and I couldn't wait until we stopped. We rushed passed Index and headed west down Highway 2. The highway winded back and forth as drivers from behind stared at me huddled in the back protecting myself from the cold wind.

We finally reached Start Up where they dropped me off at a small beat up convenience store. I slowly got up moving as fast as I could with my frozen muscles. An ache shot through my stiff legs as I hopped out of the truck bed and landed on both feet from the raised pickup. I walked up to the drivers' side door where he cracked the door open and I said, "Thanks for the ride."

"No problem. I've been in your shoes before. Just remember to help someone else out when you get the chance," he suggested in his Good Samaritan tone.

"Say, do you got some change for the phone?," I

asked. He glanced at me for a moment as if he were trying to think of something but then he turned and I heard some change jingle as he grabbed some from the ashtray. He flipped a couple of quarters my way and I caught one and missed the other. I reached down to pick it up as they sped away with a loud call of their exhaust.

I turned to the shabby old store pasted with neon beer signs and noticed a graffiti covered phone towards the back. I walked over feeling more nervous than happy. I slid a coin in and hesitantly punched the numbers in. "What the heck am I going to say?" I thought. "Hey mom what's up?" or "Hey dad how's that deck coming along?" I punched in the final numbers and it started to ring. My heart pounded and my chest tightened. "Why am I so nervous?" I thought. I couldn't put my finger on it, but then I heard my moms' voice, "Hi, sorry we couldn't make it to the phone – leave your name and number and we'll call you back". Her voice seemed stressed and tired. It beeped in my ear, "Uhhh... hey it's me, I'm stuck at a pay phone in Start Up. Uh... give me a call at..." I turned to look at the phone number on the phone and it was covered with some mysterious hard crusty stuff. I tried to scrape it off but it wouldn't come off, "Well... I can't read this number but I'm in Start Up, right off Highway 2 at a convenience store called-" I pulled my head back to read the sign and the phone ripped out my hand and clanked against the post. I picked the phone back up, "I'm at the Snack Attack Quickie Mart. If someone could come - pick me up, that would be - great." I said non-chalantly. "I'll see you soon - hopefully." I added and hung up.

I turned around and walked over to the curb and sat down. I rested my chin on my arms and waited. "This wasn't quite how I imagined things would go, but oh well," I thought.

I sat for hours watching the cars fly down the

highway as the locals stared at me as they walked by. They probably thought I was just another runaway or drifter making my way to somewhere unknown. The sky darkened and a fluorescent light clicked on above me with a buzz. My eyes closed and I started to drift off to sleep. I was quickly awakened by a loud howl of some tires screeching to a halt in the highway. I looked up to see a van popping it in reverse and I saw my mother with tear stained eyes in the passenger seat. My father sped into the parking lot and they rushed out and we embraced each other. My brother popped out of the van too and he gave me a hug. The looks on their faces brought tears to my eyes and my nervousness melted away as we climbed back into the van and went home.

I explained to my family the story I worked out before hand, of my survival while my dad called my sisters and relatives to tell them that I was alive. Questions fired at me like, "Didn't you hear us calling?" or "Did you see the search helicopters?" I answered them as truthfully as I could yet I made sure to leave out the fact that Tilauth helped me. My brother asked me how it felt to have a tombstone and live to talk about it. We laughed and we cried the whole way home.

My sisters were waiting for me when we got home and I went through the story again with my hugs and tears. Finally after awhile they let me go to sleep. My bed never felt so comfortable and I felt truly happy inside. I slipped off into a much needed sleep right after I said a little prayer of thanks for Tilauth. I was already starting to miss my new friend.

Chapter 10
The Lie

The next morning I awoke to a knock at my door and saw my grandma and some other friends and family. My niece flew in jumped on the bed and tackled me. She hugged me tightly and my heart soared. I went through the same conversations as the night before, with my hair shooting off in every direction like a wild man. My dad came in and said that we needed to head down to the police station and tell them what happened. I took a nice hot shower and put on some clean clothes.

We headed down to the station while I stared out the window thinking about Tilauth and wondering what he might be doing. "What are you thinking about?" my dad asked. I snapped out of my trance, "Nothing...I'm just glad to be back." He smiled at me in agreement and we continued to the station in silence.

At the station we walked up to the front desk and we were asked to wait in the waiting room. I watched the second hand lag its way around the clock, when a hefty man in a cheap brown suit waddled out. "Are you Neal Forester?" he said looking at me.

"Yeah." I replied.

"I'm detective Wittenberg. Could you follow me please," he asked as we got up and started for the back offices. He stopped in his tracks and saw my dad following, "Actually sir if you could just wait out here. I'd like to talk to Neal alone for a moment." My dad nodded, a little confused and headed back to the waiting room. "Thank you sir," the detective said as he spun around and I followed him through a sea of desks and fluorescent lights that loomed overhead. Several of the men stared at me with their sunken eyes from behind their steel framed desks. We shuffled across the cold white tile floor until we came to what I assumed was detective Wittenberg's' desk. He motioned for me to have a seat in the metal fold out chair as he sat down in his wooden reclining desk chair with a squeak.

"So Neal, your folks uh... picked you up last night at a small store in Start Up?" he asked. Every time he made an 's' sound a whistle would come out. Distracted for a moment by the whistle, "Uh – yeah that's correct," I replied as he studied me carefully. "Well first of all, I'm glad you're ok," he said in a feeble attempt to sound like he cared.

"Thank you," I said dryly.

"You want to tell me what happened?" He said, cutting to the chase.

I relayed to him the whole story of how I fell down the mountainside, broke my arm, sprained an ankle, bruised, and cut myself up pretty good. I told him how I was knocked unconscious for an undeterminable amount of time before waking up to my mangled body. I explained how I hopped and crawled to a nearby stream where I got water, made a small shelter, and mended myself back together before walking out of the forest.

Detective Wittenberg leaned back in his rickety chair with his chin resting in his hand and his elbow securely placed on the wooden arm rest. His large belly swung out in front of me as he swiveled back and forth in his chair scrutinizing me. He had a grey curly afro that no doubt had been styled like that since the early seventies, only presently the top was bald and the afro shot out around his head in the shape of a horse shoe. His index finger tapped his lip as he decided what he thought of my whole story.

I got the feeling that Detective Wittenberg was trying to intimidate me. His meager attempt was humoring me rather than threatening although, I was beginning to wonder if he was able to pick out the slight modifications of the truth. The detective sat forward with the squeak of his chair and he rested his elbows on the table. "Do you have any idea what it costs to fly search helicopters and send out search and rescue and police forces to look for someone for weeks," he said with a series of whistles? I shrugged my shoulders and shook my head no. "The paperwork alone on your missing person's case is unimaginable." I could feel him trying to intimidate me. "After not finding or hearing from you in over a month we have to rule out foul play, suicide, etc, etc... Do you know what your stunt has cost our department alone?" he asked

"It wasn't a stunt! I..." I replied feeling a little taken back.

"Don't give me that shit! Your arm was never broken", as his eyes glanced at it. I looked down at my arm and rubbed it with the other hand noticing that it didn't hurt.

"Look, I know it doesn't look broken - I guess... I just...heal fast," I weakly retorted.

"Look Mr. Forester, you want me to write in our file explaining that you claimed to have broken your arm, sprained your ankle and completely healed in a month because you're a fast healer," he said sarcastically.

I nodded, "Yes, because that's what happened."

"And what do you think the general public will think when the press finds out?" he said continuing to drill me with twisting hand gestures that completely annoyed me.

"I couldn't care less about what the public thinks

about it," I said with annoyance.

"Really?!?" he leaned back in his chair scrutinizing me.

"Really!"

"Isn't that why you did it?" he asked.

"Did what?"

"To get attention! Isn't that what you want... attention from your family and the public?"

"No!"

"Well, you have our attention – so what is it that's so important that we have to send search crews, helicopters, and planes out looking for you. What is it that you want to tell us and the rest of the world?" he said resting his cheek on his hand in a gesture of boredom.

"Look I have nothing to say. I don't need attention. This wasn't some stunt to get attention," I defended myself.

"Well, I'm sorry Mr. Forester, but that's what it looks like to me and I think Joe Shmoe on the street is going to agree. So...do you want to tell me the truth?"

"That is the truth!" I yelled. Other detectives in the sea of desks stopped their work and turned to look at me. He stared at me allowing me time to consider telling him the truth. A whole minute passed with us staring at each other. "I've told you the truth and I have nothing more to say. Am I being charged with something?" I asked, feeling the anger well up inside of me.

"No..."

"Then can I go?"

"You're free to go. Take my card in case you remember anything you forgot to tell me," he said handing me his card. I swiped it out of his hand and quickly made my way past the desks and through the door. The door flung open and slammed into the wall. I could feel their eyes in my back as they all watched me leave.

I was infuriated. The last thing I expected was to be interrogated like that. It takes a lot to get me angry and Detective Wittenberg went straight for my buttons. I have no tolerance for people who judge me or make assumptions about me and Wittenberg went straight for the judgments.

I went home talked to more family but I just wanted to be alone. I went to my room shut the door and closed myself off from the world. I sat in there for maybe ten minutes before I decided to hop in my car now sitting in the driveway and go for a drive. My mom called out asking where I was headed and I said, "Just for a drive, I'll be back soon." I could tell she was going to be a little more concerned as to my whereabouts from now on.

I fired up the old Jeep and headed to work of all places. I figured I'd better stop by and make sure they hadn't already replaced me. I walked in the door with a beep and the front desk person, Vangie, leapt backwards from where she was standing and let out a gasp. "Holy..." she stopped herself from swearing in front of the patients. I just smiled and said, "Hey, how's it going?" I said enjoying the shock treatment I was giving her.

"What the - How the – How are you here?" she asked perplexed.

"Don't I work here?" I said sarcastically.

"Well yes – but you're supposed to be dead. Everyone thought you were dead."

"Nope," I said simply. "Is the doc around or is he busy with patients?"

"He's supposed to back any minute from his lunch."

"Fine, I'll wait." I sat down at my old desk and peeked around. I could tell Vangie had been doing my job for the time being. Her notes were everywhere and everything was scattered in inexplicable piles. "Sorry I made a mess, I was trying to figure out how to do your job," she said looking at me expecting me to be angry. "Oh, it's fine. I'll figure it out," I reassured her.

I heard the door beep and Vangie went to see who it was that came in. I heard her say, "Uh, Doctor Pell – I think you might want to come back here for a second." There was a pause of silence then I saw Dr. Pell come around the corner with leftovers from his lunch in a plastic doggie bag.

"Whoa!" he said turning back to Vangie then back to me. "You a ghost or something," he said half joking and half serious.

"No, I'm real," I said pinching myself in the shoulder.

"Well okay then," he said turning back and forth in amazement between Vangie and me.

"Is my job still...mine?" I asked, feeling strange about the question.

"Uh...of course...well we haven't hired anyone else yet. We'll have to remove the want ad from the paper," he said still looking surprised and perplexed. His lunch bag was swinging around in circles bouncing off his thigh and bumping into the wall as he twisted back in forth in confusion. "Say, what happened? I thought the coyotes must have gotten to you?" he asked. I told him the same story I told everyone else. Vangie and Dr. Pell looked at me in astonishment. "Which reminds me doc, I was wondering if you would take a look at my arm and ankle to make sure everything's healing ok?" I asked him. "Uh, no problem - of course – I'll take you back right now," he said, giving me special treatment, that I can only assume he must have felt obligated to do.

The doc and I headed back to the x-ray room and he took a couple of pictures of my arm and he wanted one of my ankle. He did some range of motion tests, checked my vitals, and did a basic physical.

"Well your ankle seems to have healed up pretty

quickly, so it must have been a minor sprain," the doc said as he looked perplexingly at my ankle. He started to palpate my forearm and take it through its range of motion. "Do you get any pain when I do this," he twisted my wrist slightly.

"No."

"How about this", he twisted it the other direction.

"Nope," I said. He clicked on the light behind the x-rays he snapped of my ankle and forearm. We both scrutinized them carefully.

"There doesn't appear to be any fractures with any of the bones in your ankle from what I can tell," he said as he moved to my forearm x-rays and began examining them carefully. After a few moments of looking at the different angle of pictures he said,

"Your forearm doesn't appear to be fractured either." He turned to look at me with furrowed brows. He turned back to the x-ray, and moved his eyes closer to one particular shot. With a pen he made a tiny mark and said, "It appears that it may have been fractured here at one time," motioning to the area with his pen. "However, this fracture appears to be fully healed and almost unnoticeable. Have you fractured this arm before?" he asked looking back at me.

"I've never broken a bone in my life."

"Well..." he turned to look back at the x-ray. "Well it's virtually impossible for you to have fractured this bone and have it mend this fully in the amount of time that you've been gone," he said looking at me with bewilderment.

"That's weird!?!," I replied, knowing full well why the bone has healed so quickly.

"A fracture of this magnitude," he pointed to the bone again, "would need nothing less of a miracle to heal that quickly."

"Well I don't know. I am positive that it was broken. I heard a loud pop and my arm gave way and bent in an unnatural way. The pain and swelling I had, was right where you describe the fracture to have been. I pulled the arm straight by pinning my hand between my other hand and the ground," I said, adding a new lie. "So I must have reset it and it healed that fast," I said trying to give my story some credibility. Dr. Pell studied me for a long while, then turned and studied the x-ray again.

"Well I guess I don't know what to say. The idea of you resetting your own arm out in the middle of the woods isn't necessarily impossible but the fact that it was reset perfectly and it healed so quickly without a cast I might add, is unfathomable!" He looked at me for a response.

"Well I guess I don't know what to say – I guess the unfathomable is what has happened." We sat there in silence for a bit while Dr. Pell wrote a few notes in my chart.

"Well Neal, you seem to be in extremely good health, all things considering."

"Thanks doc. I'll start back to work tomorrow?"

"That should be fine. I'll see you tomorrow then," the doc said as we got up and exited the room.

I left work feeling a little unnerved about how my partially true story was going over with everyone. I couldn't change my story now after I'd told everyone the same thing including the detective.

I swung by the college to make sure I was still enrolled in my classes. It appeared that it was going to be up to each professor as to whether or not I would have to retake the class since I missed so many days. My stomach started to feel knotted up inside at the idea of getting back into the same old grind. The last thing I wanted to do was continue with my ordinary boring life but what other options did I have, I asked myself.

My mind went fluttering back to the time I'd spent with Tilauth in the forest. I longed for our

conversations and his simple company. He had a way
of taking away the complexities of life and leaving
nothing but the simple joy of living. I began to think
about how he explained to me that my mind, body, and
spirit were all messed up. He told me that it was fear
that has broken these three things far apart and this
is why I'm dying. Just then an idea popped into my
head.

Chapter 11
Old Grinding Stone

I'm going to go to where I first saw Tilauth. I drove straight to that beach where I saw him standing, so many months ago. I'm not sure what it was that I was thinking but maybe I was hoping. I was hoping that I might see him there and maybe... I guess I don't know. I guess I thought he could continue to show me his way of life. It was becoming painfully obvious that I needed a teacher of some sort. Not just any teacher, but a teacher like Tilauth. Tilauth is a teacher who could teach me how to live my life with some kind of purpose. I feel like my experience with Tilauth was just a glimpse of what I needed to put an end to my ordinary life.

On a July afternoon, I walked out onto the beach where I saw Tilauth for the first time. I walked out there and stood exactly where Tilauth stood. Scanning down the beach I could see a middle aged woman walking her chocolate Labrador, a mother sitting on a picnic table watching her three kids play wildly throwing sand at each other, and a young couple most likely skipping school, lay cuddled up to each other with their heads resting on a piece of driftwood. The other half of the beach remained empty except for a young Asian man practicing Tai Chi while balancing on a log. I watched him for a few moments as he moved slowly in a flowing motion. The wind picked up but he remained perfectly balanced, as if he were part of the log.

I glanced over to where I had fallen asleep when I first heard the words 'You are dying.' I strolled over there thinking that if I was in the right spot, I may see Tilauth again. The idea was stupid and I knew it, but I was desperate. I sat in the same spot and looked around to see that nothing had changed. I decided that I was going to lie down and try and fall asleep. If I fell asleep, perhaps this would somehow bring Tilauth to the beach. I laid down feeling the soft sand spread out behind my head as the bright sun warmed my body. The waves crashed on the shore and I felt my body relax. I must've laid there for about three minutes when I suddenly stood up. "Nothing..." I thought. "And why would there be something." I walked quickly off the beach feeling like an idiot. How can recreating a situation actually bring someone there? The thought was ludicrous. I drove home, had some dinner, talked with my mom for a bit, and then went to bed.

The next day I went to work bright and early. The sun was out and the air was crisp. Being the first one there, I unlocked the front door, flipped on the lights, and disarmed the security system. Slowly my coworkers streamed in one by one saying, "Welcome back Neal," as I began to make sense of all the piles of papers. My mind got lost in the work and I forgot about my unhappiness for a moment.

Just as I was about to break for lunch, Vangie peaked her head into my office and said, "Neal there's a phone call for you on line two." She noticed that I was slipping on a jacket and grabbing my keys, "do you want me to take a message."

"No, I'll take it," I said with a moment's hesitation. "Hello, this is Neal."

"Hi Neal, this is Janice Templeton with the Seattle Messenger," a pleasant voice came out from the other end.

"I'm sorry Janice but we're not interested in the paper. Thank you." Relentless telemarketers, I thought.

"No Neal, I'm not trying to sell you a subscription," she quickly said trying to catch me before I hung up. "uh...I would actually like to talk to you about your experience in the Cascade Mountains." I didn't say anything as I began to think about the idea of my story being in the newspaper. "I'm a journalist Neal, and I would like to do a story on what happened to you."

"I don't know. I'd think I'd rather just let it be in the past."

"Neal you don't understand. You survived in the mountains where at points it had dropped below freezing. Your story was in the newspapers and all the major TV crews where covering the events while you were missing. The public is dying to know what had happened to you. Did you know that they aired on several channels last night that you were still alive?" she asked.

"No. I don't watch a whole lot of TV," I said feeling nervous.

"Well Neal, I'd like to give you the opportunity to tell your story." My mind reeled around in circles and my stomach turned over at the thought of so much attention. But I thought this may give me the opportunity to solidify my story and throw it back in the detectives' face. "I guess I'm not really interested in creating so much racket with this whole thing. I don't like attention, especially for something so tiny," I said.

"So tiny!?! Neal what you've been through couldn't have been 'tiny'. Surviving in the woods with injuries for a month is far from tiny. You have to tell the public how you did it; otherwise they will be left to make all kinds of assumptions." This suddenly strummed a chord with me. The last thing I wanted was for people to make assumptions like the way the detective did.

"All right I'll do it," I said feeling even more nervous now that I'd committed to it.

"Great Neal, I'd like to meet with you today if that's possible?"

"Well, I've got classes after work so I'm actually pretty busy till about eleven thirty tonight."

"Are you taking a lunch break today?"

"Yeah, I was about to take one right now, actually."

"How about I meet you wherever you're going to lunch?"

"Uh...sure...I was planning on heading to Osaka Teriyaki in Lynnwood."

"I know the place. I'll meet you in ten." I heard the phone click and I got the feeling she was farther away then ten minutes.

My instincts were correct. I waited fifteen minutes after I arrived at the restaurant before I decided to order without her. My food came and I picked up the chopsticks and began eating without her.

Then the front door flew open and a woman with sandy blonde hair, a white button up collard shirt, and black pleated slacks quickly scanned the room. Her eyes fixed on me and with a smile she weaved around the tables directly for me. "Hi Neal, I'm Janice," she said as she extended a hand with long slender fingers out to me. "Hi Janice," I said shaking her hand.

"I guess you know what I look like," I said feeling a little strange.

"Neal, the whole northwest knows what you look like. You picture was strewn across every news channel in the hopes of finding you."

"I suppose so," I said as I looked around wondering if others recognized me. "Would you like something to eat?" I asked.

"No, I'm fine," she said as she waved a hand and pulled out a small tape recorder and notepad with pen. I could tell she was overworked and had little time for bare necessities like eating. "So Neal, tell me in your own words what happened."

I told her the whole story leaving Tilauth out of course. I told her about my injuries and some of the things that I did to survive. She listened intently scribbling down things in her notepad hardly taking her eyes off of me. I told her how I hitched a ride to Start Up and waited by a phone until my family came to pick me up.

When I was finished she continued to scribble down notes. Then she looked at me, appearing a little confused. "Neal, you mentioned that you broke your arm."

"Yes," I said already knowing where this was going.

"How come you're not in a cast now?" she asked.

"I had the doctor look at it yesterday and he said it was for the most part...my arm is fully healed."

"And your ankle?"

"Healed too. I think I'm a fast healer," I said in my defense.

"I see – so you have no pain at all?"

"For the most part no – I'm doing pretty good."

"Well...that's amazing," she paused as she considered everything. "So...what do you do at the doctors' office?"

"I'm the manager of their insurance billing department."

"And what are you studying in college?"

"My major is in accounting."

"What do you do for fun?"

"Well I like to hike as you know, and I've always enjoyed acting in school plays."

"Acting," she nodded as her bottom lip pushed into the upper lip in seeming surprised and interested.

"Neal are you a middle child in your family?" she asked.

"What does that have to do with the story?" I asked quizzically.

"It's just some basic background questions to help me with the piece."

"Uh... yes I'm a middle child." I hesitantly answered.

"Everything good at home, at work, and in school?"

"Mrs. Templeton, I don't see how this has to do with the story!?!" I asked feeling more uncomfortable.

"Don't worry. I just want to use it to help the readers understand who you are. When I write a piece I try to give the reader a clear understanding of the kind of person I'm writing about. It will give your story a certain credibility and readability when they can put themselves in your shoes," she explained.

"I see," I said keying in on the credibility.

I don't think people would believe me even if I did tell the truth about Tilauth and how he helped me. If I lied or told the truth I'm sure my story is going to seem like it's got some holes. "Ok...uh...my family life is ok, work's ok, and school's ok," I answered feeling like I hadn't a choice.

"Just ok," she restated my answer.

"Yeah, it's just ok. I mean there's nothing special or unique about it – In fact it's kind of...boring. There's really not a whole lot of excitement in my life aside from the experience I had in the Cascade Mountains. Life in general, seems to be about making enough money to pay the next set of monthly bills. So I'm going to college to hopefully get a higher paying job so I can pay for higher monthly bills and maybe a week long vacation per year that is, if I'm lucky. The whole idea of making it 'big' in today's world has the same amount of excitement as watching paint dry. Sometimes I think I'd rather stick a pencil in my eye than to go about life the way I do," I said suddenly realizing that I may have said too much after looking at Janice's face. She paused for an unnerving amount of time taking in what I so loosely babbled out. "Ok," she finally broke the silence, "Well I think that's everything I need. It was nice to meet you Neal and I appreciate you giving me your time." She extended her hand out for me to shake.

"Sure, it was nice to meet you too," I said shaking her hand.

"Bye now."

"Bye." I said watching her weave through the tables for the door.

I finished up my meal feeling a little uneasy about the whole interview. I shook off the feeling, went back to work, made some phone calls, finished up some paperwork, and went to my classes. Every single one of my teachers told me that I was going to need to redo the course. Missing a month of class was too much to try and catch up they all exclaimed. "Great", I thought, "there goes a big chunk of my tuition already paid, down the drain." I went home drank myself silly in front of the TV and passed out on my bed.

Chapter 12
Love and Hate

I awoke to the screaming of my alarm and a pounding in my head. I slapped my alarm in hopes of hitting the right button to bring back the silence. I sat up on the side of my bed and my head pounded harder. I winced in pain with every beat of my heart. I walked straight for the aspirin in the medicine cabinet. I caught a glimpse of myself in the mirror with hair sticking straight out in all directions and my eyes were red like a fire truck.

I chewed down the aspirin and showered in a hopeful attempt to make myself presentable for work. By the time I got dressed my headache had begun to wear off and I hopped in my Jeep and headed off to work. This time I wasn't the first one to arrive at work. Vangie, Dr. Pell, and the X-Ray tech Elly were already there. I walked in the door with a beep and saw Vangie at the front desk. She forced a smile across her face and greeted me with a, "Morning...Neal."

"Morning." I noticed Elly and Dr. Pell were both looking at me strangely. I walked passed them, "Morning guys," I said shrugging off their strange looks. I went back to my office and took off my jacket. I glanced at my 'to do bin' when I noticed a large picture of myself in the corner of my eye. I turned to see Elly standing there in a tweed skirt holding up a newspaper in front of her. "Neal, you might want to take a look at this paper if you haven't already," she said in a concerned tone.

"Damn, that's a big picture," I said pulling the newspaper closer to me. "I told the journalist that I didn't want a lot of attention with this."

"Trust me, Neal, that's the last thing you're going to be concerned about. Look at the headline," she said pointing to the large print front and center.

A Miraculous Story of Survival or a Cry For Attention? The headline emblazoned in my eyes. My heart dropped to the floor and my gut twisted into knots. I looked up at Elly briefly to see her concerned eyes, expecting me to do something.

"What the hell did she write?" I said as I sat down to read it. "It's not good Neal. She's making you out like some crazed lunatic in search of attention in some boring pathetic life. Then her voice dropped down to a whisper, "Dr. Pell isn't very happy by the way." I looked up at her to see her eyebrows lift in concern. She's quoted you saying that you'd rather stick a pencil in your eye than go to work and school," Elly said wincing at what she was saying. "She's taking what I said out of context!" I exclaimed. "It's...horse-!" I stopped myself short and continued to read the article. The article begins with;

> *Neal Forester, a college student, works in a doctor's clinic he refers to as "boring" returns from the Cascade Mountains two days ago after he claims to have survived a sprained ankle, broken forearm, and a concussion and a month in the mountains without provisions. He had no medical attention, no food, no shelter, and no treated water readily available to him. Is this all an elaborate hoax designed to create some excitement in his life and draw some attention his way? Neal has described to me that his life lacks excitement and his family, school, and job are boring. He has reportedly said, "There's really not a*

*whole lot of excitement in my life aside from my experience
I had in the Cascade Mountains." And "Sometimes I think
I'd rather stick a pencil in my eye than to go about life the
way I do." Here is his story, you be the judge.*

"Elly, this story is completely taking my words out of context!"

"It gets worse Neal, keep reading," she points back to the paper. I reluctantly turned back and continued to read the article which went on explaining the story I told Janice yesterday. After the journalist explained my story she pulled in some random doctor which said it was virtually impossible to fully heal from a fractured forearm and a sprained ankle in less than a month. The journalist then condescended me with my statement about being a fast healer. She also got quotes from the general public calling me all kinds of names from 'spoiled brat' to 'he's a disgrace to this community'. Janice commented on how I was trained in acting throughout high school and college providing me with the capability of fooling a lot of people. But the worst of it came when she got a quote from a psychiatrist who said, "It is not unusual for someone who is disappointed and bored with their life to do something elaborate like this. People who are bored and reclusive like Neal often turn out to be our next serial killers or major law offenders. People like Neal will need to step it up a notch each time progressively becoming a major threat to themselves and the general public." Horrifically the article went on explaining how much the county spent in the search efforts and were considering pressing charges for the full amount. The county was unsure however, if they could prove their case, due to the lack of witnesses.

I sat back in my chair, pushing myself away from the article as the wheels slowly squeaked. "Neal - what is the truth?" Elly asked. "I mean...what are you going to do? This article has painted you out to be the world‚s next…serial killer for God sake!."

"I don't know what I'm going to do." I said throwing my hands in the air with disgust. "I mean, what the hell can I do? This woman has completely twisted my words around. The truth is…" my chest deflated in defeat. "Nobody will believe the truth anyway." I said quietly but just loud enough for her to hear. Her head pushed forward as she struggled to hear my words. She stepped closer to me and with her piercing blue eyes she looked directly into mine and said, "Neal- you're not telling the truth? You have to tell the truth or this article is going to ruin your life. You will always be known as the crazy guy who pretended to be lost to get attention. You have to tell them what really happened Neal," she said grabbing my shoulders as she squatted down in front of me. "I promised I wouldn't say anything," I said feeling her soft eyes pierce me with concern. She paused for a moment trying to figure out why I would promise someone under my circumstances. "Well…is the promise worth keeping if it's going to ruin your life?"

"Yes…actually. I owe…" I cut myself short. "The truth is even more unbelievable than the lie…I've said too much already. Elly promise me you won't say anything I've already told you." Her hands pulled away from my shoulders. "Neal," she pleaded. "I don't think you're making the right decision – but I don't understand the circumstances. Obviously if you're willing to ruin your life over a promise – it must be really important. So I promise, your secret is safe with me but I don't think it's much of a secret since the whole world is going to think you're not telling the truth anyways."

"No – I mean about lying in order to keep a promise."

"I've never known you to be so honorable when it came to promises. But if that's what you want – I promise."

"Thanks Elly."

She wrapped her arms around me and I almost broke into tears. All the emotions in my life, and now this article was bringing me to the verge of exploding in grief. I sucked back my tears as Elly pulled away and studied me closely with her deep blue eyes. "You call me if you need anything ok?" she said. I took a deep breath feeling that if I spoke I'd lose it. "Tell me you'll call."

"I'll call." I managed to say.

"And I mean for anything - I like talking to you anyways." I glanced up to her eyes to see her smiling warmly back at me. I could feel my heart jump and pull as I saw her pretty eyes comforting me. "Thanks Elly," I said. She rubbed my shoulder and walked out of the room.

I could sense a brief silence outside my office as Elly walked out. She was no doubt silently gesturing to Vangie not to bother me. I took a deep breath and tried to push the story out of my mind. I shuffled through some papers trying to focus but I couldn't get my head away from the article.

Slumped over at my desk, Dr. Pell walks in. I immediately jump into action in a pathetic attempt to appear hard at work by moving stuff around. I could hear Dr. Pell sigh, "Neal, why don't you take the day off. Come back tomorrow when your head can be in the game." I turned my head slightly enough to see him behind me in my peripheral vision.

"Sorry about all of this, Doc. I had no idea that this would get so twisted around. I'll be here tomorrow," I said as I put on my jacket.

"Things will die down I'm sure Neal. It will just take some time," Dr. Pell said trying to comfort me.

"I hope so," I said as I walked out the office and headed for my car.

I drove straight home to an empty house and flipped on the TV to get my mind off of things. I flipped through the day time soaps until I found the Travel Channel. I watched the top ten beaches of the world count down and wished that I was at any of them.

I fell asleep on the couch for a couple of hours before waking to a loud commercial. I looked at the clock, stretched, and strolled into the kitchen to make some lunch. As I reheated some spaghetti in the microwave I heard my name come out from the TV. My heart sank at the thought and I raced back in the living room to see the news anchorman reporting the update on my story.

"Neal Forester was thought to be lost and to have most likely died in the Mt. Baker National Forest when he went hiking over a month ago. It appears that Neal has returned from the forest with a story that has local authorities questioning if he is telling the truth or if this is all an elaborate hoax for reasons unknown."

Detective Wittenberg pops up on the screen, "We are still investigating the situation and there is the possibility that Neal may be facing some charges. That is however, still under investigation."

My accounting teacher then appears on the screen, "Neal has always been a pretty good student of mine, no complaints. I guess you can never can tell with the quiet types, however. He told me that he had broken his arm, suffered a concussion, and sprained an ankle. I didn't think anything about it at the time but now I'm wondering why he seemed to be in pretty good health. His arm wasn't in a cast or anything. His story does seem to be a little fishy."

A news woman popped on the screen standing in front of the trail head that I hiked down before I met Tilauth.

"Neal was reported missing on June 9th after he told family members that he was going hiking down this trail head. Search and rescue crews along with friends and

relatives searched for a couple of weeks coming up with nothing. Temperatures had dropped below freezing most of those nights leaving the search crews with little hope for Neal's survival. After two long weeks search crews called off the search and a funeral was held a week later. One week after Neal's funeral, he makes a call from a pay phone in the small town of Start Up off of Highway 2. Neal told authorities that he had fallen off the trail, broken his arm, sprained an ankle, and suffered a major blow to his head knocking him on conscious. He then claimed that he managed to survive by mending himself back together and walked out of the forest, where he then hitch-hiked to Start Up. The hole in Neal's story is not only is his tale a miraculous one of survival, but doctors say that he couldn't have possibly healed as fast as he claims. This has left the authorities extremely speculative and many search and rescue crews upset.

An elderly man dressed in a flannel shirt, suspenders, jeans, and a beard appears on the screen. "I volunteer for Search and Rescue every time someone goes missing out here in the Cascades Mountains. I donate my time and put my blood, sweat, and tears into each search. I spent two weeks straight in the rain and cold in those mountains searching for this joker and this is the thanks I get!?! It's bull$#?!" The network bleeps out his profanities.

I turned off the TV and sat on the couch in complete awe of what was happening. "This can't be," I thought. Just then the silence was interrupted by the phone ringing. I dragged my lifeless body to the phone, "Hello..." "Is this Neal?" a rough voice hammered through the phone. "Speaking..."

"You're a spoiled rotten piece of shit. You go to hell."

"Who is this?" I hear them hang up. I checked the caller ID to see the words Unknown Listing.

This is insanity. I had no idea that this whole thing would get blown this far out of proportion. If Tilauth knows anything about this, I'm sure he'd be sitting there laughing his guts out. I could actually see his deep eyes watching the whole thing and giggling like a child. This thought infuriated me to no end. I started to wonder if Tilauth knew that this would happen and had somehow planned the whole thing like some oversized elaborate prank. I could hear his giggling inside of me and I got more pissed off.

I spent the next couple of hours thinking about Tilauth and wondering how he could have pulled it off. My mind banged around many different possibilities and all that was left was Tilauth snickering at my misfortune, whether he planned it or not. Every moment passed and my agitation grew to anger with every thought. I decided to stop thinking about it and try and catch up on some sleep. I unplugged the phone and passed out on the couch. I fell into a deep sleep and disappeared from the world.

My dreams swirled with long giant pieces of tensile and kids playing on bikes. I could feel the childhood freedom and the impression of flexibility that a child has. You can throw just about anything at a child and they will bounce back stronger. As humans grow older they become more rigid with age and less resilient. I awoke feeling refreshed and decided to embrace my situation rather than to reject it. I will start by plugging the phone back in.

The moment I plugged it in, the phone rang. The ring startled me and I hit my head on the bottom of the counter. I got up rubbing my head grimacing out profanities as the phone continued to chime away. I took a deep breath and picked up the receiver and said nothing. Then I heard a familiar voice, "Neal? Are you there?" I could hear a tinge of concern in her voice. "I'm here Elly." I said.

"Thank God. I've been calling you over and over again and your answering machine doesn't pick up. I was beginning to think that something may be wrong."

her voice sounded relieved.

"No, I'm fine. I unplugged the phone cuz..." I stopped myself from explaining everything. There was a moment of silence and I could tell she was trying to put things together. "Well I'm glad you're ok. Well maybe not all ok but at least not...something terribly wrong." she stumbled through her words.

"No I'm fine. I took and nap and actually I feel pretty good. Well, all except for my head. I smacked it on the bottom of the counter when the phone rang as soon as I plugged it in." I rubbed it feeling a goose egg of a bump beginning to form. "Ohhh, I'm sorry. I didn't know." she said.

"It's ok."

"So what are you doing right now?" she asked.

"Well, I'm rubbing my head and talking to you." I said sarcastically.

"I...I know you're talking to me." she laughed. "What are you doing in say the next ten minutes?" she decided to be more specific.

"I don't know." I said looking around the house for something that I was supposed to do.

"Well do you want to head out for a few drinks?" she asked.

"Sure." I said quickly.

"Good, shall I pick you up?" she asked.

"I can pick you up Elly, it's no problem," I offered.

"Ok." I could sense a hidden burst of excitement in her voice.

"So is this, like a date then?" I asked, enjoying making her feel uncomfortable.

"Uh...well no...it's like a date but it's not actually a date."

"So it's like a date?"

"Uh...Yeah."

"So does that mean we're pretending to go on a date?" I asked digging at the issue.

"Uh...sure." her voice quivered with nervousness.

"All right, I'll be over in ten for our pretend date."
I said. She finally laughed a little and said, "Good, I'll
see you then."

We hung up the phone and I quickly changed my
clothes and cleaned myself up. I drove over to Elly's
house and knocked on the door. Her sister answered
it. She stood tall in the doorway and smirked at me
obviously knowing what I was going through. "Hi
Neal," she said opening the door wider to let me in.
"Hi Eve, how are things?" I asked.

"They're good, and you?" a sudden panic look
spread across her face as she tried to pull back her
words.

"I'm good, all things considered."

Her face relaxed. "Well...that's good," she said.
"Elly" she yelled up the stairs, "Neal's here." She
turned and motioned for me to come in and have a
seat. I sat on an old beat up couch. The house was
filled with healthy plants and old hippy décor. Elly's
mom was an old hippy raising three girls by herself.
The house was simple yet very cozy and clean.

Elly came down the stairs with her eyes glancing
at her feet as she gracefully placed each foot on a
stair. Time seemed to slow down in my head like it
does in the movies and soft sound of a flute echoed
through my head. Her eyes pulled up to meet mine
and she smiled softly sending shivers down my spine.
She reached the bottom of the stairs, "Are you ready
to go?" she asked. I stared at her in silence with an
obvious gawking expression. I managed to snap out
of it before embarrassing myself too horribly, "Yes, are
you ready?"

"More than ever...let's go." she said as went out the
door and jumped in the Jeep.

The Jeep rattled off. "You look nice." I said
complimenting her.

"Thank you, you don't look so bad yourself."

"Thanks, but I feel like shit."

"Well you look pretty good, all things considering."

"Thanks." I said smiling at her.

"How does 'The Sail Inn' sound for drinks?"

"I couldn't think of a better place," I said. I could see her fidget in her seat in the corner of my eye. "You okay?"

"I'm fine. I guess I'm just a little nervous," she said as she flashed me a nervous smile.

"Yeah?"

"Yeah."

"I suppose I'm a little nervous too," I said realizing that I felt nervous and to comfort her.

"What do you have to be nervous about?" she said smiling at me as she pried to the heart of things.

"I suppose the same reason why you're nervous," I said avoiding the question.

"And how do you know what I'm nervous about?" she said grinning from ear to ear.

"Well I don't suppose I really know but I assume it's because were going on this pretend first date."

She laughed. "We are a couple of weirdos, you know?"

"Yeah, especially me. I go out in the mountains, get lost, come back and lie about it, and then I go on this massive rampage killing people in hopes to get attention," I said sarcastically. We both laughed.

We walked into the seaside smoke-filled bar with dozens of taps. It was crowded but we managed to find a small table in the corner where we could hang out and talk. The bar was filled with some familiar faces from my high school years and lots of seaward fisherman and their weathered faces. The few people that I recognized gave me quick glances looking away quickly. I could see them in the corners of my eyes as they whispered to their friends and they'd look by pretending not to look. I decided to ignore them and give my full attention to Elly.

The waitress came up, a sandy blonde heavy set girl I remember seeing in the hallways at high school. Her eyes peeked up at us, "Do you guys need dinner menus?" she asked. I glanced at Elly as she shook her head no. "We'll have just a pitcher of Red Stripe." The waitress suddenly recognized me and thought about saying something, but quickly changed her mind and walked away saying, "I'll be right back with that pitcher."

Elly watched as people recognized me from high school or from the TV. The gossip spread around the bar like wildfire. We sat there in silence waiting for the looks and gossip to dissipate. My head hung low as to not draw attention to myself.

"You know, we could leave," Elly said, noticing all the commotion developing around the bar.

"It's okay. They'll find something else to talk about when they realize there's nothing to talk about," I said to put Elly at ease.

"Alright." she said with a smile.

The waitress quickly dropped off a pitcher and glasses saying, "Cheers" and quickly walked away. She was no doubt very busy. I poured our glasses and we sipped the beers silently. The nervous silence was now setting in, so I quickly scoured my mind to think of something to talk about.

Her eyes pressed me quizzically, "Don't do that." she said.

"Don't do what?" I asked wondering what it was I was doing.

"Don't try to think of something to say. I don't like forced conversation. Let's just let the conversation come to us."

I was a little surprised, and didn't realize that I was that transparent. "Okay, let's let the conversation come to us." So we sat there in silence feeling a little more comfortable.

I began to look around the bar and noticed that the

looks had subsided a little and people went back to their drinks. The doors were open allowing the salty sea air breeze through and helped to clear out some of the smoke. The walls were covered with a dark worm wood and the windows were slanted outward like the cockpit of a ship. There were also little circular windows outlined in brass as if we were sitting in a ship. All we needed was the creak of the ships frame and the slow rock back and forth. Instead, all I heard was the sound of people's voices murmuring accented by the subtle sound of Wooden Ships, by Crosby, Stills, and Nash playing on the jukebox.

"I like this song." I said.

"Me too...my mom used to play these guys to put me to sleep."

"Yeah? You're not going to fall asleep are you?" I joked.

"No." she smiled. We talked for the next hour or so about our likes and dislikes from music to places we want to travel. We did the typical thing people do when they go on a first date. We got to know each other better. We talked about all those personal things we never talked about while we were at work. I could feel the attraction grow between us as we realized that we were very similar in many ways. Our differences however, only drew us closer. My heart felt like it was leaping out of my chest as the spark of a relationship brewed on the horizon.

Elly sat back in her chair smiling, "I'm buzzed." she said. I grinned and noticed that my tongue felt a little numb.

"I'm not too far behind." I looked up at her eyes which were blazing into mine and I looked down quickly feeling more nervous than ever. We sat in silence for a moment and I could feel her studying me carefully.

She finally broke the silence, "I'm not just saying this because I'm buzzed," she said looking towards the table as if embarrassed about what she's about to say. "But…I've had the biggest crush on you for the longest time. Son of a bitch, I've shouldn't of said that," she quickly changed her tone squeezing her eyes shut in regret. A smile spread across my face that I couldn't stop.

"No, I'm glad you said it. I'm flattered, you hid it well. I didn't suspect anything until earlier today at work."

She looked at me relieved and the tension fell away. "Oh, I was an emotional wreck when I found out you were lost and then they declared you dead. Your funeral ripped me to pieces and I didn't want to tell anybody why. Then I saw you at work and I nearly had a panic attack thinking you were a ghost. But now that you're alive I thought; what's the point of harboring my feelings. So here I am laying it all out on the table for you to see. You are in my thoughts all the time and I wonder what you would do if you were right there with me. I used to pretend that you were by my side with everything I did and I tried to imagine your reactions," she paused to see me smiling uncomfortably. "I'm sorry, I'm saying too much. I'll stop. I've got to stop drinking or you're going to run away thinking I'm some psycho chick infatuated with you," she sat in her chair pressing her lips together to in hopes to prevent anything else from escaping from them.

I smiled at her, "You're fine Elly. And the feelings are mutual." She did her best to hide her grin and decided to cover it up by sipping her beer.

The next few moments we spent hiding our excitement from each other by talking small talk. I watched how her hair laid softly against her cheeks and her eyes would make me shy away every time she glanced directly at me. Of the many years I worked with her I never knew she had any interest in me. I always thought she was stunning but I never thought she would give me the time of day. Now here we sit like a couple of love sick puppies gawking at each other. Everyone in the bar seemed to disappear and the loud mumble of voices turned to utter silence as she spoke. I forgot all about my problems in the media, the charges that may be brought up against me by the state, and my adventures in the woods with Tilauth. My only thoughts were about Elly and her eyes. She would smile at me and I'd feel my heart sputter. She looked directly in my eyes and shivers ran up and down my spine. I can't remember a time when a girl ever made feel so ridiculously silly in love.

That's when my mind reeled backwards over my thoughts and I said to myself, 'whoa, did I just use the word love?' I scratched that word from my mind quickly and dismissed it as a slip up. "Regardless," I thought "love or not it was the closest I've ever felt to actually being in love."

The minutes slipped away like seconds and I hung on every word. My heart sank at the thought that I would have to drop her off at home and spend time away from her. A couple of guys walked by our table and I didn't even notice that one of the guys called me some derogatory name. If it wasn't for Elly flashing him a scowl I wouldn't have even noticed. "Don't worry about them Elly. I don't care anymore what people think," I said calming her. She grinned at me and said, "We should get going. We've got to get up early tomorrow for work." It suddenly hit me that we work together and I will be able to see her tomorrow. Strangely, for the first time ever, I actually looked forward to going to work. "Yeah, we should probably get going," I said.

We stood up putting our jackets on and the crowded bar slipped back into my awareness as we worked our way to the bar so I could pay our tab. After a few minutes of standing shoulder to shoulder in a sea of drunks and cigarette smoke I paid my tab and we pushed our way out the front door into the open sea air. I could smell the salty air in my lungs as I took a deep breath. Waves gently lapped against the shore of the Puget Sound while we walked back to the car.

I looked down at her to catch her looking at me. "Thanks, Neal for coming out with me," she said with a grin.

"No, no thank you," I said with a British accent.

"That's what I love about you. You're so candid and animated. You make me laugh."

"Well I'm glad to be here for your entertainment. However my services do require a fee," I said with a smirk.

"And just what kind of fee are we looking at?" she said quizzically.

"I will require at least one kiss on the cheek," I said again still maintaining my British accent.

"Well I'm not so sure you've earned such a hefty reward," she said playing along. I laughed out loud the way a Brit would laugh by restraining it to a quiet chuckle. "Well Miss. Elly you'll have to let me know when I've earned my bounty so that I may collect," I said. Half way through my sentence I saw a shadow move near the back bumper of a car next to me. I whipped my head around after I passed the car and saw nothing.

"What is it?" Elly said.

"I thought I saw something." I turned my head forward again to see a fist with a glimmer of brass knuckles hit me squared in the nose. I heard Elly scream, which was quickly muffled.

The blow knocked me off my feet and I felt the pavement slam into the back of my head with a load pop and ringing filled my ears. Stunned, I managed to focus few seconds later to see guy with a baseball cap, dropping to his knee onto my chest. The air forcedly pressed out my lungs as both of his knees slipped down to each of my shoulders.

I heard Elly's muffled cries break free of the hand over her mouth as she screamed, "Let me go!"

"Keep that bitch quiet!" the guy on top of me said with a raspy voice. I could tell he was trying to not draw attention to himself. I instinctively threw my hips and legs forward to wrap them around his face and pull him off of me. But my attempt fell short and my knee slammed into his back. His knees pressed harder into my shoulders. "Brian, sit on this fucker's legs."

That's when I saw Brian come from behind me and jump on my legs. I noticed four other guys that were standing silhouettes in the street light. A big fatter guy held Elly. He leaned his back up against the side of the car with his left leg wrapped around both of her legs to keep her from kicking. His left hand covered her mouth and his right arm wrapped around her holding her arms down. The fat guy's bumbling hand let go of her arm and grabbed her breast, which she quickly used her free arm to whiz up and hit him on the forehead.

"Ouch, you fuckin' bitch!" the fat guy said. He whipped her around and slammed her face down on the trunk of the car. I heard her moan slightly as she was knocked out cold.

"Leave her alone you stupid..." I yelled but was interrupted by a fist slamming into the side of my face.

Blood began to pool up in my left eye so that I couldn't see anything out of it.

"You shut the fuck up, you piece of shit excuse for a human being. I saw your dumb ass on the TV. How about I just save our world from one more dumb ass like you and shut you up for good?" I could hear some of the guys behind me chuckle like excited teenagers about to throw their first punch and declare their manhood.

"Leave her alone." I managed to mumble out.

"Oh, don't you worry. We'll take special care of her." the guy on top of me said in a maniacal tone. "Alright you guys, it's either now or never," the guy above me said. In one of my eyes I saw a scrawny built guy hover over me. He leaned forward obviously new to this and spit in my face. "You're a piece of shit," the guy muttered. He swung towards my face but I turned at the last second and his fist skimmed my skull and slammed into the pavement.

"Ahhh, you fuckin' asshole," he whimpered as he clutched his fist. He quickly disappeared behind the guy on my shoulders and I suddenly felt four sharp blows to my ribs as he kicked the toe of his boot into me. My ribs and chest writhed in pain as I struggled to get my breath. Another husky built guy hovered over me.

"Hold his fuckin' head!" he said. And the guy on top of me held my head still by grabbing on to my ears. His fist quickly and repeatedly slammed into my nose which felt like putty. I could feel the blood fill my sinuses and trickle down my throat. I began to involuntarily cough, sending blood out onto the guy holding me down.

"Fuckin' shit!" he exclaimed. "This fucker's a bleeder," he said with hint of excitement in his voice. "That's how you do that shit," the husky guy said as he turned away from me to the guys standing behind me. I heard the laugh as my shoulders dug into the pavement and my nose and left eye throbbed in pain.

Just then I felt two more sharp blows into my ribs as the scrawny guy must have felt inadequate. My body contorted uncontrollably and I sent more blood sailing into the air as I coughed uncontrollably.

"Wait a second," the guy on top of me said motioning to the next guy in line. "I want this fucker to know that were going to take good care of his girlfriend." He twisted my head sideways and pressed my ear into the pavement so I could see the fat guy covering Elly's mouth restraining her. Tears streamed down her face and my heart sank at the thought of what was about to happen. The fat guy slammed her forward over the trunk of the car and began to unbuckle his pants with one arm while holding her down with the other arm. Elly began to cry "No, no, no, no..." until she ran out of breath. "Somebody cover her mouth," the guy above me ordered. The scrawny guy ran on the other side of her covering her mouth with one hand and slid the other hand down groping her breast. The fat guy violently pulled her khaki pants down and she let out a muffled scream. He grabbed her underwear and pulled it directly back with a quick ripping sound. He backed up gazing at Elly's back side, "Oh yeah, I'm going to enjoy this sweet piece of ass."

A new found energy swelled up inside of me and I twisted quickly throwing the guy above me off balance. I managed to slither out from under him like an animal, and I came up quickly, socking Brian square in the nose. He fell back unconscious after my fist sailed through him like he wasn't even there. I spun around and kicked the other guy that was on top of me in the ribs, who was trying to scramble to his feet. He fell to his side, and I kicked him again, this time my foot slammed into his face. His head flew back unnaturally and I heard a loud pop. I seethed at the mouth like some enraged beast. Just then a sharp blow hit me in the head from behind and I turned to see the husky guy hit me again in the left eye. I heard a tinging noise fill my ears and my body went limp. After that there was an undeterminable amount of time where everything went blank. I can't remember what happened during that time.

What I do remember was when I came to. I opened my eyes but I could still only see from my right eye. I was now lying belly down with my head cocked to the left. From what I could tell two guys were sitting on top of me, one on my back and the other on the back of my knees. The guy was so heavy I could hardly breathe. I assumed it was the fat guy that sat on me now. I struggled with every breath as my right eye began to focus on what was in front of me. I could hear laughing amongst the guys and the horrific sounds of grunting. I saw Elly completely naked, slumped over the trunk of the car. Blood ran from her nose and her cheeks were soaked in tears. Her hair was balled in some guys fist while he thrusted himself in Elly's lifeless body. Her eyes stared unresponsively into oblivion. "She must be unconscious," I thought. The man continued to thrust himself into her as blood streamed down her legs.

I tried to yell but only coughed up blood. Another moved in on Elly and then another. Her body did not move and her eyes remained lifeless. I struggled to fight back but I couldn't break free. When they were finished they began to shove rocks and sticks inside her. I closed my eyes in horror with my face smashed against the ground. How could people have so much rage to do such things? Who put this madness inside these people, I asked myself. One of the guys leaned down and began to whisper in my ears. "You like what you see you piece of shit? You want attention? Well now you got it." The smell of booze managed to seep in through my bloody nose. "Your girlfriend is one fine piece of ass." he whispered hoarsely in my ear. "You don't deserve a piece of ass like that. When we're finished with her we're going to beat the fuck out of you. We're going to beat you so hard you will wish you never lived." He grabbed my head and shoved my cheek into the pavement. "Look at her you twisted fuck. Does that turn you on?" his voice eerily calm. "I bet you like seeing your girlfriend fucked like that." he said. I struggled to breathe but felt like giving up and dying. I didn't want to see another day.

I heard the fat guy that sat on me speak up. "Hey man, is she fucking dead?" I cried out, only this time a noise came gurgling deep from my throat. "Keep that fucker quiet, God damn it!" one of them said. "I'll keep him quiet." the guy who was whispering to me said. He stood up, "get off him Jackson." I felt the fat guy get off me and I could suddenly breathe except for a sharp pain in my ribs prevented me from breathing deeply. A quick and sudden blow slammed into my ribs as the guy kicked me. Suddenly I felt blows coming from all sides as my body skidded across the pavement like a rag doll. It seemed as if every guy kicked me all at once. My body went numb and I caught a glimpse of Elly one last time covered in blood lying naked over the old car before a boot slammed into my face and I lost consciousness. Silence filled my mind and I thought this was going to be my last memory on earth.

Chapter 13
The Awakening

The strange thing about being unconscious is that all time and place seems to disappear from existence. When one finally comes around they are not sure where, when, or even who they are. Yet when one wakes up from consciousness they almost instantaneously forget what they may have dreamt about just a second ago. The same thing happened to me when I came to. My eyes slowly peeled open to see a blurry outline of someone's big head hovering over me. I could smell stale coffee on their breath as they slowly came into focus. It was Detective Wittenberg hovering over me like some kind of mad man, only I didn't recognize him at first. I lurched backwards on the hospital bed, sending the tubes flying and rattling. A sharp pain spiked through my ribs and I winced in the pain. "Take it easy Neal. No one's going to hurt you," Detective Wittenberg said. My eyes squinted at him and I looked at my arm with the tubes and my chest in a cast. I looked back at Wittenberg trying to figure out who he was. He must have noticed my confusion and realized that he was going to need to reintroduce himself. "Neal, I'm Detective Wittenberg. We spoke when you returned from the mountains," he said in hope of some recognition.

It all came flooding back to me.   Suddenly I remembered Tilauth healing me and taking care of me in the woods. I remembered the reporter and the news that was ruining my life. I remembered Elly and our date. Then a surge of panic struck like an electrical shock across my entire body and I wondered if it was a dream.

"Elly?!?" I hoarsely whispered. Wittenberg face remained focused on me without saying a word. "Where's Elly?" I said with a shakiness in my voice. Wittenberg leaned forward,

"Neal, I need to ask you some questions about what happened a couple of nights ago?"

"What day is it?" I blurted in confusion.

"Neal, you've been out cold for the past two days. The doctor says you have several fractured ribs, a broken collarbone, wrist, nose, a partially detached retina, and a dislocated shoulder. You suffered a major concussion that was causing so much swelling around your brain that the doctor had to drill a hole in your skull to allow the excess fluid to drain. Doc says you'll live but it's going to be awhile before your up and running around. Your family has been staying here overnight since you got here. I told them to wait outside a few minutes because I wanted to talk to you when you first came to. I want to ask you about the other night while it's fresh in your mind," Wittenberg said with his usual whistles upon every 's' sound he made.

My head fell back onto the pillow and began to throb in pain. I didn't care about how messed up my body was, "Where's Elly." I asked more sternly.

Wittenberg's eyes looked down "Neal...she didn't make it. The doctors didn't get to her in time." I turned my head towards the window and felt a burning begin in the back of my eyes. "She bled internally and died long before the paramedics arrived. Neal I need to know what happened that night. I need to know who did this. You're the only one I have as a witness. Another guy has been paralyzed from the neck down and is still in a coma. The doc has no idea when or even if he'll come out of it. Neal, you have to tell me what happened that night." I could feel his eyes piercing into me as I stared out the window. I heard everything he said, but I didn't want to. I stared out at the grey skies, ignoring him. The pain of Elly's death was seeping into me like someone slowly pushing a dagger into my stomach. I fought hard to resist the tears, but one trickled out from my right eye and streamed down my cheek. Wittenberg finally sat down in his chair, realizing that he may be pushing too hard.

"I'm sorry to hit you with this as soon as you wake up but it's extremely important. The sooner I understand what happened, the better chance I have of catching whoever did this to you and Elly."

We sat in silence for a moment as I wiped the tears from my cheek by rubbing it against my shoulder.

"Sir..." I managed to squeeze out through the lump in my throat. "Everything within me wishes that I would've died that night." I turned to look at his face. "Sir, I tried to help her." The tears began to stream down my face uncontrollably and I turned back to the window to avoid his questioning eyes.

"Neal...I want you to tell me specifically what happened from start to finish, everything that you know."

I swallowed a few times to soften the lump in my throat so that I could talk. After a few minutes of silence with Detective Wittenberg patiently waiting for me to speak, I managed to start from the beginning. I relayed the whole story back to him swallowing gently to diffuse the lump in my throat. He got me a cup of water and I continued. I told him every detail except for the way I felt about Elly. I felt vulnerable enough telling this man (whom I didn't trust after the last time I spoke with him) about the personal things. But it didn't matter, he managed to pry out the feelings I had for Elly along with all the gruesome details of what happened that night.

When I finished telling him the story, he leaned forward in his chair and stopped the little tape recorder he had sitting on the food tray in front of me. He scratched his temple as he took in the whole story. Every scratch seemed to move his afro like a giant helmet. Wittenberg finally spoke after a long silence.

"I don't think you should feel guilty or responsible for what happened that night. You've done more than most people ever would've done or could've done. You paralyzed that guy and put him in a coma." I interrupted him from saying anything more.

"Well, it wasn't enough now...was it?" I said staring at him plainly. His eyes looked down at his feet as he searched for what to say. "There are no words that I can say to ease your pain. I wish that there were but there are none. I deal with a lot of people that have lost someone close to them and there is no training in my profession to help people deal with their pain and loss." I turned my head from the window to see him do his best to empathize. It was the first time I saw him as an intelligent person. Before I always saw him as a simple minded black and white person, now I could see that he actually had an ounce of feeling in him.

Wittenberg hit record on the tape recorder and set it back up on the tray. "Neal...so how many guys would you say attacked you and Elly that night?" he asked. "I don't know...maybe seven or ten. It felt like I would see someone new as it all progressed." He stopped the recorder again and stood up. "I'm gonna do my best to get to the bottom of this Neal. I'll let your family in on my way out. Here's my card. If you remember anything else, I don't want you to hesitate to call me." He laid his card down on the tray and walked out. My family came rushing in with hugs and kisses all around.

I spent the next month in the hospital doing physical therapy and slowly mending myself back together. A psychiatrist visited me one day and asked me if I minded if he sat down and listened to my story. About half way through the story I realized that he was yawning and starting to fall asleep. I then cut out all the details and shortened the story down to nothing. He then gave me some useless advice of not allowing my self to feel it too much to prevent myself from being overwhelmed. He recommended that we meet again but I declined and told him to leave. He hesitantly left with his pride tucked between his legs.

Dr. Sarong, my attending physician, came into my room later that day. "I thought the psychiatrist would be good for you. Emotionally healing yourself often helps speed up the physical healing," he said.

"Yeah well, that guy was an idiot and if I was you I'd find another psychiatrist to refer to."

He smiled at me, "You're doing pretty good overall and I'm going to recommend you for release tomorrow."

"Thank God, I don't think I can take another day in this hospital."

"I'll check on you tomorrow to see how you're doing and let you go if all looks good. But just cause I've released you doesn't mean you're free to go about whatever you want to do. I want to see you in a week to check on your progress. We'll take that cast off you when I see the bones have mended real well. You'll need to continue to do your physical therapy exercises too." He hung my chart back down on the end of my bed. "I'll see you tomorrow buddy." He left the room and I fell into a deep sleep.

Chapter 14
The Stupor

The next day I was released and I went home. After a few months I got the casts removed and tried to feel normal again. The pain of that night still rang furiously in my heart and in my dreams. I awoke just about every night in a cold sweat after a series of violent nightmares. They always had me viciously killing the guys that killed and raped Elly. They always killed Elly no matter how hard I fought them.

Weeks passed and I slipped deeper and deeper into a depression. I drank myself into oblivion every night. My daily routine included waking up around ten, I'd watch TV for a few hours, start drinking around three, drive around to the local bars, drink, and I'd sit there alone scanning the crowd for any recognition of the guys that killed Elly. Dr. Pell laid me off saying that it would be for the best. I didn't argue because I knew that I would be completely useless. Everything at the office would remind me of Elly and that night anyways.

I never saw the guys from that night. I'd scan the bars listening to the different voices and imagine what their silhouettes would look like under a street lamp. Occasionally I'd find someone that sort of sounded like one of the guys. I'd stare at him from across the bar until I caught his eye. I guess my hope was to see their reaction when they realized I was staring at them. If they didn't quickly look down in cowardice or leave the bar in a hurry, I would assume they were probably not the guys. None of the people I saw acted in this way though. They all probably just assumed I was gay for staring at them. In my drunken depression I didn't care at all what people thought of me. Deep inside of me I wished I was dead. Drinking numbed the guilt and the pain temporarily.

Seven months passed in a drunken blur, the nightmares continued and I avoided sleeping as much as possible. My life and health was slowly slipping away and I didn't care. Nothing felt like it would cure my pain the way death would; only I hadn't the courage to kill myself all at once. So I continued to drink myself into a stupor to numb the pain and to kill myself slowly deadening the hurt I felt. My family never said a word, unsure of how to deal with my problems. I stopped talking to my friends and became that shadow that lurked in the bars every night. I grew a long beard to disguise myself from recognition and gave up trying to find Elly's murders. Detective Wittenberg got nowhere with the case. It remains on his desk as open and inconclusive.

One day blurred into the next and I got a notice that my unemployment benefits were about to run out. That's when I got to thinking that I needed to do something. I either needed to pull my life together or end it right then and there. The latter sounded agreeable but I hadn't the audacity. Yet pulling my life together would be like trying to fly to the moon in a beer can.

That's when I remembered what seemed to be the happiest moment in my life. I remembered the days I spent with Tilauth and how he helped me heal myself and how he showed me a different perspective on life. I thought back to those days and my heart lifted inside of me and the weights of pain was forgotten for a moment.

Every bone in my body knew that I had to find him. I had to find him and see if he could help me. If there was anyone in the world who could help me it would be him. No doctor, friend, or family member could help me with the issues I was facing. Tilauth was the only answer I could think of.

Chapter 15
Picking Myself Up Off the Floor

I awoke early the next morning, fueled up the Jeep, and took off to the mountains. As I drove the rattling rig down the highway a moth landed on the inside of the windshield directly in front of me. I rolled down the window to swoosh it away. I flicked it lightly with my fingers and it sputtered out of the window. I looked at my fingers and they were lightly covered with a speckled dust that glittered in the sunlight. I didn't understand it at the time but that moth made me feel strange. I shrugged the feeling off as nothing and sped through the farmlands of the Skykomish River flood plains. I went through Monroe, Sultan, Start Up, and turned up through Index. I went down the road where I was picked up by those kids. I kept driving until I found the last place where I saw Tilauth.

I parked the old Jeep deep in the brush off the road and threw my back pack filled with food, a tarp, and a sleeping bag. I slid down the river bank to the Skykomish River and looked around half expecting to see Tilauth. The sky was clear and the sun shined down on me warming my bones. The river growled in front of me as it twisted around the boulders. Tilauth, of course, was nowhere in sight. Here I was standing in the very spot I last saw Tilauth and I suddenly remembered the date. It was to the day exactly one year that I last saw Tilauth. I was also stunned to realize that it was exactly one year ago that my life started to fall apart.

I sucked in the misty air and felt at peace for the first time in a long time. With my water proof boots, a pair of wool pants, a T shirt, small back pack, and my long beard I trudged up river in the direction Tilauth and I came from one year ago. I felt like a hermit returning home as I slipped up the ravine.

The tricky part is going to be remembering where Tilauth and I came down. Tilauth followed deer, rabbit, and other little critter trails that blended into the environment. I recognized some of the more prominent rocks that we passed by and some of the old growth trees the stood out from other places. This made me feel confident that I was still on the right path.

As I pushed on up the ravine, eyes down to negotiate my footing on the boulders, I noticed something move just ahead of me. I stopped dead in my tracks and looked up to see a coyote staring back at me. We stared at each other for a few minutes until he quickly disappeared into the forest. I stood there a few minutes trying to decide if I should keep going forward or wait to give the coyote plenty of space. I didn't want the coyote to think I was hunting him, and in a moment of feeling cornered he turns on me and takes me out. I had no gun and no knife. All I had was a pack full of food. Great, he could eat me and have my pack for dessert if he likes.

I decided to push forward, only at a slower rate. Moving cautiously, I keep my eyes peeled for any movement. I got to where the coyote went into the woods, and I looked deep into the forest. I scanned the area for him but saw nothing. Upon closer scrutinizing, I realized that this was where Tilauth and I had made camp. A little stream ran by that dumped into the Skykomish River. I decided that this would be a good place to set up camp again. I threw up my tarp and slung out my sleeping bag. I looked around and could barely see where Tilauth and I had made our little shelters made of debris. With my pack strung from a branch way up in a tree, I stoked up a small fire and sat there watching the flames lick the night air. That's when I felt the urge to have a drink, only I didn't pack any. I sipped some water instead and shrugged the urge off, knowing there was nothing I could do about it. The fire died down and I fell asleep in front of it.

I had the same nightmare I always had, and I awoke sweating and kicking the dirt. I spun around in the darkness regaining my senses. I suddenly remembered why I wasn't at home in my bed. I looked at where the fire was and could see a few faint coals hanging on with there last breath of life. With a stick I sputtered up the fire to put it out completely. In the flicker of sparks and light I saw a glimpse of an animal that was on the other side of the pit. It finally registered in my mind as the coyote I saw earlier. My heart raced and I hollered at it in hopes of scaring it away. But I could see nothing in the blackness and I heard nothing running away. Quickly I poked the coals in hopes of see the animal again. The sparks swirled and a small flame flickered revealing an empty campsite. A gasp left my lungs and I breathed easy again. I crawled into my sleeping bag listening to every noise the forest produced. Needless to say I didn't sleep very well. I jumped to my feet several times in the middle of the night to every little noise. Anyone who has ever slept in the forest knows that it always makes all kinds of noises in the middle of the night. It is left to our minds to conjecture the author of those noises. And in my state of stress the noises had to have been made by some large man eating beast. However, I somehow managed to fall asleep despite all of the racket that goes on in the forest at night.

I awoke the next morning to the first rays of sunlight beaming down into my eyes like the flashlight of an inquisitive cop questioning my ability to drive. I squeezed out of my sleeping bag and peed for what seemed like an hour. I didn't want to get out last night to pee for fear of the man eating beast that would surely eat me whole.

I gathered up my things and pushed on in the direction Tilauth and I came down a year ago. Some things seamed recognizable but most of the time I felt like I was guessing as to what direction we had gone. I started to grow more wary when I didn't recognize anything. But I pushed on not knowing of the right way. I moved slowly, back tracking half the time in hopes of seeing something recognizable.

My body became ripped and torn as I trudged through thorns and shrubs. It was a hot day and the sun streamed through the trees like diagonal pillars of light. I drank a sip of my water and noticed that I was running low. With the stream well behind me I remembered a trick that Tilauth showed me the last time we were walking around and I was thirsty. He told me that in the morning you can take your shirt and wipe down the morning dew that collects on the leaves. The shirt works like a sponge and you can squeeze the water out into a container. I however would need to wait until tomorrow morning so I sipped my water conservatively.

After hours of walking I stepped into an alder tree grove that looked vaguely familiar. I spun in a circle in hopes of getting an idea of where I should go. A blue jay squawked away loudly in a tree with its scratchy cry. It dropped from its branch and soared up to another tree in the distance. He let out a few more squawks before flying out of my sight. I wiped the sweat from my brow on my shoulder started to walk in the direction the blue jay flew. I figured I had nothing to lose and no other indications of where to go. This direction led to a thick wall of blackberry bushes. I popped a couple in my mouth that weren't quite ripe yet. The sour taste filled my mouth and I spit them out. When I looked down at the half chewed berry I noticed a small crawl space in the bushes. This had to be where Tilauth and I belly crawled under the brush. I looked around and things seemed mildly familiar but I couldn't be sure. It was all so long ago and nature is constantly growing and changing.

I slipped off my pack and pushed it in the crawl space in front of me and began to slither on my belly. I moved like a little inchworm moving one segment of my body and rotated it forward up to my head. I pushed my pack forward with every inch. Some small birds sputtered out of the brush above me tweeting away like mad.

"I bet its not too often that the see a human crawling around down here," I thought. I pushed forward inch by inch until I finally reached the other side. I slithered out and pulled some of the thorns from my clothing and brushed the dirt off. Slinging my pack back over my shoulders I looked around for anything familiar. It all seemed so monotonous; tree, bushes, and dirt. It looked the same as anywhere else in the forest.

No direction seemed right to me. So I guessed and aimlessly headed in any direction. It crossed my mind that I could get seriously lost out here and die from the elements of nature but I didn't care. Returning home without finding Tilauth was not an option. "I have to find him. I have no other choice," I thought. If I was going to return to some sort of normality, Tilauth was the only guy that could help me do it.

I popped out in a small circular meadow surrounded by fir trees. I looked around and nothing felt right. In fact it felt horribly wrong and completely unfamiliar. The smell of wet dog filled my nose as I scanned the area. Just then a deer leapt up from its bed in the tall grass and sprang forward hopping through the grass at lightening speed. It disappeared under the fir trees as my heart pounded in my chest. That deer scared me half to death. I instantly turned back around and headed in the same direction I came from. Returning to the place where I slithered out from the brush I headed in a different direction that seemed better to me.

The trees got taller and older as I winded around the ferns. The ground rolled up and down over mounds of old fallen trees like forgotten graves. Things suddenly looked very familiar. This was the forest that I walked around while I healed from my fall. The old shelter had to be just ahead. I started to run and I even called out Tilauth's name a few times. I sprang over logs and whipped around the old trees as if I where in my back yard. Then I saw the old shelter and yelled Tilauth's name again. I came to the old door and whipped it open forgetting to knock in all my excitement. I couldn't believe that I actually found the old place again.

The inside was dark, cold, and empty. All that remained was a small log round Tilauth used as a chair and the skeleton of the old bed I slept in for those several weeks. In my disappointment I peeled off my pack and sat down just in front of the old shelter. I looked around for any signs that Tilauth had been there recently. The painful truth of the matter was that it looked as if no one had been there in a year. It looked as if the only person that had been there was me.

The sun sent beams of light through the old trees creating a fairy tale appearance. The birds sang from all different directions giving me the sense I was sitting in a cathedral listening to a concert. A few whipped by my head as they went about their daily activities. I sat there watching somberly hoping that Tilauth would just pop out of the bushes the way he usually did. He loved to startle me by being right beside me without my knowing it until I would turn around and nearly jump out of my skin. The thought of this spread a smile across my face as I reminisced. I didn't really realize it until then, but I really missed him. I knew him for only a short while but I learned more from him in that short while than what felt like I learned in a lifetime. I could tell I was feeling desperate and in the moment I felt abandonment and a tear slipped from my right eye. I took a deep breath and wiped the tear from my eye. I was tired of being sad or angry. I didn't want to feel those things anymore. I began to forcefully stifle my emotions and make myself feel like a lifeless rock of strength. I breathed deeply pretending that none of this mattered to me. I was aloof and unfaltering in my new way of being. I stood up, threw on my pack, and decided that if I'm going to continue on with life then I will need to be stronger. I cannot be so fragile in life, that a small breeze will send me flailing out of control.

With that I turned to look at the shelter one last time, then continued back to the Jeep. I walked straight back to my rig now knowing the unmarked path very well, stopping for a night at the camp. I hadn't realized it then but, I didn't see one animal on the way back. I did however hear the yelping of the coyote the night I camped along the river. Other than that I don't even recall seeing any bugs. I thought it strange as I drove my Jeep down the winding road but I didn't care. I felt great. I felt confident, strong, and most importantly I didn't feel sad or angry. These were feelings I was glad to be absent of.

I drove back home and began what I have come to know as the numb period in my life. I started taking classes again at the college and got some meaningless job working retail near the Alderwood Mall. I picked up a second job that started at four am every morning frying doughnuts in a local grocery store. My schedule was filled with doughnut frying from four to ten in the morning, classes from noon to four, and retail from five to nine at night. Somewhere in between I'd fit in homework. I was so busy that I didn't have time to think about being sad. For the most part I never thought about Elly, that night, the guys who raped and killed her, or Tilauth. I hadn't the time and they were no longer a part of my new way of being.

I became a social recluse and rarely spoke to friends or family. Everyone was happy to see me putting my life back together. No one ever brought up Elly or the time I was up in the Cascade Mountains. I could tell that many people were thinking about it but I didn't care. If someone did bring it up I would surely change the subject quickly to maintain my feeling of strength and solidity. Luckily, no one brought it up and I hadn't a reason to bother with it.

I got my bachelors degree graduating with a 3.5 grade point average. I could now choose my pick of the litter of colleges around the country. I however, had a big chunk of money in savings with all the work I was doing and the minimal expense from a non-existent social life. I was heading in the direction of becoming a certified public accountant but was reluctant. Somewhere in the back of my mind, crunching numbers in front of a computer screen all day everyday didn't sit well with me. I decided to go on sabbatical for a year with my savings and hopefully during that time I would figure out what it was that I wanted to do with my life.

The big question was, where would I go? I hadn't the slightest idea.

Chapter 16
Sabbatical

I quit my jobs, collecting any vacation pay I had owed to me and packed my Jeep for the year-long journey. Having never done anything like this before, I wasn't sure how to pack exactly. I threw in winter and summer clothes in two large garbage bags, packed a tent, sleeping bag, tarp, ropes, my passport, and strapped my kayak to the top of my Jeep. I said my goodbyes the night before and headed out just before sunrise.

Before I knew it I was headed northbound up I-5 towards Canada with the sun rising up over the Cascade Mountains on my right.

The off road tires droned away on the highway as I passed through Everett, over the Skagit River, and through Bellingham. Upon crossing the border into Canada the border patrolman asked me what my business was in Canada. I lied knowing that they wouldn't want to hear that I was aimless in my journey and said,

"I've got a friend that lives in Vancouver and we plan on doing some kayaking out of Tofino". He peered in my Jeep for a second noticing the camping gear and he then glanced up at my kayak strapped to the roof.

"How long you 'spose you're going to be here in Canada?" he asked.

"Oh, we planned on being back from kayaking in a week, so I should be heading back in about eight or nine days."

"Okie dokie, you have fun." he said as he slapped the side of the Jeep, suggesting that I was free to go.

I headed north up Canadian Highway 99 before veering north east on Highway 1. I wasn't sure if they called it an interstate since they didn't have states or was it rather an interprovidence? That didn't sound right to me as I zipped passed the signs that had the number one with the outline of a maple leaf, so I decided to just call it Highway 1. I started to climb deep into the mountains with shrouded giant Douglas firs, cedars, hemlocks, and Alder trees. The mountains skewered into the sky like giant snow-capped needles. I slipped through the towns of Chilliwack and Hope before turning due east on Highway 3 stopping only for gas. I was determined to get some miles behind me before I would stop and rest. The mountains slowly changed from jagged snow peaks to rolling timber covered hills.

I passed through strangely named towns, lakes, and rivers like Okanagan, Osoyoos, Salmo, Kootenay, and the town of Yahk where I finally pulled off the road and parked the Jeep in the bushes. I walked away from the road and threw down my sleeping bag in a clearing. The night sky sparkled with stars through the cracks of the ponderosa pines and I hoped that the weather wouldn't suddenly change and start raining in the middle of the night.

I slept like a rock despite my new surroundings. It usually takes me hours before I can fall asleep in a new place. But I fell asleep from the moment my head laid down and didn't wake up until morning to a choir of birds and a thin layer of dew on my sleeping bag.

Brushing my sleeping bag off and scratching the

sleep from my eyes, I walked back to the Jeep. It was going to be a beautiful September day. The air was crisp with a slight nip in the air, but that would be gone soon with the crystal clear blue skies overhead.

I pushed on down Highway 3 until I reached Cranbrook, where I finally grabbed something to eat at a local diner. I shoved down some greasy breakfast food and felt the freedom of not having to go to work or study for finals along with the rock now in my stretching stomach. The Jeep carried me through forest lands and farms over lakes like Lake Koocanusa and towns like Fernie before climbing up over the Rockies. The poor rig was taking a beating but it kept ticking away. Coming down from Crownest Pass the old Jeep had a chance to take a break as I popped it into neutral and coasted along.

I suddenly started to feel like I was going the wrong way. "What the heck was I doing in Canada anyways? I'm free to go wherever I please and I choose to drive around Canada," I thought to myself. Canada is beautiful beyond words but I had no purpose being up here. I then decided to take the first highway I saw going south, which was Highway6. I cruised down the highway to Pincher Creek, where I pulled into a service station because my Jeep started making this deep growling noise. The front end came to a grinding halt when I stopped in the front of the gas pump. I filled up the tank and went inside to the attendant. She was the spitting image of Elly and my heart leapt out of my chest. She smiled at me but I didn't move. I couldn't feel my legs or my hands and my face must have looked absolutely frightened.

"Is there something the matter sir?" she said staring at me with concern. Her voice was the only thing that sounded different yet it still took me a moment before I could talk. "Are your alright sir?" she asked.

"Uh...n-n-no." I stammered as the shock and flashes filled my mind of the night Elly died.

"Is there something I can do for you?"

I managed to spit out the words despite the dryness in my mouth, "My Jeep out there is…making a horrible noise. Is there someone here who could take a look at it?"

"Yeah, I'll have Jimmy take a look at it." she got on the phone, punched a couple of numbers. "Jimmy, could you take a look at the Jeep in front. It seems to be making a strange noise." She hung up the phone, "It'll be a few minutes so you got some time to kill."

"Thank you." I said, trying to calm myself down.

I walked out in front of the station and leaned up against the wall around the corner away from the attendants' sight. I took some deep breaths and tried to regain my composure. The whole night began to flash through my mind and my body began to tremble and shiver uncontrollably. I sat down on the concrete curb and buried my face in hands. I stood up again immediately and walked in circles, trying to slough off the emotions. I shivered like crazy and I began to roll my shoulders in a meager attempt to calm myself. I took some quick deep breaths and finally managed to keep myself from having an emotional outburst of tears. I swallowed several times to smooth out the lump in my throat and sat down on the curb again burying my face in my hands.

An orange bellied robin tweeted overhead drawing my attention away from myself and to my surroundings. I glanced around to notice a dark skinned old man sitting in the passenger side of a parked pick up truck. His hair was long and silver and I could tell he was either Mexican or Native American. However, his mannerisms seemed too relaxed in his environment to be a foreigner. What struck me strange was the way he was looking at me. He wasn't looking at me but rather through me like the way Tilauth used to look at me. I looked away in embarrassment knowing that he must have been watching me the whole time as I walked back and forth trying to calm myself. I could see him in the corner of my eyes still staring at me unwaveringly.

Just then a younger man, dark skinned, black hair, wearing blue jeans, cowboy boots, and a flannel comes from the service station tapping a pack of smokes on the heal of his palm. He walks right by me without even noticing me sitting on the curb. He hops in the driver seat of the pickup with the old man. I could see them talking to each other and motioning to me sitting on the curb but I couldn't hear what they were saying. The driver appeared to be arguing with him but the old man seemed to be standing his ground.

The pickup truck fired up with a chugging roar and the transmission clicked as he shifted it into gear. I stared at the ground in front of me trying to act normal (whatever that means, nothing feels normal anymore). The truck roared towards me and pulled up along side of me with the old man leaning out of the window with one elbow. I looked up to see him looking me over. I started to feel a little uncomfortable as he stared at me. "The Earth Maker wants me to tell you that he's been watching you," his feeble voice said over the rough idling of the truck. "He tells me that you need to go south; the direction of the Red Road. Listen to your heart...that's where the Earth Maker talks to us. So go south and you'll find what it is that you're looking for." The driver leaned forward to see me sitting on the curb with a perplexed face. "I told you he wouldn't have any idea what you're talking about," he said to the old man. The old man ignored him and gave me a nod then started to laugh a raspy 'he he he' as they pulled away. The truck chugged away and sped up the highway going north.

"Go south, Red Road, listen to the Earth Maker, I will then find what I'm looking for?" I said aloud summarizing what the old man said to me. If I had never met Tilauth I would have surely dismissed this old man as crazy. Earth Maker must mean God but I had no idea what the Red Road meant. South sounded good to me but what was it that I was supposedly looking for? I went on this trip to get clarity. Clarity on what it was that I was going to do with the rest of my life. Is that what I will find if go south? I asked myself. The old man must be some sort of sage or shaman for his tribe. I couldn't imagine the average person taking a glance at some stranger acting like a freak in a parking lot and know what it was they needed to hear. A raven croaked from the branches of a giant maple on the hillside behind the station. I stared at the large black bird and its long slender beak as it croaked again.

Just then the service attendant came strolling around the corner, "There you are," she said. I saw her face again and managed to force a smile. She looked at me concerned noticing my awkwardness "Is everything ok?"

"I'm fine, it's just that…you remind me of someone is all."

"Well I hope she's pretty," she smiled.

I smiled back, "She was very pretty, yes." My heart began to jump at the thought that I was even talking about Elly. The sun shone down on the attendant's face and I had the strongest urge to leap forward and wrap my arms around her and say how much she meant to me and how sorry I was that I didn't save her. I began to fight the lump in my throat and fend off the tears. She realized that something wasn't right about who she reminded me of and decided to change the subject.

"Your Jeep is ready. Jimmy said that all you needed was some new bearings. It's a good thing that you stopped when you did or you would've ended up stuck somewhere and your wheels would've went sailing off in all different directions. So it was a quick fix and it only cost you twenty dollars to replace them," she said as we walked back into the service station. I paid her for the gas and the bearings and hopped back in the Jeep, firing the old girl up. I turned back to see her reading a book behind the counter. I watched her for a moment, knowing full well that it wasn't Elly but the resemblance was like looking at a ghost. A tear slid down my cheek and I felt the grief again.

I gassed it and sped off heading south down Highway 6. The giant Rocky Mountains loomed skyward on my right, rolling hills of timber to my left, and the U.S. was in front of me.

After about an hour of driving I pulled over to watch one of the most amazing things I had ever seen. A herd of wild elk grazed calmly on a grassy knoll along side the road. I got out of my car to hear them calling each other back and forth. They didn't seem to mind my presence as I sat on the front wheel well of my Jeep. Their calls were eerie sounding as they jutted their chins forward, letting out a high pitched screech that dropped in tone suddenly and disappeared. Some calves wandered around the knoll with their mothers always keeping a close eye. The herd was like one tight knit family watching everyone and everything, including me. The sky was turning golden as the sun began to slowly sink in the west.

I jumped back into the Jeep and pushed south. After finally reaching the border, the U.S. border patrol took one look at me and told me to get out of the car. I had a feeling that this was going to be quite the hassle. The officer told me to stand in this one particular spot and that I couldn't move. He put on surgical gloves and began to rifle through my bags. Every little compartment in the Jeep was checked and double checked.

Because of the lax laws on certain drugs in Canada the U.S. doesn't hesitate to take a person like me aside and practically strip search them. Because of my age, the fact that I was alone, male, and had camping gear, this was a typical profile for a drug smuggler. I sat at the border for what had to have been two hours while the officer tore my car apart. They brought out the dogs and everything to sniff the tires, my bags, and me. I had visions of the movie Midnight Express and kind of chuckled quietly. The officer turned to me quickly after inspecting my underwear.

"What the hell is so funny?" Not realizing that he had my underwear in his hands at the time I chuckled, "Uh...nothin' sir," I said with a smirk as the laughter within me began to build. "You know this is serious business. You could be smuggling terrorist bombs or illegal drugs into this country and it would be my ass if you slipped through under my watch."

"Sorry sir, you're right sir, it isn't funny." The officer slowly turned back to my car and continued to rifle through my stuff as I waited patiently.

Finally the officer let me go and I headed southbound along the borders of Glacier Park in Montana. I stopped in St. Mary, Montana at a hotel where I took a much needed shower and grabbed a bite to eat at some rustic restaurant and had a buffalo burger for the first time. I sipped a beer with my burger as I sat at the table by myself. There's something about sitting at a table by yourself that makes others curious about you. People stare and seem to wonder what your story is. I ignored them, finished my burger and went back to the hotel.

Chapter 17
Nonsense and No Sense

The next morning, I decided to take the scenic drive through Glacier Park since I was there and it headed in a southerly direction. The drive along the mountainside, with cliffs straight down right up along side the road was breath taking. I could see mountain goats crawling around on the rocky terrain above. At one point I saw a Grizzly Bear up the mountain side through my sun roof. I pulled over and got out to watch the large beast lumber along, slowly sniffing around rocks and logs. I snapped off a few shots of the scenery and kept pushing forward.

After the park I continued south through Kalispell, Elmo, and drove through the Flathead Indian reservation. The hills rolled with golden grasses as I crawled along the small highway to Plains and then to St. Regis. The small highway brought me into Idaho where I winded down the St. Joe River Valley. The mountains pushed up on all sides as I slithered down the valley like a drop of water in the St. Joe River. I checked my map and realized that I was now actually headed west rather than south. I saw a highway in St. Maries that turned south, and figured I'd make the turn there. When I reached St. Maries it was already night again, and I wanted to find some place to sleep. I grabbed a bite to eat at the Pizza Factory and pulled into the IGA grocery store parking lot. I didn't want to pay for another hotel, so I tilted the seat back, locked the door, and tried to fall asleep.

I couldn't sleep because of all the kids that streamed in and out of the parking lot all night with their oversized lifted Chevy trucks. It was the weekend, so the local kids were bound to have some fun by drinking booze out of their Big Gulps, revving their engines, laying down a track of rubber, or spinning doughnuts. I could hear them screaming at each other in their drunken stupor.

This all started to give me flash backs of the night with Elly and I. Just when I was about to leave, they all found a place to party up in the mountains, or at least that's what I heard one of the drunken girls yell, and they all took off. Finally, it was silent and I drifted off to a nonsensical dreamland.

Pardon the drifts of the mind - bandits of foretold - unanswered questions of delirium. Ask the penny piper to hang on the words of every bird. These are the mysteries of the gates you precede. Lengthen your soul to circumvent the universe. You are not alone. These are the strange words that stream through my mind just before I fall asleep. Usually these words are accompanied by pictures in my mind that also seem to lack any reason. For example, my mind flashed a vision of a Red Wagon that held a passenger dressed in all green. The passenger rode this wagon at high speeds down mountain sides, dodging large pine trees. The vision would change in a flash to a few rabbits jumping down railroad tracks;trucks billowing up steep mountain roads while grinding their gears.

This is what happens when I fall asleep, or at least when I can remember it. Usually I'll fall asleep and forget everything I saw and heard. This time the last nonsensical words I heard made me shiver. The words 'you are not alone' echoed through the very core of my being. Startled, I opened my eyes to see a coyote standing on the hood of my Jeep staring at me through the windshield. My head pressed back into the seat in an uncontrollable effort to move away. The coyote's head dropped and his body spun around before leaping off the front of the hood and trotting away from me. He trotted down the now deserted Main Street. He stopped in the middle of an intersection and turned to look at me over his right shoulder. His eyes pierced into me just before he bolted right and headed up a road and disappeared behind a building. There was a center light that swung above the intersection blinking red. My ears were very acute and I could actually hear the buzz of the light when it flicked on.

At that moment I heard a loud tapping noise on the window next to me. My body jolted in fear, and I awoke to the sun shinning in my face. Confused and still in a sleepy haze, I squinted my eyes and blinked repeatedly. The coyote must have been a dream, I realized. A loud tapping noise rapped on the window again and my head spun around quickly to see a police officer starring at me. "You want to roll down your window, son?" he yelled through the door. I fumbled around for the window crank still trying to figure out the difference between dream and reality.

The window came down with a squeak. "Did you spend the night here son?"

"Uh...yes sir, I did," I said rubbing the sleep from my eyes.

"Can I see some identification?" he said.

"Yeah...sure." I lifted a cheek to realize that my wallet wasn't in my back pocket.

I panicked for a moment before I remembered taking it out and putting it in the back seat. I turned around and reached for it to see it still resting on the seat. I pulled my license out and handed it to the officer. He was an older guy with a peppered mustache. He took a look at the license and walked back to his patrol car without a word. After a few minutes he came back, handing me my license.

"The store manager at the IGA informed me that there was a car here that was left abandoned. I don't think he realized that someone was actually sleeping in it. Anyways, it's illegal to park here, unless of course you're doing some shopping."

"Sorry about that sir, I just needed a little sleep after being on the road for so long."

"Not a problem son. Next time consider getting a hotel room or maybe a campsite."

"Thank you sir."

"You have a nice day," the officer said as he tapped the Jeep twice and walked back to the patrol car. I fire up the engine, which turned over a few times sounding like a dying cat. The officer peered at me through my side view mirror. I cranked it over again as it slowly and barely roared to life. The officer climbed into the patrol car after it started and he pulled out onto the street in front of me.

I let the old Jeep warm up as I watched the patrolman head to the same intersection I saw the coyote. In my dream it had headed north up Highway 97 according to the sign. I remembered the old man said to 'go south', which went the opposite way as the coyote. I pulled out to the intersection and looked in the direction the coyote ran. The red light hung above blinking. I looked in the opposite direction and my gut felt unsettled. The direction of the coyote felt like a longing. I remembered how the old man had said to follow my heart... A loud horn blazed behind me as I sat there with my indecisions. I quickly turned right and headed in the direction of the coyote. This direction for some reason just felt right to me. I headed north up 97 through rolling golden farmlands scattered with lone ponderosa pines.

The highway suddenly started to venture down

steeply through ridges scattered with pines and cedars. Several wild turkeys walked along the hillside in front of me as I winded down the highway. A very large golden eagle was swooping down at them, pestering the group. I could hear the turkeys crying out through my open windows as I drove by. "The eagle must be after some of the young", I thought.

The highway winded down by Lake Coeur d'Alene to the small town of Harrison, where I stopped to eat some breakfast at Rose's Café. I watched the locals stroll in and out as I slowly ate my French toast. They found me more interesting than I them. I was definitely the unknown person in this small town of 230 people. Everyone was very pleasant to me, nodding and smiling as they passed by my table. This small town was nestled on the water's edge of Lake Coeur d'Alene and my table had a view over the lake. The late summer left the ridges looking dry in the height of fire season. The water of the lake appeared like an oasis in these semi-arid mountains of the Rockies. Oddly, this area for some reason felt a little like home to me. I had no idea that this corner of the world was going to be home for me for awhile.

I paid for my breakfast and hopped in my Jeep. It was going to be a hot day, I felt the surge of heat when I opened the door. Windows down, I pulled out of the small town of Harrison and popped out where the Coeur d'Alene River dumped into the lake. I crossed over the old bridge and turned right onto Blue Lake Road. I stopped at a boat launch and walked down to the waters edge to wash my face. A giant sign exclaimed "Warning!" explaining the high concentrations of pollutants in the river from mining. I opted to not wash my face, and instead glanced out over the slow moving river. It had two banks, with lakes on both sides and a road going through the middle. I jumped back in my Jeep and continued east on Blue Lake Road. The road was like a land bridge with a lake on one side and the Coeur d'Alene River on the other. Mountains sprang up from the waters edge, giving me the feeling I was driving through a fairy tale. Osprey swooped down, snagging small fish from the lakes as I drove down this strangely mystical road. The osprey's giant nests rested on top of just about every electrical power pole that strung along the road.

The pavement suddenly ended and the road climbed up a ridge. The gravel road reverberated through the Jeep with a loud rattle. The old rig sounded like it was going to shake to pieces. The road split several times and I just took the one that felt best to me. I ended up bouncing along some forest service road with some of the largest ponderosa pines I'd ever seen. I winded down the road for what seemed like hours going up and down in the mountains. I thought that there would be some good camping out here and I could stay and explore the area at my leisure. As the road winded up a deep valley shaded with old cedars and mountain ridges I rolled up the window feeling a chill in the heat of the day.

As I rounded one of the turns I came to a skidding halt. Out in front of me on the road was the coyote from my dream last night. My heart pounded in disbelief. He had the same markings as the one from my dream. We stared at each other for a moment until I blinked my eyes to make sure I wasn't imagining him. When I opened my eyes, he was gone. I scanned the forest around us but couldn't find him anywhere.

I relaxed back in my seat assuming that I must have imagined him. I pressed forward down the dirt road turning down different forest service roads listening to my heart. I began to worry if I was going to be able to remember how to get back.

The road got more primitive and the Jeep slowly maneuvered around fallen trees and large potholes. I finally popped out on top of a ridge where the road came to an end. I had a 360 degree view of mountains, lakes, valleys, and not one single house or sign of human life. I turned off the Jeep, got out, and looked around absorbing the awesome view. I decided to set up camp right there.

I threw up my tent and dug a small hole for a fire pit. The ravens were cawing all around the ridge while I set up. I gathered some fire wood and cooked myself some dinner. The ravens continued to croak and caw while I ate and relaxed into my new surroundings.

It didn't take long before the sunset majestically set over the mountain peaks and it was just me and the fire light. The light flickered off the pine trees and I scooted closer to the fire to keep warm. A breeze howled up the ridge and I wrapped my sleeping bag around me.

"What the heck am I doing way out here," I thought. "There isn't another human being for miles. I'm looking for the answer to where and what I'm supposed to do with the rest of my life." I thought. "Why in the world would the answer I seek be on a ridge somewhere in Northern Idaho?" The truth of the matter was I didn't know where to look. Northern Idaho is just as good a place as any I guess. Somewhere deep in me I wished I could talk to Tilauth. Intuitively I knew that he could get me going on the right foot. I was feeling pretty messed up inside and I knew it. I just didn't want to admit it.

I hunkered down for warmth and looked out over the mountain ridges. A few lights specked the ridges here and there but they were few and far between. The night sky was speckled with stars that twinkled down upon my lone camp sight. I began to think that this must be one of the few places on earth that hasn't been completely exploited by man. "I wonder if this place was any different a hundred years ago," I thought to myself. "Maybe you should go and find out?" a voice broke the silence. Startled, I jumped straight up into the air sending my sleeping bag flying.

"Who's there?" I spun around and saw nothing but the flickering light from the fire on the trees. A soft familiar chuckle began to echo out from the bushes.

"Where are you?" I said still panicked.

"I see you're still just as jumpy as ever." a voice came out from my right. This time I knew who it was but I couldn't believe it until I saw him for my own eyes. Tilauth stepped out of the bushes still chuckling,

"I had a feeling you'd find me," he said.

"Holy shit it's you!" I said astonished.

"What, no 'hi – how are you' just a 'holy shit' uh?" he said smiling at me. I walked over to him still amazed and hugged him.

"It's good to see you Tilauth. I've thought about you a lot," I said. "Say how did you find me out here?" I asked.

"Actually the question you should be asking is 'how did you find me way out here?" he said with a twinkle in his eyes.

"What do you mean?"

"I mean how did you find me?"

I looked at him perplexed, "I guess I just started driving, following my heart I guess?"

He smiled at me in his knowing way, "Good," he said simply.

Tilauth sat down next to my fire and I sat back down too. I looked at him in disbelief. "I didn't think I'd ever see you again. I began to think that you were just a ghost in my life. You mysteriously disappeared that day we were walking down the river and I figured I'd never see you again. I went home and..." I suddenly remembered everything that happened to me, from the accusations by the reporter and that night with Elly. My eyes redirected to the fire to hold back the grief. There was something about just the thought of telling Tilauth of all the happened to me that made me want to start crying. It felt like he would be the only person that would understand what it was that I went through. He listened to me quietly smiling. Somehow, I got the feeling that he already knew.

"What did you mean when you said that I should go find out?" I asked changing the subject quickly.

"You were wondering what it was like here a long time ago," Tilauth said.

"Well yes...but I didn't actually say that out loud. How did you know what I was thinking?"

"There is no separation between you and me. In fact there is no separation between anything. The sooner you realize that the better." A moth swirled around, playing chicken with the flames. It almost got snatched up by one of the flames before it swirled around and landed on the log next to me. It raised its wings quickly and slowly lowered them again and again. I watched the moth as it did this as if it were using the fire heat to dry its wings. Tilauth watched me watch the moth as if he knew something that I didn't.

"You are not separate from anything Neal," Tilauth said as he glanced at the moth.

"Tilauth, you have to teach me." I blurted out.

"Teach you what?" he asked.

"What you know. Teach me what you know."

"You don't even know what it is you want to learn."

"Well no...but I know that you know something that I want to know... I'm sick of my life. My life is painful and I'm scared to death...I'm scared to death that it will just be ordinary. I-I don't want to go through life and end up on my death bed saying to myself that my life was ordinary. I don't want to grow up, get a nine-to-five job, get married, have kids, retire, and die. The whole idea sickens me."

A deep yellow, almost orange, moon began to rise just over Tilauth's shoulder as he listened to me intently. He didn't say anything for the longest time while the crackle of the fire filled the air. Tilauth looked to the fire, and I could see the reflection bounce off his eyes.

"The moth seems to think that you're ready," he said, without looking away from the fire. The big question here is, do you think that you're ready?" his eyes shifted upward to me with a blink.

"I'm ready – I'm so very ready," I exclaimed.

He nodded his head slightly. "I must warn you. If I teach you – you will no longer see the world the same way you do now. You're entire foundation will be turned upside down. After that happens you cannot turn back. Many people want to turn back for countless reasons, fear being the most common. Basically what I'm asking is - are you willing to die?"

Naturally, I was taken aback by his words. "Well, I don't want to die. But, I want to live and learn." I stared at him, suddenly feeling a little uncomfortable.

"What I'm talking about is embracing this moment of who you are right now. When you embrace yourself in the present moment, your idea of who you are will die. I'm not speaking of the physical death of your body. Nobody actually ever dies. This is the great illusion that has been swept over your eyes. You will understand this more when you embrace yourself and the present moment," he said.

"I guess I don't fully understand...but I do know that what you are talking about is what I feel I want to learn."

"Good, then I will teach you," he smiled at me. I grinned and sighed in relief. The fire began to die down and Tilauth threw on a small piece of wood. The flames flared up instantly, and began to crackle as the sap popped under the heat. The moon was now much higher in the sky, and now shown a silvery white color.

"Tilauth, I've seen some horrible things since I last saw you." He held up his hand to silence me.

"You and I are not separate, Grandson." This was

the first time he called me Grandson. It made me feel comfortable and at ease. "The circle of life has no end," he continued. "Tonight is not the night to deal with these horrible things you speak of, however. Tonight calls for us to enjoy each other's company."

I smiled and agreed with him. "So what are you doing out here?" I asked.

"The same thing that I was doing when I was in the Cascade Mountains; living," he said with a smile.

"How long have you been living out here?"

"I'm not sure, but this will be the second winter I've spent out here. Maybe somewhere around a year or so," he said as if it was of no concern to him.

"Don't you get lonely out here by yourself?"

He laughed his usual chuckle. "I'm never alone, so I guess I don't get lonely." The idea of being out in the wilderness by myself for over a year strangely sounded tempting, but I knew that the sting of loneliness would set in for me sooner or later.

"So do you have a shelter around here somewhere?"

"Yes, it's about eight miles from here. But I like your spot – I think we'll make a shelter here. Tomorrow I think we should build a tepee like the way the old ones did on the plains. It will be good for your training." I nodded in approval.

We were silent for most of the night after that. I crawled into my sleeping bag and fell asleep next to the fire. Tilauth pulled out a bear skin and covered himself. He laid his head back on a balled up piece of hide and we fell asleep.

The next morning I awoke to the sunlight shining in my eyes. I looked over to see that Tilauth was no longer there. A strange fear pounced through me and I wondered if I had dreamt the whole thing. I looked at were Tilauth had laid and tried to decipher the impressions on the ground. I saw nothing that revealed his presence there. But then again I was no tracker. I rolled up my sleeping bag and shoved it in the Jeep. I looked around beginning to think that it could have been all a dream. I sat down on a rock and basked in the sun and tried to remember the details from last night.

Just then I heard a strange scuffing noise. I turned to see Tilauth dragging two tree poles that where three times him in length.

"Grandson, you're awake," he said as he dropped the poles on the ground.

"Yes, I am." feeling relieved to see him and to realize that I wasn't dreaming. "Good, give me a hand with these lodge poles."

Tilauth and I gathered up some lodge poles for the tepee, set, and strung them together. I gazed up at the skeleton of the tepee noticing its simple design. I'd never set up a tepee so this was quite the learning experience. It was surprising how quickly it all went. The efficiency of the plains tribes was intended for quick tear down, transport, and rebuild. This was necessary because these tribes would move to different locations depending on the season and the abundance or lack of food. They knew that if they over depleted an area of food and other natural resources they would not be able to return to the area to camp for a long time.

Tilauth and I headed out from camp to go collect some hides that Tilauth had at his other camp. We were going to use the hides to line the outer part of the tepee.

It didn't take long before I was staring at the trail directly in front of me to watch my footing on the uneven ground. I found out that this is the most common mistake people make when they are walking in the woods. I finally brought my gaze up and realized that I was by myself. I turned my head around to see where Tilauth went but I couldn't see him anywhere. Did he go down a different trail while I, being the idiot, went down the wrong one?

In my moment of confusion, I got a hard slap across the back of the head. The smack was so hard that it threw me off balance and I landed on all fours. I spun around onto my feet grabbing the back of my head with one hand. There stood Tilauth, smiling like a little kid.

"Your first lesson; always pay attention, never leave the present moment." He laughed and kept on walking in front of me.

I had no idea how he'd gotten behind me. But now I was bound and determined to keep my eyes on him the whole time. I followed behind him rubbing the back of my head. I watched nothing but him; he was not going to leave my sight no matter what. It didn't take long for Tilauth to figure out what I was doing.

We walked a couple of miles when all of a sudden a rock comes from out of nowhere and hits me square on the forehead.

"Ouch…where the…" I spun around trying to figure out where the rock came from. Tilauth just smiled at me chuckling softly. "It's not funny, it hurts," I said rubbing my forehead.

"Oh, that's not what's funny. You're what's funny. I said pay attention, not only to one thing, but to all things," he said as he continued to laugh and turned back around and walked down the trail. I continued to rub my forehead and checked my hand to make sure there wasn't any blood. I could hear him still chuckling to himself.

He was starting to infuriate me. I had no idea how he hit me with that rock, but he did. I decided to suck up my pride and try and learn whatever it was that he was teaching me. I looked all around now trying not to let anything pass me by. This however, was very exhausting. Trying to pay attention to everything we passed by and trying to always keep him in the corner of my eyes was not only challenging, but it was beginning to bore me. I kept at it as much as I could.

Nothing slipped by me without me knowing about it.

Not only was I struggling to keep my awareness but I was also struggling to keep up with Tilauth. He was like a ghost that glided along the landscape without effort.

When we finally reached his camp, I collapsed on a log next to his small hut. His hut was half underground and half above ground. The roof was layered with pieces of cedar bark. Tilauth went straight in and I managed to get up from the log and check out his shelter. He had made a small bed for himself to sleep in, a primitive chair, and a large flat piece of slate stone that he must have used as a table. A small fire pit was dug in the center, which he had lined with rocks. In the center of the roof above was a small hole to allow the smoke out.

"This is a pretty luxurious shelter," I said. Tilauth smiled without saying anything. He was rolling up his hides and tying them in a bundle with some primitive rope that he had made no doubt. He also grabbed some bladder skins which he handed to me to carry. He slung the hides over his back like a back pack, and grabbed a big bundle of food he had stored away. Without a word, he started back down the trail and I followed wishing that he would rest so I could rest. "Obviously he wasn't tired," I thought and I pushed on behind him.

We walked for about an hour and I did my best to pay attention to everything. On the way back, however, I was much more lax because of my fatigue. But even if I wasn't tired, I don't think I would have caught what was about to happen. Tilauth was in front of me and slightly on a decline in the trail. My eyes were looking right at him when I swear he literally disappeared into thin air. I couldn't remember if I blinked or what, but somehow he slipped away in a split second.

I stopped immediately in my tracks and began to look around wildly to avoid being hit in the back of the head. I saw nothing in every direction I looked. "Come on Tilauth," I called out. "I know you're around here somewhere." I cautiously walked a little further down the trail towards where Tilauth disappeared. I spun my head around in circles to see him before he smacked me. He was nowhere in site. I listened closely as I looked around trying to hear any noise he might give off. I heard nothing.

Despite my frantic searching he still managed to smack me in the back of the head. I spun around again rubbing my head and instead of seeing him standing there laughing, there was no one. Thoroughly confused I kept spinning around in hopes of seeing him. "You are truly as blind as they come," his voice seemed to come out of thin air. I spun around again trying to pin point his voice when he smacked me again on the back of the head. This time he hit me a few times which threw me on my back trying to avoid the smacks. That's when I realized where he was. Lying there flat on my back rubbing my head I could see straight up into the trees. He was sprawled out across a branch above the trail. His face smiled down on me like a child who has just won the game again. He laughed again as he silently slipped down from the tree and helped me to my feet. The hides he had on his back were resting in the nook of the tree branch. He pulled them down as I brushed the dirt off.

Tilauth looked at me and noticed that I was beating myself up inside.

"Don't be too hard on yourself, Grandson. My teacher did the same thing to me. His name was One Who's Heart Stands in the Middle. I however, knew him just as Grandfather. He was named One Who's Heart Stands in the Middle because he never took a side during disputes. He hated to quarrel and never wanted to let anyone feel like he was against them when others fought. But his peaceful nature didn't stop him from hitting me on the head."

"What am I doing wrong?" I asked. Tilauth gazed upon me closely and then looked out into the forest. He seemed to be thinking about what he was going to say. This was something I was starting to get used to. He never seemed to blurt out anything without thinking about it first. "Everyone has blind spots in their awareness and you are no exception. In fact, Grandson, you have developed some very large blind spots. Directly above your head is one blind spot. Your eyes are not the only things that can go blind. Your ears can go deaf, and your sense of touch, taste, and smell are also lacking," he said as he turned down a different trail and we started making a steep descent.

The trail meandered near a stream where Tilauth walked over and knelt down. "Hand me those bags you got," he said pointing to the bladder bags I had slung over my shoulders. He filled up one of the bladders while I watched. He secured the end of the bladder and set it down on a rock next to him. I handed him another and I started to fill up the next mimicking him. We filled all the bladders. He tied them together and strung a set over my forehead as the bladders hung down my back. He slung some more over my shoulders and I felt the weight press down on the heels of my feet.

"You didn't think I was going to do all the packing did you?" he said, smiling at me.

"Well...no," I said realizing that I hadn't been doing much labor.

We made our way back up the trail and all the way back to camp. My neck and shoulder muscles burned from the weight of the water. I set the bladders down, stretching my neck and shoulders.

"That's going to be the one downfall to having our camp set up on top of the ridge. Water is a ways away and straight uphill. But it will be good exercise," Tilauth said smiling.

I helped Tilauth secure the hides to the tepee and

dig a small fire pit in the center. He sent me out to gather up some firewood. As I gathered the wood I was randomly pelted by a large array of pinecones and small rocks. I knew it was him but I could never see him. I gathered the wood while a rock, pinecone, and sometimes a small stick would sail through the air and hit me just about anywhere on my body. One time he hit my hand as I reached for a piece of wood and he hollered out, "Not that piece, it will stink up our tepee when it burns." His chuckle filled the forest all around me and I couldn't for the life of me seem to find him.

When I came back to the camp he was sitting up against the trunk of an old ponderosa pine as if he had been there the whole time. I stacked the wood feeling frustrated with myself. I got a small fire going in the old fire pit from the night before, all the while Tilauth sat quietly against that tree staring out across the mountain tops. He seemed to be thinking about something so I didn't want to disturb him.

The fire cracked and popped and Tilauth finally got up from his tree. He cooked up some food and we ate in silence. I kept stewing over the fact that Tilauth can dance circles around me and I can't even catch a glimpse of him.

Tilauth noticed that I was internally beating myself up and asked, "So what's bothering you?"

Feeling frustrated beyond words, "Do you enjoy making me look like a idiot?"

"You're not an idiot, and yes I do enjoy making you look like an idiot." I glared at Tilauth with eyes of fire. "I'm kidding, you need to lighten up. You'll give yourself an ulcer at this rate."

"How do you run around the woods pelting me with pebbles and things and I can't see you anywhere?"

"What are you talking about?" he said playing dumb.

"I know it was you."

"Alright, you got me," he said, clearly toying with me.

"You know I'm not enjoying being the brunt of your jokes."

"Oh, they're not jokes," he said matter of factly. "You're so rigid and structured. You need to relax because I'm serious about that stomach ulcer. And you will find that I'm almost never joking. Even when I am joking it is usually for a serious reason."

"And for what reason might it be that you find it necessary to pelt me with pebbles?"

"To help you see."

"To help me see?" I repeated him.

"Yes, to help you see. You walk through your life looking through a drinking straw. In other words, you only notice the things put right in front of you or wherever you point your straw. I can throw little things at you and dance circles around you, as long as I don't set myself in front of your tiny little straw. I'm trying to get you to put it down and see." The fire light flickered across Tilauth's face, which seemed to make his eyes twinkle.

I rummaged over the idea of looking through a straw, imagining the tiny pinhole it creates when you look through it.

"So how am I supposed to put down the straw?" I asked. Tilauth points behind me by jutting his chin forward. I quickly turned around afraid of what I might see, to see nothing but darkness. This began to startle me given the thought that something may be behind me and I can't see anything because my eyes are adjusting from the fire staring at the fire. "What is it that I'm supposed to be looking for?" I asked.

"Nothing," he calmly replied. "You're supposed to be looking for nothing. That is the whole point," he stated.

"I'm sorry Tilauth; I guess I do not understand what it is that you want me to do?"

"That's your problem. When you ask me 'What am I supposed to be looking for?' this is the same thing as asking me 'Where am I supposed to point my straw so that I can see what it is I'm supposed to be looking at?'" Tilauth watched me as I assimilated what he was saying.

"Okay," I said.

"Don't point the straw anywhere, but rather let it go. As your eyes adjust to the darkness I want you to look at things like the way an owl might. I want to you remember its large round eyes. It can hunt for a small mouse in a large field of grass by sitting up in a tree. With its dish-like face and its large rounds eyes, the owl becomes extremely sensitive to sounds and movement. This is an absolute necessity if it wishes to succeed in hunting in the middle of the night. It never knows when and where a mouse will appear from one of its holes, so it can't look at one spot or the owl will miss dozens of opportunities. It's big eyes look at the entire view at the same time. So by utilizing its peripheral vision, it can see the entire scene all at once. In this state of viewing, the owl's eyes become hypersensitive. Once it notices a small movement say off in the lower left corner of the scene, the owl will then turn and focus on the movement to identify the maker of the disturbance. This is when it looks through the straw and focuses on something specific. After it has identified the creature as a mouse the owl then can plan his plan of attack."

So in silence I stared at the forest behind me, slowly trying to widen my vision by staring straight ahead yet still absorbing what I could see in my peripheral vision. Once I got my eyes to manage to look at the whole scene, everything started to blur slightly.

"This doesn't seem right. Everything is all out of focus," I exclaimed to Tilauth.

"That means you're doing it right. Keep at it," Tilauth reassured me. So I continued to look at the blurred scene, blinking, and constantly reminding myself not to focus on anything specific. This was a little challenge for me but I kept at it. Suddenly I saw it. First it was a couple of branches moving from a slight evening breeze. I focused on the branches for a second then widened my focus again. Then there was something on the ground that made a slight movement. My eyes quickly focused on it to see that it was just a leaf that flipped over in the breeze. Then something swooped down towards my head. I changed my view to the sky to notice that several bats were swooping around catching insects in flight.

"Whoa! This is pretty amazing!" I said astounded. Tilauth said nothing, but I could feel that he was watching everything that I was watching. Off to my right there was a slight twitch under the brush. I focused in on the area to see a black and orange towhee pecking away looking for a bug to eat. He rustled the debris around suddenly making lots of noise.

I must have stared at this new scene for an hour catching all these small movements in the dark, before I finally turned around to see Tilauth grinning behind me. He nodded in approval.

"That is what it means to put the straw down, Grandson," he said.

"I can't believe how much can be seen in just this small section of the woods. We are completely surrounded by all kinds of things that I had no idea were here."

"You keep practicing and you'll see even more." A small chill ran down my back and the hairs stood up on the back of my neck when he said, 'more.' The way he said it made me think that there is still plenty that I was missing.

"Your eyes are not the only things that make up your awareness," he said softly. "Your ears, nose, tongue, and skin help you to absorb your surroundings. I want you to turn around again and look through the eyes of the owl." So I turned around and waited for my eyes to adjust to the darkness. "Now pay attention to every sound that you hear nearby. Imagine the big flimsy ears of a deer. The ears of a deer are what saves them from any stalking prey. As a large mountain lion closes in on a deer, the predator is bound to make a slight noise at some point. It will be this noise that gives the lion's presence away and the deer may be able to escape. Listen to the layers of sounds that surround you. Start with the sounds you hear nearby, and work your way further out layer by layer."

First I heard my breath going in and out ever so slowly. I never really realized the sound of my breath until now. I suppose I was used to it since I'm breathing all the time. Then I noticed the occasional crack and pop from the burning cedar in the fire. My eyes noticed the branches moving slightly and I could hear a breeze a rustling through the trees. I kept expanding outward like the layers of an onion noticing pockets of silence and pockets of noise. I was surprised that I could hear the drone of tires on a remote road that had to be fifteen miles away as the crow flies.

Tilauth turned me around to face the woods to relearn all five senses. Each time I was astonished to discover how much I was missing. I started to feel a little embarrassed with how obvious this all should have been for me.

"How did I go through life not noticing what appears to be the obvious Tilauth?"

"You, like most people in the world, have lost the need to be aware. In a commercialized world where businesses desperately fight to grasp your attention through bright lights, big taste, and a catchy song, many have become numb. I think if I lived in your world, I would become numb too."

"What do mean? You do live in my world," I asked.

"Not the same way you do, Grandson" Tilauth responded. I then realized that Tilauth seems to live far away from all civilization all the time. In fact I've never seen him even near a town, let alone in it.

Chapter 18
The False Spirit

Elly's face popped in my mind with a flash, first it was perfect and unharmed, then it flashed again in the same instant with running makeup, dirt and blood smeared across her face. Her hair was wet and clung to her neck, forehead, and cheeks. Her face was contorted in pain and disfigured from abuse. "Help me, Neal!" she cried. From the darkness spun the face of Brian coming at me with a hiss, his neck contorted unnaturally, and his eyes were bleeding. I recognized him as the one I put into a coma and paralyzed. Brian's mouth opened violently and a dark malevolent beast shot through it with a trembling growl.

I lurched backwards sending an elk hide that covered me flying through the air. I scrambled to my feet, realizing my surroundings. I was inside the tepee and must have been dreaming. In the faint glow of the dying fire I began to scan for Tilauth. He was not in his bed where he normally slept. My eyes scanned around the tepee where I found Tilauth sitting up against his back rest next to the door. The wind whipped around the outside as the hides around the tepee flexed and slapped up against the structures poles. Tilauth was looking at me in complete silence. He looked at me a little differently than normal, however; he seemed to be looking at me with a deep concern. His eyes pierced through me and I felt everything that he felt. I could feel his deep concern and compassion for me, and I could strangely feel his sights focused on my feelings about Elly and the guys that killed her. I don't know how I knew this, but I did.

His eyes then moved back to my bed and then returned to me standing over it. His head tilted slightly motioning for me to look at my bed. I looked down to see someone lying in my bed. My eyes squinted and I realized that it was me. A panic shot through my spine and my eyes opened to see the smoke hole spiraling inside the roof of the tepee. I turned to see Tilauth sitting by the door but he wasn't there. I quickly scanned to his bed to see him lying supine with his eyes closed breathing quietly.

I rolled onto my back and watched the faint glimmer from the fire flicker along the tepee walls. I felt a tear stream from the corner of my eye as a sting of emotion soured throughout my body in the remembrance of Elly's death.

"Grandson." I heard Tilauth speak quietly from his bed. I turned to see him lying there peacefully, the same way I saw before. He opened his eyes slowly staring at the roof of the tepee, "You are haunted by your past, no?" I felt a sudden pressure build up behind my eyes and they swelled with tears. I fought the onslaught of grief and managed to answer quietly, "Yes." There was a silence for a moment while Tilauth thought through his words. "By ignoring your past, you've unknowingly chosen to carry it with you everywhere. This has resulted in dangerously depleting your energy. A false spirit has attached itself to you and is feeding on your weakness, fear, and anger. Not to mention the spirits of your past are lingering around you because you've called them here."

I lay in silence listening to what Tilauth was telling me. I didn't fully understand what he was saying but I could feel the truth. It struck deep within me and my grief grew tirelessly. The tears were now streaming from my eyes without resistance. With all the time that has now filled between now and that dreadful night, it still felt like it was yesterday. My body convulsed and shook uncontrollably with emotion.

All this continuous hurt started to upset me. I was tired of crying and tired of feeling like a failure. A rage began to swirl inside me and the tears stopped. I wanted to hunt down and kill every one of those guys for what they had done to Elly. I began to fascinate on how I would do it. I imagined myself sitting in the corner of a bar sipping a drink waiting for one of the guys to come in.

Unknowingly he would enter and I would wait patiently until he went to the bathroom or stepped outside for a smoke. Once they were in a secluded place I would quickly and silently sneak up behind them and slit their throat, leaving them to die with a glimpse of my avenging face as their last site in this world.

The anger built upon itself, leaving me feeling empowered over the hurt of my grief. I fantasized with every aspect of the hunt for Elly's murders. Each one of them I would successfully find and kill. Nothing would stop me. I was immortal until each and every one of them was killed.

As I laid there fantasizing my vengeance, I suddenly felt like I was being watched, and rolled my head over to see Tilauth looking at me the way he normally does, by staring through me.

"This false spirit has a strong hold on you, Grandson. False spirits are not something to take lightly. They can and will consume you if you continue to feed them the way you are now," he said to me with a concerned look.

"What do mean by false spirit?" I asked.

"A false spirit is just that. They are a spirit that

whispers false truths into your heart. What the spirit says is false but to them it is a truth. If you listen and follow the truths of a false spirit they will consume you to the point where you are no longer. They will consume every ounce of life energy from you, and you will be forced to look to others to feed from. The false spirit grows in unimaginable strength as it not only consumes you, but tries to consume everyone around you. It is nothing to fool around with. The false spirit that is with you has already grown to astounding strengths and the only person to blame is yourself." Tilauth's eyes were serious studying me with concern. "The only way to combat a false spirit is to not fight them with fear or anger for this only helps them to grow stronger. You kill them with your love and understanding, Grandson. You will need to face this false spirit soon, Grandson or you will be lost to its false truths."

"Tilauth, I'm tired of being sad. In fact, I'm tired of my life and this world. I don't have the energy to love some false spirit," I said feeling annoyed.

"Exactly Grandson, the false spirit has taken away your energy because you allowed him to. There is going to come a time where you will need to face this false spirit or you will endure the darkest of days until then. It will only get worse, Grandson."

I felt so angry inside and Tilauth's words only seemed to antagonize me even more. I knew that something was wrong with the way I was handling things, but I could see no other options. Tilauth left me to swallow his words and I rolled over and fell asleep.

The next morning was cold and the winds whipped up the south ridge twisting through the trees. I stood on a rocky ledge as the Coeur d'Alene River meandered slowly through the valley filling the bowels of Lake Coeur d'Alene. Along the river lie the scattered lakes of Swan Lake, Blue Lake, Thompson Lake, and Anderson

Lake.   Occasionally I could hear the distant echo of cows mooing from a remote ranch. I practiced using my five senses in the light of day, noticing everything from little insects to the shimmer of sunlight reflecting off the river below. It was difficult to hear much whenever the wind would pick up, but it strangely seemed to carry noises from afar. It almost seemed like I was imagining it, but I just shook it off.

I had practiced for an hour when I suddenly felt like something was behind me. I quickly turned around to see Tilauth standing there looking out at the same view I was. He glanced at me in the corner of his eye and smiled softly, "You are learning quickly, Grandson," he said as his face marked a sign of approval, "Come help me with some of the morning chores." We walked back to camp and I collected firewood, while Tilauth gathered some wild edibles to eat. Tilauth showed me how to make a wooden bowl by burning it slowly with pieces of coal from the fire. While my bowl burned slowly he showed me how to make all kinds of things from tools to string using the things that surrounded us.

It was just what I needed. I could still feel the anger inside me but it was silenced by the tasks at hand. The busy work made feel calm and peaceful, and I forgot for a moment that I even knew Elly and the dreadful things that happened to her and me.

I scraped the new charcoals away from my forming bowl with the sharpened rock I made earlier. Tilauth walked over to look at my work. "Your bowl is coming together nicely, Grandson," he said as he studied my work. "Tonight you will meet your false spirit," Tilauth said plainly and walked away without another word.

I watched him walk away and a surge of nervousness shot through my body. What could have he possibly meant by that? As I mulled over this idea my apprehension grew and the bushes near by rustled and it sounded like something got up and ran away from me. Startled, I jumped up to see what it was, but saw nothing but the swinging of a branch or two. The hairs on the back of my neck stood on end, and I suddenly felt like I was being watched only I couldn't see anything. Cautiously, I knelt down and continued to work on my bowl again, keeping a watchful eye on my surroundings.

Just before sunset, when the golden rays of sunlight beamed through the trees drawing long shadows across the earth Tilauth called me over to sit with him. I sat down next to Tilauth with our backs resting against a fallen log.

"Dusk is a good time to confront a false spirit," he said calmly. Your false spirit has been lingering around here all day. I forced him to leave you alone so you can clear your heart a little bit before confronting him. Now, the most important thing to keep in mind is to not give in to fear or anger. These things feed a false spirit and they will easily consume you." Tilauth paused for a long time. "Stare off into the woods directly in front of you. Relax your mind and breathe slowly. Allow your eyelids to close halfway but open enough to see out from under them."

I tried to breathe slowly but my apprehension was building, and I started to feel anxious. There was something about the unknown that was driving me crazy. I had no idea what to expect but perhaps a floating ghost. The idea of seeing a ghost terrified me given that I'd never seen a ghost or at least not that I could remember. "Relax, Grandson. Don't allow fear to consume you. The false spirit can see your fear and he will seize your weakness. Fear gives the false spirit power because you believe that they have power over you. They do not have power over you unless you believe they do," Tilauth said calmly. I kept telling myself that I was not afraid even though I was completely terrified. Tilauth was asking me to do things I had no idea how to do.

The sun continued to sink and the shadows stretched further across the earth. I expanded my awareness using all five senses and this seemed to calm me a little. The light grew dimmer and my eyes felt as if they were blurring. I blinked several times and it went away but would come back a few moments later. I looked over at Tilauth who was sitting there calmly looking into the woods. He jutted his chin to the bushes in front of us in gesture to tell me to keep looking. I turned and continued to hold my attention on the woods and the bushes began to blur again. This time I didn't fight it. I just let the blurry spot be there. Suddenly the whole scene seemed to blur and shift but I continued to focus on the forest.

My insides began to feel something in the bushes that was watching me but I couldn't see anything. Suddenly the bushes rustled loudly and I jumped up ready to run. "Sit down, Grandson!" Tilauth said but I couldn't move. My eyes were glued to the bushes and I could feel something horrifying lurking out there. Every inch of my body shook with fear. "Do NOT give into your fear," Tilauth commanded but I couldn't bear the thought of this thing, whatever it was.

Abruptly, the most ghastly looking beast lurched from the bushes towards me with an earth shaking growl. In an instant state of panic I jumped up and ran maniacally through the woods in the exact opposite direction of the hideous creature. I ran in the darkness ripping through the shrubs. Thorns dug in deep and tore at my clothes and skin. I didn't care, for I could hear the beast smashing through the bushes behind me. When I ran twigs snapped and behind me I could hear what sounded like trees snapping. The beast growled and I could feel it vibrate in my chest. I could feel my legs running but they couldn't go fast enough. I leaped over logs and bushes with amazing agility that I didn't know that I had.

Then just as quickly as it started it stopped. I

couldn't hear anything behind me at all and I finally began to slow down. I came to an abrupt stop, my chest heaving and turned around to see nothing. I half expected the beast to lurch out at any second and consume me with one gulp.

But I could hear something faint off in the distance. I quieted my breath to hear it better. To my utmost shock I could hear someone laughing. I listened harder to see if I was hearing correctly.

Not only could I hear laughing, but it was the all familiar belly laugh of Tilauth's. He was laughing at something that I must have missed. I made my way back towards the laugh feeling a little more at ease yet confused. Surprisingly, the camp was a lot closer than I imagined. I walked in to see Tilauth doubled over laughing like a child. Tears streamed down his face and he laughed harder as I got closer to him.

"Do you mind telling me what's so funny?" I asked feeling like I was possibly the brunt of one of his jokes.

"You of course," he said managing to get out between one of his laughing fits.

"I see...and just what is so funny about me?"

He laughed even harder and had trouble catching his breath. "You were running...," he broke out in another laughing fit. "You were running around in circles," he managed to finally get out.

I sat down on a log and waited for Tilauth to finally get a hold of himself. "I'm sorry, Grandson; it's just that you kept running around our camp in a giant circle trying to get away."

Tilauth noticed that I wasn't finding any of this funny and regained his composure. "I laugh because I have been in your shoes, Grandson. My teacher laughed at me when I ran, only I didn't run in circles," he said laughing a little more. "You see, today is the day I realized why my teacher laughed at me. It's because he knew what it was that I was running from."

"And just what was it that I was running from exactly?" I asked.

"Yourself," he said simply. "This is why it is so funny." I offered no gesture of a laugh or a smile. "Someday you will understand, Grandson."

"I see. Well, there was no way that I was running from myself," I argued.

Tilauth chuckled again.

"I know that it is difficult to understand right now but you will eventually. You see the world is made up of energy. Your scientists have already discovered this when they looked at the atom. All atoms are made of energy and everything is made of atoms. What scientist can't explain yet is why and how this energy that makes up atoms seems to know exactly what another atom is doing miles down the road. My people have known about this phenomenon for a long time. My people call this the Circle of Life. A circle does not come to an end but rather keeps going around. You see, Grandson, there is no breaking point or beginning or end to the world we live in. It is from the world of spirit that we were derived from. In the spirit world it is common knowledge that we are all part of the same circle or great oneness. The illusion is the separation between you and the false spirit or any other being. The reality is the continuous flow of the Circle of Life. This is why it is important for you to get to know your false spirit. The false spirit is you consuming yourself with fear and anger. There is no one to blame except yourself." I sat in silence listening to what Tilauth was telling me. What he said made sense to me but I was having difficulty applying it to what just happened. I couldn't comprehend understanding that the false spirit was myself.

"Grandson...the false spirit that you ran from tonight is a collection of your false spirits. I never expected you to do anything other, than what you did tonight. I did the same thing you did the first time I came face to face with my false spirit. People spend a lifetime feeding and nurturing their false spirit to become the worst thing imaginable. You are no different." Tilauth sat in silence appearing to be listening to something I couldn't hear. "You are almost ready to go on your first vision quest. But the spirit tells me you must first learn more about the physical world before diving into the world of spirit." Tilauth peered at me and waited for a reaction or a question but I said nothing.

"Let's build a fire and heat up some dinner. You've had enough for one evening. Tomorrow I'll begin teaching you more about the physical world. Your false spirit will have to wait. You do not have enough energy yet to take it on."

Chapter 19
Physical Education

The whole idea of having a false spirit made me nervous; however, this was beginning to become the norm when I was around Tilauth.

The next morning, I awoke after a good sleep feeling rested and restored. The sun shimmered down on our ridge, melting the frost from the late night chill. I started a small fire to take the nip out of the early morning air. After a small breakfast of dried fruit and a couple of fire roasted eggs that Tilauth found early that morning somewhere, I started firing away with questions.

"So what is it that I need to start learning?"

"Well for starters, you're soft, like an old woman. You watch too much TV. It's time to put some muscle on your jiggly body," he said as he poked my belly.

"Hey!" I said, pushing his finger away from my belly.

"Ok, jiggly boy, let's get started. Let's go down the valley and get some water."

I grabbed the empty bladders and we headed down the valley at a quick jog, jumping over logs and dodging mud puddles. The whole way, Tilauth kept reminding me to practice my awareness using my five senses. He smacked me on the head with his hand, a small rock, or a stick every time I lost focus. It was very difficult to hold my awareness while physically exerting myself. Tilauth's reminders were getting annoying, and beginning to hurt mentally more than physically.

When we reached the bottom of the valley, I filled the bladders with water and tied them off. After I filled them all up, Tilauth nodded.

"Good, now let's get going." He started up the trail, leaving me behind with all the water. I began to throw them over me, feeling the weight cut deep into my shoulders. My back strained to keep my balance as the water shifted with every step. Tilauth was a good ways up the trail waiting for me. I struggled with every step, feeling my muscles burn in my legs and back. I ached all over. Sweat trickled down my face and my chest heaved with every awkward step.

Tilauth nodded in approval, "Good work, Grandson, now push harder." I looked up at him with a glare and began to walk a little faster. Tilauth followed behind me making sure I pushed myself harder with every step of the way.

By the time we neared the top of the ridge, my legs wobbled uncontrollably and the bladder straps felt like knives cutting into my back. I clumsily lifted the bladder sacks off my shoulders and hung them in a tree next to camp. My shoulders felt like they were flying without the weight. I collapsed to the ground feeling the blood surging through my burning legs. Tilauth poured me some water from the bladders, which I drank like a slobbering fool.

"Don't waste it, Grandson, or you'll have to turn around and go back for more." I rolled my eyes at the thought of going down again and drank a little more cautiously.

Tilauth made me get up and stretch, having me move my arms around in different patterns. I mimicked him going through the motions. The stretching was slow and reminded me of a time when I saw an old Asian man doing Tai Chi on a beach back home. My muscles burned and ached with every movement, but they began to relax a little. I did, however, begin to notice a change in my awareness. Everything seemed more vibrant and acute. The light off the trees jumped out with colors of green and brown. The sky seemed to reach down and stretch all the way into my heart. The air was fresh and crisp in my lungs. Every ebb and nuance of the forest was brought to my attention with the utmost clarity. It is difficult to explain, but Tilauth's eyes seemed to mold me like a piece of clay as we moved through the stretches. I wasn't sure if the sensations I was having was from the stretches, Tilauth's eyes, or both. Regardless, I enjoyed the feeling of hypersensitivity.

Chapter 20
Elementary

Tilauth finished with the exercises and I stretched out over a log and let the sun beat down on my exhausted body. Tilauth went about the camp, doing little things here and there. I listened to the sounds of nature as I relaxed, allowing my muscles to recuperate.

With my eyes closed, it wasn't long before I heard something strange. Or rather it was the lack of what I heard. The forest around me grew silent and I could no longer hear Tilauth rustling around. In a split moment a surge of panic shoot through my body. With eyes still closed, I shielded my chest with my forearms. In the same instant I opened my eyes to see a long pole strike my forearms. The sting from the thwack throbbed in pain. At the other end of the pole stood Tilauth, grinning.

"Good, Grandson. Now get up and defend yourself." I jumped up, thinking that Tilauth must be losing his mind. He tilted his head ever so slightly, motioning to a pole lying on the ground next to me. I quickly picked it up, feeling the fear shoot through my body.

Tilauth began by striking his pole at me in several directions. He went slow enough to give me time to react and block his strikes with my pole. "Focus on the present moment, Grandson. Don't be afraid of what might happen in the future. There is no past or future in the world of spirit, only now. It is now that makes the past and future. If you want to own and create your past and future, you do it now in this moment and time. There is no other time but now. The moment you deviate from the now you will fail to create your future and be responsible for your past," he said as his pole sailed towards me again and again making a loud cracking noise as it collided with my pole. "I want you to focus on relaxing your body as you move. Every breath should be sent to an area of your body that needs to be released of tension. A body that is relaxed and calm will react quicker because it is in the present moment. A body that is tight, is afraid of the future and is resisting the present moment. Breathe and relax, Grandson, and do what instinctively comes to you. You already harness within you everything you need to know. Be present, and that instinctive knowledge will come through without thinking."

Tilauth's rhythm began to get erratic, striking slow then fast then slow again. I reacted to his strikes as they came in. My shoulders tightened with the faster pace and I tried to breathe and relax. My legs burned from hiking up the ridge with all the water before. I tried to get them to relax but they continued to burn with pain. Tilauth came in with several quick strikes and I began to panic. I blocked the first quick strike but his pole slid down and crushed my fingers. The next blow tapped my pole knocking it out of my hands and I cowered in a ball throwing my arms up to block the next blow. His pole collided with the side of my head smacking my ear. I was knocked off my feet and hit the ground with a shrilling ring in my right ear.

Tilauth's pole spun around like a baton before he set an end down into the ground next to his feet, standing it upright.

"You did well, Grandson, but you began to drift from the present moment. That is why you are now on the ground in pain. Had you not thought about your climb earlier today you wouldn't have panicked. I saw your mind drift and I took advantage of your weakness." Tilauth smiled at me as I rubbed my ear trying to dull the sting. "Take no shame, Grandson, you are doing very well."

I made my way back up to my feet and picked up my pole. Tilauth continued to teach me how to stay in the present moment. He showed me how to hold the pole and how to defend and strike. We kept at it for hours as I focused on relaxing my body with a slow breath. My form got better; however, Tilauth would periodically humble me with a few stinging blows.

"Breathing is one of the most important things when doing any sort of exercise. Breathing deep into the belly using your diaphragm will keep your energy balanced. When you become stressed, Grandson, your breathing and energy is all in your shoulders. As your opponent, I can then recognize the opportunity to knock you over because you are top heavy. I can also work you with the pole faster and know that you will tire before I do," Tilauth said as I tried to catch my breath. "You need to focus your attention on breathing deeply and slowly. This will keep you balanced and give you endurance." I nodded to his advice as I stooped over resting my aching muscles. "Take a break and drink some water, Grandson. I'll make us something to eat."

I doused myself with a little water to wash the sweat from my body and drank for what felt like the first time in my entire life. I collapsed on the log again feeling every muscle ache with pain. After resting I helped Tilauth with dinner. We ate in silence.

After we ate dinner we relaxed around the fire, listening to the cedar pop and crackle. The night air was eerily still and the forest was quiet.

"Why does this night seem so strange?" I asked.

"You are wondering why the forest is quiet?"

Tilauth said as he glanced up from the fire for the first time that night.

"Yes, the air is still and I haven't heard a noise."

"I'm glad to see that you haven't stopped practicing your awareness, Grandson."

"I'm afraid if I do stop I'll get thwacked on the head or something," I said. Tilauth began to laugh one of his whole-hearted laughs. I loved to hear him laugh, especially when he wasn't laughing at me.

"The animals are still and quiet because a storm is coming. Most animals that are normally out and about have found a place to bed down for the night."

"How do you know all this?" I asked.

"Because my teacher taught me to never let up on my awareness; otherwise my life would slip by… unnoticed." Tilauth responded as he rested a piece of wood on the fire.

"Tell me about your teacher," I asked.

Tilauth smiled at me as he sat back, making himself comfortable. "My teacher's name was One Who's Heart Stands in the Middle as you know. I called him Grand father however, others called him Hanunquuush. I'm not certain where the nick name came from or what it means for that matter. Regardless, he was a pleasant man, treating everyone well. He didn't lose his temper much. In fact, I can't remember one time when he was angry." Tilauth paused to try and think of a moment. "He was handsome and mysterious. Some women were absolutely infatuated with him. His good looks would catch their eye, and then he would reel them in with his charm. Hanunquuush never really opened up completely to the women who loved him. That is how he would drive them mad. They always wanted more, and I think he liked the attention."

"How do you say his name, Hanunquuush?" I said stammering out the pronunciation.

"'Ha' as in hu-ddle, 'nun' as in a catholic nun, 'qu' like saying 'qu-iet', and 'ush' as in sl-ush.

Hanunquush." Tilauth repeated.

"Hanunquush." I restated.

"Good. You know, your spirit reminds me a little of Hanunquush." Tilauth said, smiling at me. "For the most part, he was a peaceful man, but he was also a strong and lean man. In other words, if you were his family or friend, he would defend you to his death if someone threatened you. He was also a miraculous healer and seer." Tilauth paused for a moment. "It is not polite to talk about someone who has passed away. It is better to talk to them directly or to at least acknowledge their presence when you talk about them."

"What do you mean talk to them?" I quickly asked, feeling uneasy.

"When you talk about someone that has passed away, their spirit becomes present. You can upset a spirit if you talk about them without actually listening to them or talk directly to them. It is simply considered rude. However, in your case, Hanunquush understands that you are learning, and do not know how to see or hear from the world of spirit. Hanunquush's spirit is with you often, as with the many teachers before him. You are now part of our lineage, which means that you will someday become a teacher too. Their spirits are constantly protecting and teaching you." Tilauth paused to let me gather up the idea that I wasn't alone. "You see, last night when you were running around in circles trying to escape your false spirit; well, it was the protection that was placed on you that did not allow the false spirit to consume you. This does not mean that you are invincible. It just means that your spirit will be protected only when it matters. Your physical body can still be harmed; however, your spirit will not be consumed."

"I see." I paused for awhile and thought about having someone watch over me. It made me feel a little strange thinking that they see me with everything I do, and yet it also made me feel at ease knowing that someone like Hanunquush was there to protect me if something horrible goes wrong. "So do spirits see my every move and thought?"

"No, they only see the things that matter and your thoughts are heard like prayers to the spirits that they apply to. If you feel that certain things that you do and think are personal, then they are protected by your spirit's individualism and other spirits have no right to them."

"Ok." I said feeling a little relieved.

Tilauth smiled, "It's ok, Grandson. I felt the same way before I became aware of the spirits around me."

We sat in silence for awhile. I began to think of the false spirit I ran into last night and it reminded me of the night Elly died. My gut twisted with anger and grief.

"Tilauth, I'm still..." My throat squeezed tight and it was difficult to breathe. My body began to tremble uncontrollably.

"Grandson...I know that you are still struggling with your past. When the time comes for you to vision quest, you will begin to find some of the answers you are looking for." Tilauth stood up and put a hand on my shoulder to offer some compassion. "It's getting late, Grandson. You have a busy day tomorrow, and I want you fully rested."

That night I slipped into a deep sleep. I was so exhausted that I didn't wake up to the thrashing winds that nearly picked the tepee off the ground and sent it sailing down the ridge. Tilauth told me how the thunder shook the ground and the rains never ceased until early morning. There was so much rain that a small stream cut its way through one side of the tepee. When I awoke Tilauth had been up most of the night keeping things dry and keeping them from blowing away.

My muscles were so sore from the day before that

when I stood up, I nearly fell back down. Tilauth laughed as I struggled to stand and walk.

"Drink plenty of water, Grandson...it will help with the soreness." I went outside in the fresh morning air and took a deep breath. The air smelled of wet soil and everything dripped down into the muddy earth. The sun peaked out occasionally from behind large cumulus clouds offering a brief opportunity to dry things out.

My legs ached in soreness and I drank hesitantly. The last thing I wanted to do was haul another load of water up the ridge. "Drink as much as you want, Grandson. I collected a lot of rain water last night to extend us for awhile. Today I will let your muscles heal and rest. Tomorrow we'll jump back into working off the extra insulation around your belly."

I spent the day learning simple survival skills, like how to build a fire using two pieces of wood. Tilauth also showed me how to make some snares and deadfalls to catch both large and small animals. He said it was important to know and understand that mother earth has provided everything necessary for survival. Human beings have forgotten how to live on the Earth the way the Creator intended, were his words. So over a period of about nine months I learned how to build both temporary and long term shelters. I also began to learn the vast uses of what seemed like an infinite amount of plants in the area. Tilauth showed me how to skin and gut the animals I caught. I tanned the hides and made them into clothing using the sinew from the animal. I also ate many plants and animals that my stomach has never seen before. I learned the many different styles to weaving baskets from cedar and other plants in the area. With my increased awareness, Tilauth showed me how to listen to nature's rhythms. I also started to become a very proficient tracker. Not only could I identify what animal made a particular track but I could also tell its sex, speed, the direction its head was turned, and its emotional state.

I was practicing or learning something every waking moment. I would wake around six in the morning and not fall asleep until ten or eleven at night. I'm guessing, of course because I left my watch in my Jeep and never bothered to pull it out. Time had vanished in my world; I ate when I was hungry and slept when I was tired. I was starting to feel like I could take care of myself no matter where in the world I was. The feeling was absolutely liberating. I began to wonder how I could have gotten by without the knowledge that Tilauth has bestowed on me. I sopped up everything like a dried up sponge.

Occasionally, I would make a trip into the small town of Harrison and make a phone call home letting them know that I'm ok and having fun. My family didn't ask too many questions and I didn't offer many answers other than I am out seeing the world. Even though I hadn't traveled far I was experiencing what felt like life for the first time. I was beginning to experience the one thing that seemed to be lacking in my life; living.

Chapter 21
Invisibility

Over the months Tilauth worked me hard physically during the day, and I practiced my survival skills at night like making arrow shafts, knapping stone, and shaping my bow. It wasn't long before I started to see muscles that I didn't know I had. Tilauth taught me more fighting techniques like grappling, a martial arts style of fighting, tomahawk and knife throwing, and the art of invisibility. I learned that the art of invisibility requires unbearable patience and a calmness that only exists outside of oneself.

It was now fall and the tamaracks were a brilliant bright yellow. The air was turning cold again and I occasionally wondered about the outside world. I felt like I was slipping out of a society that no longer applied to me. When I return home I began to wonder what had happened in the world; would the U.S be at war, did California collapse into the ocean, who died, who was born, did the world find peace, or was the world conquered by some power hungry dictator. I kind of felt like everyone in the world was, or rather should be, growing and coming to the same enlightenment as I was; however, that I later understood to be a big misconception.

One morning I sat in the camp building a fire. Tilauth left in the middle of the night on one of his excursions. I warmed myself by the fire stretching my legs and back. I dug out some dried fruit I had stashed away and began to work on a winter hat I was making from the hide of a coyote. As I worked a strange feeling stirred through my stomach. I felt as though I was being watched but every time I looked up I saw nothing. My gut told me it was to the right of me but I could see nothing. To the right were a couple of ponderosa pine trees and a small yew tree. There was almost no undergrowth so there was little place to hide. I stared and stared at the area but saw nothing. Nothing moved and nothing made a sound. I continued to work on my hat but couldn't shake the feeling. Finally, feeling annoyed I got up and slowly walked to the area. There was nothing there and I was beginning to think I was losing my edge. I stood before the small yew tree and looked up into the branches to see nothing but branches. Just as I was about to head back to the fire something grabbed my ankle and pulled it out from under me at lightening speed. My foot spun so quickly out from under me that my cheek slammed into the cold wet ground before I could catch myself. The impact knocked the air out of my lungs and I struggled for breath. I turned to see Tilauth standing over me chuckling the way he always did.

As I struggled to grasp my breath, I looked around to try and figure out where he was hiding. Nothing offered him a cover to blind him from my view.

"Where did you come from?" I struggled to say with my first breath.

"Right there." Tilauth said pointing to the ground at my feet. "In fact you nearly stepped on me. You should watch where you're going," He said with a smile.

"Very funny. How did I not see you?"

"I moved to your blind spot where shadows are in

your mind," Tilauth stood over me, looking proud of what he'd done. His face and clothes where muddy from his camouflaging. He helped me get back up and I brushed myself off.

"So tell me how you did that."

"Everyone has blind areas in their vision; however, your blind areas have been shrinking with your increased awareness. This forced me to be extremely patient, very cautious, and it also forced me to shift my perception point to a place of invisibility."

"Perception point?" I asked.

"A perception point is a name that I've given to a pin point place where all energy is entered through and departed through. Every energetic being has a perception point, and by moving my point I can rearrange my energy makeup to an infinite amount of possibilities. So by moving my point to a specific place, I was able to reorganize my energy to appear invisible. I was also paying attention to your perception point. By studying yours, I could influence it both physically and energetically."

"So if I have this perception point, how do you influence it?" I said critically.

"One way to influence it is by scaring you. By scaring you, I can dislodge it from its normal comfort zone. This allows me to then more easily influence it with my intentions.

But this is jumping ahead and I don't want you to try and bite more than you can swallow. First and foremost you need to become aware of your own perception point before you can start influencing others."

"So I can turn invisible?" I asked, feeling like I was on the brink of becoming some sort of superhero.

"Yes, and you're capable of much more although, it's not as simple as saying the magic words and presto. Moving your perception point requires you to have and or tap into a certain amount of energy. If you are depleted of energy and you have a purpose that is selfish, you will have a very difficult time moving your perception point. By having a purpose that is unselfish, you can receive energy from the great universe of life to assist you in moving your point."

"So where is my perception point now?" I asked.

"I'm not going to just show you, I want you to find it." Tilauth said sternly.

Tilauth told me to sit next to the fire comfortably where I could stay warm. He then had me go through some breathing exercises and muscle tensing and relaxing exercises to get me into a relaxed state of mind. Once relaxed he told me to point to the place where I imagined my perception point to be. I then pointed to a place just to the left of my sternum in my chest.

"Very good, Grandson, you are absolutely correct. Now I want you to imagine a place where that perception point should be to make yourself invisible." I sat for a moment and could only see one spot inside of me that seemed correct. I pointed to a place on the lower lateral portion of my right rib cage. "Very good, Grandson, this is the point where you will sometimes find invisibility. This point can vary during different circumstances; however, under the circumstances you are in now that is the point of invisibility. Now I want you to move your point to that spot following the path that seems right to you."

I pictured in my mind the path necessary to move my perception point and began to imagine it was moving along that path. At times it moved slowly and almost felt stuck. But I continued to push it there following the squiggly path to the point of invisibility.

When I imagined it arriving at the point of invisibility I heard Tilauth say, "Good you're there. Now I want you to hold it there." This surprised me because he obviously was able to track this movement of which I felt like I was just making it all up. "Now open your eyes," Tilauth said softly.

I opened my eyes to see him sitting diagonally from me. Everything seemed normal; however, just a little different in ways that are difficult to explain.

"I want you to go for a walk slowly into the woods all the while constantly focusing on holding your perception point at the place of invisibility. I got up and slowly walked into the woods away from our camp. "Focus on that point, Grandson," Tilauth called out from behind me. I walked out slowly into the woods observing my surroundings. It took everything within me to keep my perception point at the place of invisibility. I reached a place that was a good distance from camp and stood there for awhile. The area had lots of wild animal tracks from deer to wild hares. I saw some sparrows hopping and flying around from branch to branch doing their normal activities. They didn't seem to notice me but then again they didn't ever seem to have much of a reaction when I was around normally. I sat there for a long time focusing on the point. I started to grow tired and my attention began to drift to meandering thoughts that had nothing to do with invisibility. Just before my thoughts could drift very far I heard Tilauth yell, "Focus!" His yell sent the sparrows into a startled panic, which sparked the craziest experience I'd ever had. A sparrow flew right into the small of my back. I turned around to see the poor creature on the ground flopping around maniacally. I studied the bird for a second as it regained its composure and then flew away, nearly hitting me again.

My heart jumped in realization that the sparrow, the master of maneuverability in flight, did not see me and flew directly into me. And then almost did it a second time when he flew away.

I quickly made my way back to camp astonished and amazed. I saw Tilauth sitting on the log tending to the fire. He saw my face and I could tell he knew exactly what had happened. After the whole experience I felt exhausted yet I hadn't done anything physically exerting.

Tilauth noticed my tiredness, "Your energy is lacking. This is why it is important to have a purpose that is unselfish. In this case, you had enough energy to learn something new. The next time you will have to find a way to make your purpose unselfish. We can work to rebuild your internal energy; however, this will take some time. For now focus on finding that selfless purpose." I nodded, as I began to search my mind for any reason that could be defined as selfless. The selfless purpose was difficult to come up with. I needed to find a purpose that serves something or someone other than myself.

I spent the rest of the morning exercising and practicing the fighting techniques Tilauth had been teaching me. After working up a good sweat I headed down the valley to the lake. As I strolled down a series of deer and elk trails I focused on expanding my awareness. At the same time I tried to be conscious of where my perception point was. I noticed that when I expanded my awareness my perception point seemed to move a little more freely.

A couple of ravens cawed away as they swooped from branch to branch nearby. Their voices echoed across the valley, giving me a relaxed feeling. As I walked I tried to figure out a possible scenario when I would be able to move my perception point with selfless purpose. The trees slipped past me like patient giant people watching me as I passed by deep in thought. The only circumstance I could imagine utilizing selfless purpose for invisibility was to save someone. Like for example say I needed to save a child who had been kidnapped. I could render myself invisible to the kidnappers while I snuck in and freed the child. Such a scenario seemed highly unlikely to me, and I was beginning to think that I would never need the ability to make myself invisible under a selfless circumstance.

When I reached the lake I dreaded the moment of feeling that cold nip when entering the water. I stripped my clothes and tried and work up the nerve to jump into the frigid waters. The wind suddenly whipped around and my muscles quickly tensed up to resist the fall chill. I stood on the shore with my arms wrapped around me tightly gazing over the waters.

I wondered if this physical change had affected the placement of my perception point so I quickly checked its placement by scanning my body with my mind. I was surprised to find that it had moved from where it was before. That's when it hit me. Tilauth had mentioned that the movement of the perception point has infinite possibilities. I quickly scanned my body to see if there was a place where I could change the temperature of my body by placing my perception point there. As I scanned my intuition guided me to a specific spot. I focused all my energy on that spot.

When I successfully moved my perception point I no longer felt the cold air whip around my body. Without losing my focus I held that point and continued into the water. To my utter surprise, the water felt fine. I lunged all the way in and felt comfortable. The water was cold but I felt fine. I quickly did my bathing routine, struggling to hold my perception point. I remembered how exhausted I was from the last time I moved my point so I bathed extra quick to get it done before I couldn't hold it there any longer. I threw buckets of cold water over my head to rinse and I felt the sting of the cold water. I could no longer hold my perception point. Once I finished with the last bone chilling bucket of water I dried off as quick as possible and got dressed. I was so tired that I was actually panting.

I quickly got dressed and felt much warmer and I laid back to take an obligatory rest. It didn't take long before I actually fell asleep for a few minutes in my exhaustion.

I awoke feeling a little disoriented because I didn't plan on falling asleep. I wasn't a hundred percent sure how long I slept because the sun was behind the clouds and the daylight hadn't changed much. I made the long and arduous climb back up the ridge slowly. First off, I didn't want to break out into another sweat and render my bath futile. Secondly, I hadn't the energy to move quickly up the ridge.

I slowly hobbled back into camp and flopped down on the log near the fire. Tilauth watched me closely as I laid back on the log to rest. I could feel his eyes examining me and I was too tired to care. I passed out again for an undeterminable amount of time. Falling asleep was never an easy task for me however, in my fatigue there was no opposition to keep me awake for my normal hour spent trying to fall asleep. I awoke to Tilauth hovering over me with an eye of concern.

"Grandson, your life energy is nearly gone. This is why you're having trouble staying awake."

"I moved my perception point again to learn how to withstand the cold waters when I bathed. When I was finished I was so exhausted I passed out asleep."

"I know, you were gone for some time. When I went to check on you, you were asleep next to the lake. I just let you sleep and figured you'd be back when you were good and rested."

"How long was I asleep for?" I asked, feeling like there was a gap in time that needed explaining.

"Well, you left yesterday afternoon and didn't bother coming back until the next day, which is also in the afternoon," Tilauth explained. "Now you fall asleep again for about an hour before I woke you up. You'd probably sleep till next spring if I'd let you," He said starting to chuckle. "You're like the toad that hibernates. Are you trying to hibernate?" he laughed again. I sat up scratching my head yet still feeling very tired. "I hadn't realized that I slept for that long. To me it only felt like a few minutes."

"There is no time or place in the world of spirit. When you start moving your perception point around, time and place can get distorted as you are now beginning to understand. You also need to understand the meaning of selfless purpose, Grandson."

I was feeling bewildered and was trying to recollect the entire day that I missed.

"I can't figure it out Tilauth. There doesn't seem to be anytime when I would have selfless purpose, unless it's under circumstances that I doubt would ever happen," I said, feeling annoyed.

"Geeze you're grumpy when you're tired," he said laughing. "In order to understand selfless purpose you need to understand who you are completely. The answer lies in the Circle of Life. You are everything and everything is you. There is no separation, only the illusion of separation. I know that you don't fully understand what I'm saying because you haven't experienced the complete self yet." Tilauth sat down and looked at me for a moment. "I think the time has come where you are ready for a vision quest. The vision quest will help you sort out many of the problems you are facing, that is, if you want to face them, of course." I looked up at Tilauth and felt a sudden surge of fear and relief. The vision quest frightened me but I knew deep down inside that it was the next step. The idea of seeing that false spirit again sent shivers up and down my spine.

"I think I'm ready. I will be honest with you Tilauth, the whole idea quite literally frightens the hell out of me."

"That is normal. You'd be insane if you were not afraid or you probably wouldn't need to quest at all." Tilauth paused a moment to listen to the wind. "The spirits tell me that the time is right."

Chapter 22
The Sweat Lodge

I slept hard that night, despite the large amount of sleep I had the day before. I was exhausted and it seemed to take a long time to recuperate from moving my perception point. The next morning after Tilauth and I finished our regular chores Tilauth started the preparations for my vision quest. He went through some guidelines for me to follow and some 'what to do if's.' The gist of what I was supposed to do was spend four days and four nights in a small five to ten foot diameter circle, eat nothing, go nowhere, and do nothing except be present. I don't know what it was but the whole idea made my body literally shake with nervous anticipation. Maybe it was because somewhere deep inside me I intuitively knew what was in store for me.

After talking with Tilauth for sometime about the quest he told me to go out and find the place where I was to quest.

"How do I know when I have found the right place?" I asked.

"Follow your heart, Grandson. There may not be bolts of lightening coming down from the sky when you find the correct place, but it will simply feel right to you. Your heart will let you know."

I started down the north side of the ridge with some water and supplies that Tilauth said to take and leave at the site once I found it. I walked all the way down to the stream where we collected our water. Nothing seemed to feel right, so I kept walking. Every once in awhile I'd come across a good place to set up camp, but it didn't feel right. I headed up the other side of the valley crossing a small meadow littered with white tail, mule deer, and elk antler sheds. The meadow seemed like a great place to explore, but it still didn't feel right to me. I made my way up the ridge crossing an old logging road that hadn't been used since the early 1900's. The road was grown over with ponderosa, yew, and pine saplings. As I continued up the ridge it began to narrow with steep edges on both sides. It funneled into one trail that was littered with elk tracks. The trees closed in and I felt a change in my gut. Stopped in the middle of an elk trail I looked around;this was to be my quest site. My heart raced as a surge of fear shot through my body. My head spun with a dizzy sensation. The ground was hardly flat and there was moderate tree cover from the weather. This wouldn't be my first choice to set up camp, but my heart said it was the right place. I tied up my gear and water into a bundle, wrapping it in a tarp I had stored in my Jeep to keep things dry. Through the pine trees I had a slight view to the south, where I could see the east portion of the ridge where Tilauth and I were camping.

I made my way back to camp where I saw Tilauth securing some hides to a small dome like structure that couldn't fit more than four people comfortably.

"Hello, Grandson, it is good to see you," he said to welcome me. I walked over to examine the structure more closely. It had a small door like an igloo that forced me to get on all fours to peek inside. The inside was pitch black except for the light skewering in through the door. Inside the structure was a small pit directly in the center. The dome was shaped by main support saplings where one end was embedded into the earth and the other was bent over and strapped to another sapling on the opposite side of the structure. Smaller branches where then bent and strapped perpendicular to the main support saplings to give it added support. I crawled out to see Tilauth finishing up with some of the last touches.

"What is this for?" I asked.

"This is a sweat lodge. We will be using it to prepare you for your quest." Tilauth pointed to the large fire that was burning in camp. "I've been heating up some rocks in the fire ever since you left. They are just about ready now... Drink plenty of water, Grandson, you're going to need it." I looked at the large fire and could see some of the rocks inside glowing a brilliant red and orange. Tilauth went inside the tepee where he grabbed a long slender bundle wrapped in elk hide. He emerged and walked silently over to the sweat lodge. I sat in front of the fire silently listening to the murmur of Tilauth saying some prayers. He emerged from the sweat lodge and silently came over to the fire, where he plucked a coal and placed it into an old abalone shell. It instantly began to smoke as it burned the herbs Tilauth placed into it. He silently walked back into the lodge. Smoke billowed out from the door and I could hear Tilauth singing a song in his own tongue. The sound was so stunning that it sent chills down my spine. I could not understand the words he sang because they were in a different language, but I could feel the passion in his voice.

I sat next to the fire silently drinking my water when Tilauth emerged again. "The lodge is ready, Grandson." He handed me a long stick that had some antlers tightly secured to one end to resemble a pitch fork. "Get me fifteen large rocks out of the fire and place them in the center of the lodge," Tilauth asked.

Sparks swirled to the darkening sky as I finagled the antlers around a large glowing rock. The heat of the fire seared the hairs on my arms as I hoisted each one out of the fire and placed it carefully in the center of the sweat lodge. I had a pretty good idea that I was going to sit inside the lodge and sweat but I had no idea what this ceremony entailed. The fire wafted a raging heat as I struggled to fish out the last five rocks. When I finished, Tilauth instructed me to strip down to nothing and go into the lodge.

Tilauth had placed a large container of water, some cedar, yarrow, a drum, and an eagle's wing just to the right of the door. Tilauth crawled in after me and sat next to the things he had placed there earlier. He shut the door and everything went black except for the glowing rocks in the center. Some of the cedar and yarrow was placed on the rocks and it popped, cracked, and smoked. The entire lodge filled up with the smell of cedar and yarrow. The heat warmed my skin, which felt good at first, then started to feel uncomfortably hot.

He started with some prayers in his native tongue and some in English. The drum began to strike quickly and Tilauth's voice cried out in a song that seemed to shake my very being. Water splashed on the rocks and the heat intensified ten-fold. It felt as if my skin was beginning to cook. I breathed slowly and managed to stay calm. More prayers were said and songs were sung before the door was suddenly opened.

A rush of cold air swept in and surrounded my lower body first as the hot air escaped out the top of the door. Tilauth sat quietly looking at the rocks. I mimicked him and stared at the rocks. Tilauth had me bring in twelve more from the fire. When I finished I entered the lodge and sat down where I had sat before.

Before I knew it, the door was shut again and Tilauth was throwing on more water. The heat seared into my lungs and my breaths grew shallow. More prayers and songs were sung while I tried to relax and be present. I stared at the rocks and noticed that they changed shapes. First I saw the coyote, then an alligator, a fox, a frog, and an antelope. All was completely black except for the red glowing rocks in the center of the lodge. The door whipped open again and Tilauth asked me to go get some more rocks from the fire.

I staggered out of the lodge drenched in sweat. I poked around in the fire with the makeshift pitch fork and pulled some more rocks out of the fire one by one. Tilauth told me to drink some water before I came back in. I happily gulped it down, realizing that I was very thirsty.

On all fours, I crawled back into the scorching hot lodge. With the door still open the heat was almost unbearable. Tilauth closed the door and the lodge went black except for the glowing rocks in the center. They cracked and popped with a sound like little hammers hitting steel ever so lightly. Tilauth put some herbs on the new rocks to smudge them. An opening prayer was said and Tilauth sang another beautiful song. Water splashed over the rocks with a bubbling sizzle. The steam wrapped around my body like a hot hug that left my skin searing. I endured the discomfort and listened to Tilauth's prayers. When he finished he asked me to say a prayer. The lodge filled with silence and I struggled to regain a comprehensive mind to speak. My mind seemed to shift and blur between reality and fiction. When I came to the present moment I felt the pain on my skin again. I breathed slowly and began to pray. "Creator...may you hear my words. I've gotten lost somewhere along the way and I wish to find myself once again. Some things have happened in my life that I'm having difficulty...understanding. There is so much anger and sadness within me. Tomorrow

I will go on a vision quest to find my true self once again. I have so many questions and so little answers. Please protect me and guide me on this quest. All my relations." I prayed the words but I felt like I didn't even think about them before they came out. They seemed to just pour out of me without thinking.

Tilauth opened the door and asked me to get the rest of the rocks and leave one in the fire. After retrieving all the rocks except one the center of the lodge was a large pile of red rocks. Tilauth closed the door again for the final round. He said some more prayers and honored and welcomed the winds of the North. Nothing is overlooked in Tilauth's sweat lodge ceremony. He honors the entire circle of life recognizing that everything has an important role. By the final round I'm driven to lie on the ground and breathe the air that is cooler near the Earth. The door is finally opened and I stagger out of the lodge slowly feeling dizzy and disoriented. I lay on the ground, staring up at stars. Tilauth gave me a full bladder of water to drink and pour over my body to wash the sweat away. He said that the body releases toxins through the skin in a sweat lodge ceremony and it is important to wash those toxins off to prevent them from reabsorbing back into the body.

After I washed myself and drank my fill, Tilauth silently motioned for me to go to bed. He said no words will be spoken until I return from my quest.

"This is what brought me to the initial frightening moment," I thought to myself.

I now lie in this tepee somewhere in Northern Idaho. The air is cool as it trickles in under a small crack at the base of the tepee. My eyes are wide open and sleepless. The thought of facing my false spirits frightened me to no end. "I wasn't ready," I thought and my mind raced with what if this happens or what if that happens. My body trembled in nervousness. I tried to close my eyes and sleep but my mind was filled with busy concerns. Tilauth crawled in the tepee later and instantly began snoring the moment his head hit the pillow. Each snore drove me nuts with envy.

Chapter 23
The Vision Quest

It seemed like the moment I finally fell asleep Tilauth was prompting me to awaken. He nudged my shoulder without a word and I turned over to see him looking down at me plainly. I got up, put on some warm clothes, and Tilauth silently motioned for me to head off to my quest site.

The sky was still black and the stars twinkled above. The moon was bright and made the trail easy to navigate. By the time I arrived at my quest site, the sky had started to lighten and the sun was threatening to rise over Swan Peak behind me. My quest site seemed to stare back at me as I stopped for a second to look at it. It would be four days before I could look at it again from this direction. With only a moment of hesitation I walked into my quest site hesitantly. My emotions began to shoot off in all different directions and I instantly began to weep. Somewhere inside of me my soul has been waiting my entire life for this moment. I wept in joy, sadness, fear, frustration, and relief all at once. It was a confusing moment that couldn't be explained other than I felt that I was there for the ride. I couldn't stop the tears from flowing even if I tried, so I just let myself weep with all I had. Finally, my emotional state began calm down. The sky brightened as the sun rose behind me however; I could not feel the warmth of the sun yet because I was shadowed by the peak of the mountain. The air was frigid and remained so until about eleven in the morning, I imagined when the sun finally shone down through the trees.

I spent all morning praying; welcoming each direction in the circle of life and letting them know what I wanted out of the quest. It was only moments after my prayers that I started to talk to myself without realizing it. Every question I had for life was getting said out loud. I began to pretend that I was having a two-way conversation with myself where I'd ask a question and try to answer it and reason with myself. I felt like I was losing my mind, but I didn't care because no one could see or hear me. No one was there to judge or criticize me so I let it all out. I argued with myself for hours on end and I pretended the trees and bushes were my audience. I explained things to those trees so that they could understand.

I talked about issues with things that I'd done in the past to people that I wasn't proud of. I talked about my fears, my doubts, the reasons why I have taken the paths I'd taken in the past. I also talked about my big questions about religion. Being raised in a conservative Christian home, I wanted to know what was true and what was false. Religion surprisingly was my biggest hurdle. My frustrations brought me to tears as I struggled to find the answers. I hadn't realized how much religion was playing a role influencing my life. I wept for the answers; I wanted them so bad.

In a moment when I lied hunched over on the ground weeping, I heard a sequence of high-pitched chirping. I looked up with my tear-soaked eyes to see an eagle circling directly above me. It circled twice and flew west. I didn't know what it meant, but it gave me the reassurance that someone or something was listening. That was all that I needed at that time.

My mind grew clear and I began to talk out loud again. This time I calmly answered every question that had been haunting my thoughts all my life. It was the strangest feeling but I could answer any question I could possibly imagine. I didn't even have to really think about it, the answers just flowed out of me like a babbling brook.

I thought briefly for a moment, "What if I'm wrong with one of my answers?" I laughed to myself at this thought because I knew that this was not possible. Not only would I have to lie to myself, which I found out I have done a lot in the past, but I would know that I'm lying to myself because I can feel it. In a moment of clarity it is impossible to lie to one's self because it only leads to confusion and frustration. My intuition made it clear what is true and what is false and that was the only thing that I could completely trust in life.

Each answer led to the answer to another question and another question. My joy grew with every answer, as I felt a large weight being lifted off my shoulders. Time flew by as the self dialogue went on and on. The trees were my imaginary students and I was the teacher explaining every question that I could possibly imagine coming up. I kept going on and on like this for hours.

I suddenly grew aware of my surroundings and realized that it was night already. I finally sat down in my circle and realized that I had been standing for hours answering my questions and everyone else's pretend questions. My body was exhausted and I felt the nip in the air. I bundled up with blankets and listened to nature as night set in. Occasionally I'd hear a branch snap or a rustle in the bushes and I'd turn around expecting to see a false spirit lurking over me. I dismissed every noise to be from a small bird or animal and pretended to not let it get to me. It wasn't long before I passed out unintentionally for an unknown amount of time.

I awoke to a loud crinkling noise and the thud of footsteps. My mind reeled back and forth as I suddenly realized where I was and I jumped onto my feet, spinning around to the noise coming from behind me. The sky had just begun to lighten and I could barely see a branch swinging back and forth behind me. There was nothing there that I could see but there was also no doubt in my mind that something was there. I must have kept an eye on the forest behind me for a good full hour before the sky got bright enough that I could see. I half expected a bear, mountain lion, or a worse, a false spirit to be hiding in the bushes waiting for me to turn my back to proceed stalking me. I finally realized that if I was going to continue with my quest I was going to have to make sure nothing was lurking in the bushes. So I left my quest site to urinate and ensure that there was no danger.

I cautiously walked behind my quest site, about ten feet, to see my tarp that I had tied down a couple of days ago, with a dry change of clothes in case I got wet. The tarp was slightly rustled up and fresh elk tracks were everywhere. I felt like an idiot when I realized that my rope to hold down the tarp was strung out across an elk trail. I had essentially made a trip wire unintentionally and spooked the elk when it got caught up in it. The tarp rustled loudly and no doubt frightened the elk more than I was frightened. I walked back to my site after urinating, leaving the rope strung across the trail seeing it as a good deterrent for other large animals from suddenly walking over me in the middle of the night.

The rest of the day wasn't nearly as exciting. I spent most of the day fighting off boredom and trying to stay focused on my quest. I mostly tried to stay present and observe my surroundings, which is what Tilauth had told me to do when I got bored. I watched birds come and go cutting in and around the branches and trees. I prayed about every ten minutes, to keep my mind focused on the reason for my quest. I lacked the need for answered questions because they were already answered. Time crawled at an unnoticeable pace. A chipmunk let out a loud and long chirp before running across my feet as if I weren't there. The small animals of the area seemed to get used to me and treated me like a rock in the landscape. I constantly flicked off ants, gnats, and mosquitoes. The mosquitoes were especially worse at dawn and dusk. The valley echoed with a drone of millions of mosquito wings in the morning and evening. I fought them off ferociously, smashing them every chance I got. At first I felt bad, thinking that I shouldn't be killing animals, especially while on a vision quest. This guilt quickly dissipated when I realized that if a bear were to come along and attack me, I would definitely fight back. I wouldn't just allow the bear to eat me because I didn't want to hurt the bear. So I continued to kill the biting gnats and mosquitoes, acknowledging that they take a risk when they feed off of me, some succeed and some fail. "This is all part of the circle of life," I thought.

I spent most of my day getting used to the new person I'd become. I was no longer feeling like I was walking around life blindly. I now knew the effect I had on others and the truth about myself. I was beginning to realize what the circle of life meant, which is what Tilauth had been explaining to me all along. I remembered him saying that I'd lost myself because I didn't know who I was. It was becoming painfully clear just who I was. I was a piece of everything, and everything is a piece of me, and I knew this because I could feel it. Every time I hurt someone emotionally or physically, I hurt myself worse. Every time I helped someone and offered something constructive for someone, I helped myself. I started to realize that my environment was a direct result of my actions to everything. I was the one to blame when someone had ill intentions towards me. I was the one to blame when I was blaming everyone and everything else. In the circle of life there was no separation, just the illusion of the separation. What I thought was reality was actually the illusion.

In my newfound clarity I truly listened for what seemed like the very first time. I looked at the two trees closest to my quest site that I had been talking to for hours on end and I could actually feel them. I could feel and see their entire life, from beginning to end. They showed the time lapse of their life and the changes to their surroundings. I suddenly felt unworthy of being bored, as I had only been in one spot for a couple of days and these trees had never seen another spot their entire life. I could see their entire past, with highlights during tough storms and winters. Their deep connection to the earth and patience humbled me to no end. They also shared with me their wisdom. They knew I was coming before I came. They knew this because there is no time or place in the world of spirit. The trees explained to me that the past and the future are reflections of the present moment. In other words, it is in the present moment that we create our past and influence our future.

I looked around at the many things around me, feeling them, seeing them, and listening to them. I learned things from the rocks, the chipmunks, the clouds, the ants, the plants, the birds, the earth, and anything else I could set my eyes on. The rocks are the oldest things on the planet and hold the history and wisdom of all that has ever come to pass. The heart beat of the rocks are unimaginably slow, requiring me to slow down to a calmness I've never experienced. The ants are busy creatures, searching constantly for food and shelter for their livelihood. They live their lives as if every moment depends on their survival. The chipmunk is just as busy, but remains playful and lighthearted. That lightheartedness is something I'd forgotten in my all my seriousness. I tried to keep a light heart through my quest and if I came down hard on myself, the chipmunk would scurry across my feet to remind me. His long chirps sounded like he was laughing at me every time I got too serious and strict.

I also took the time to talk to Mother Earth, and found out she is much stronger than I had ever imagined. I always saw the earth as a fragile thing, easily influenced and destroyed by man's pollution and destructive nature. On the contrary, the earth will continue on, long after man has destroyed everything on the planet, including himself.

I looked at life in this new light, coming in contact with my surroundings for what felt like the first time. It was hard for me to imagine what life would be like without the questions and uncertainty I had before I started my quest. Wisdom was set right out in front of me for the taking whenever I wanted it. It was this way because there is no separation in the circle of life, and every question had an answer that resided within me. And 'Who is me?' I would ask myself. I am a piece of everything known and unknown and everything known and unknown is a piece of me.

The first day I felt tested, and a piece of the old self died. The second day I settled into my self and let the wisdom pour into me. I wondered what the third day had in store for me.

That was when I remembered Tilauth telling me that on the third night he would remove a protection he placed on me and I would face the false spirits in my life. He must've noticed the fear in my face and reminded me that I would only be presented with the false spirits that I could handle. This comforted me, but I couldn't shake the feeling I had when confronted by my false spirit many months ago.

The second day finally comes to an end with the sun shining brilliantly in my eyes. My stomach growls and gurgles and begins to cramp and I drink some water to ease the cramping. The second night was the first time I got really hungry and I began to day dream about some of the restaurants back home. My mind drifted from pepperoni pizza to chicken in a lemon cream sauce with pine nuts and a Greek salad. Thinking about food only made my hunger pains worse. So I tried to change the subject. I stared off into the night attempting to stay awake and present as much as possible.

I said a few prayers and felt the nip of the night air enclose around me. Bundled in a blanket my body felt weak and vulnerable. I tried to stay focused on the present moment but my mind slipped away to moments I cannot recall. I speculated that during most of these unaccounted for moments I was having visions. I later found out from Tilauth that these blank spots are normal and I will remember them when I'm ready. These moments will seem to come out of nowhere when I'm doing something that may hold significance to the forgotten portion of my quest. I will then all of a sudden remember the forgotten moment and understand it when it is appropriate.

Tall standing summer grasses swayed all around me as the breezes whipped through the prairie. I hunkered down low and turned to my left to see my close friend Keith squatting down in the tall grasses holding a remote control. He was wearing a police uniform like myself that we were using as disguises. To my right sat a young boy that I had just met a few days ago. He held an old Colt Revolver he stole from his dad a couple of days ago in his right hand. He was wearing his normal everyday clothes because Keith said that he couldn't get him a uniform. I looked down to notice that I had a .45 semiautomatic pistol stuffed in my holster. Keith also had a pistol stuffed in his hip holster. I remembered the young boy begging Keith for a uniform but Keith adamantly denied him. Keith said he tried but was unable to get one for him especially one in a smaller size.

There was a slight moment of confusion that entered my mind, and I wondered how I got myself into this mess. Before I could think anymore, I heard the rattle of an old car coming down the dirt road. Keith signaled for us to squat down deeper in the grass to keep us hidden. Dust billowed up behind the old black Cadillac on the hot sweltering day cruising at high speeds. Sweat trickled down my forehead as I hesitated for a moment, trying to figure out a way out of this situation. It didn't take long for the car to come rumbling in front of us and I knew that it was too late to back out now.

Keith raised the remote control and flicked a switch. The old car's front end popped and broke with a small explosion. The whole front axle tore away from the car and it came to a sliding halt, kicking up enormous amounts of dust. Keith jumped up with shotgun in hand and the kid and I followed close behind. We arrived at the car, surrounded by a large cloud of dust. Keith opened the front driver's side door to see that nobody was in it.

His head whipped around to me, "There's nobody in the car!" he exclaimed. We frantically started to look around to see if the guy had crawled into a ditch or something. It was difficult to see anything at all with so much dust. I walked through the ditch with my .45 drawn and ready to shoot. That was when I saw two black boots facing me. I quickly looked up to see a police officer in a dark blue suit pointing his gun at me. He quickly pointed his gun down when he realized that I appeared to be another officer. He pointed a finger to the air silently swirling it in circles then pointed it in the direction of the car. I quickly mimicked him and pretended to approach the scene with caution. Our weapons drawn and moving cautiously the dust finally began to settle. I suddenly realized that the entire car was surrounded by police officers and Keith was circling in opposite of me mimicking the officers at his side. The young boy was trying to open the trunk of the old car when he realized his predicament. It wasn't until now that I realized that Keith must have foreseen this possibility and knew that someone had to take the fall if we were to be caught. My heart sank in my realization that this boy was just a boy.

The young boy stood in front of us as the officers formed a perfect circle around him with Keith and me pointing our weapons at him like the rest of the officers. The boy's big eyes shifted quickly from officer to officer in terror. His eyes met Keith's and Keith offered him no help.

One of the officers said calmly yet with force, "Drop your weapon son, it's over."

The young boy's eyes shifted around the circle, no doubt looking for me. His eyes met mine and I could see that he was silently asking for my help. My heart felt like it was being torn to pieces, but I couldn't do anything, I didn't want to go to jail. When the boy realized that I wasn't going to offer any help, his eyes began to swell with tears and they ran down his dust covered cheeks. "Drop your weapon now, son!" another officer called out. But the boy remained looking at me longing for me to do something for him. I remained firm and continued to point my gun at the young boy.

With his eyes glued to mine he raised his gun and pointed it at his temple.

"No…." I yelled, but it was too late. The revolver fired and he fell to the ground limp.

I jumped up yelling "No!" but nothing came out because I was without breath. I quickly realized where I was. My heart was pounding and tears were streaming down my cheeks. The night air was cold and I remembered that I was on a vision quest. I couldn't shake out the picture of that boy staring at me just before he shot himself. I felt responsible and selfish. I wept for an hour as I felt the boy's fear and pain.

As the night progressed, I realized that this vision, among several other things, was a big lesson about complacency. Complacency or going with the flow brought me to that predicament. It was Keith 'the leader' that I followed, even though deep in my heart I knew it wasn't the right thing to be doing. But Keith was not to blame. I could only blame myself for being complacent. This is what put the young boy in the predicament. The young boy saw my selfishness and complacency and shot himself because of it. This is the vision that made me weep uncontrollably.

The night lingered on as I slipped in and out of consciousness. I awoke early the next morning with my face covered in dried tears and dirt. My body stunk from the lack of bathing, and my clothes were covered in dirt. The sky grew grey and dark and I pulled out my tarp as the rain began to come down. It wasn't long before the sprinkle turned into a downpour and I sat on the ground with the tarp wrapped around my head like an old native woman in the desert.

On the third day, new ideas came flooding into me. With my clarity and new found wisdom, I wanted to put it to use. I wanted everyone to discover what I had discovered. It came clear as day to me that everyone is searching for answers in one way or another. That is what I wanted to do for others. I began to hash out the thousands of possibilities in my head on how to help people find the answers they're looking for. My head spun in circles with idea after idea. I started to get stir crazy. The boredom of sitting in one place was driving me nuts. My stomach growled and cramped up every once in awhile, but for the most part I didn't feel too hungry.

Eagles and hawks kept circling above my quest site, which made me feel pleasant and at peace. I ached for the moment when I could walk out of my quest and head back to camp. I felt like I got everything I needed and didn't want to continue anymore. Despite my desires to leave I stayed and continued to pray for clarity and direction in my life. The rain finally began to slow down to a sprinkle as I sat in my quest site in a silent stillness. I was jarred to my surroundings with the rustling of some low growing bushes about ten yards in front of me. My heart began to pound at the thought of what kind of animal would feel so confident in the forest to make such a racquet. Most animals are quiet and very careful as the make their way through the forest; only animals that are at the top of the food chain tend to be loud and careless.

I tried to remain calm as sticks snapped and popped. Finally, a large furry beast ripped through the brush and instantly took site of me. The large black bear stared me down as I remained in my quest site, motionless. Bears have terrible eye sight, but an excellent sense of smell. What concerned me most was that the bear didn't smell the air he was just looking at me as if he already knew what I was. It was as if he knew why I was there too. His eyes looked deep into my soul as if he was trying to tell me something but I couldn't understand the language.

My heart spun with the feeling of cautiousness. It felt like the bear was watching out for me and I just missed a close call that I wasn't even aware of. The bear spun around on his hind legs and headed down the ridge to my left. I watched his fury rump disappear back into the brush just as loudly as he appeared. It wasn't until after he disappeared that I realized I was shaking from fear. Then it struck me; Tilauth warned me that the third evening he would remove any protection I had from the false spirits. Tilauth taught me awhile back that he used certain animal spirits for protection. The bear was one of the protector spirits that had just come to let me know that he was leaving me.

My eyes quickly scanned my surroundings half expecting a false spirit to already be stalking up to me. The sun was setting, and most of the clouds disappeared, enabling long shadows to be cast through the forest. I sat up at attention, waiting for the false spirit to pounce on me at any moment. I heard nothing and saw nothing. The forest seemed normal and continued about its normal everyday tasks. Squirrels shot back and forth across my site as the ants fervently continued to try and climb me. I brushed them off paying little attention to them. I remember Tilauth telling me not to fear the false spirits because they feed off the fear. So I pretended not to be afraid even though I couldn't help but remember the moment that hideous beast chased me through the forest. I felt as if the worst thing imaginable was tearing at the integrity of my being.

Now I'm about to come face-to-face with the beast again, only now I feel vulnerable and lonely. Tilauth removed the protection and now it was the false spirit and I going one on one.

The day shifted to night as I began to get tired of waiting for the beast to show itself. The drone of mosquitoes finally began to subside and I stopped slapping myself to smash the persistent little bugs. The drone of mosquitoes was replaced by the subtle chirping of crickets. I listened to the singing crickets and relaxed forgetting about the false spirits altogether.

It was at that moment when I decided to forget about the false spirits that the crickets suddenly stopped. I could hear them way off in the distance but the crickets around me fell dead silent. A cold breeze etched ever so slowly towards me. The hairs on the back of my neck stood straight up and I lost my breath. My heart began to pound so hard in my chest that it felt like it might crack through my ribs. My body surged with a jolt of adrenaline as I knew what was about to happen.

Before I could look around to see if something was lurking up to me I realized that I was already face to face with my worst fear. The beast's skin was pale white and hairless, with long slender legs and arms. It squatted in front of me with its featureless face a foot away from mine. Its pale skin had only depressions where the eyes should be and an almost infinitesimal lump for a nose. Its mouth was a flat slit that stretched across its face motionless. His head began to slightly tilt like the way a dog does when it's trying to figure something out. His eyes opened abruptly from what I thought was just skin. I fell back involuntarily as my heart beat so fast I thought that it might burst in my chest.

His long slender arms stretched out and it crawled up over me like a spider and hovered over me on all fours. His black shiny eyes examined me as if he were trying to size me up. His mouth opened with a hiss and I could only see the infinite blackness that resided within. He began to whisper as he breathed in and out creating an eerie sound that shot fear into the center of my bones.

"You can...see me?" he hissed as he hovered over me.

"Yes," I stated as the fear grew inside me.

"You...are...afraid of me!" he hissed as he inhaled with every other word.

"I'm not afraid of you," I quickly replied.

"Your heart...says...that you are," he said as his head tilted to peer deeper into me.

"You don't know my heart," I began to squirm under my skin. He began to laugh in such a way that it seemed to fill the whole valley with his laughing echo.

"You see everything but...you know...nothing!" He quickly got off of me and turned his back to me in a squatting position. His head turned to look at me over his shoulder. "I can see...your anger." His eyes closed and once again looked as if his face was covered in a pale plastic wrap. His body began to vibrate unnaturally and a flash of darkness shot around me.

I looked around to see that all the trees were dead and charred from fires. The air was thick with a burning sensation as it entered my lungs. The sky was a deep amber color from all the smoke that blocked out the sunlight. A puddle at my feet was black and thick like tar. I felt a strange sensation as if something was behind me. When I turned around I saw more of the tattered landscape with burning fires everywhere. Next to a charred stump in the distance I could barely see the same false spirit that hovered over me earlier. In a blink he was standing only few feet away from me. He appeared larger and stronger this time. "You are...me," he hissed. His hand shot up at an unnatural speed and covered my eyes so that I could not see.

I awoke to the sun shining down on me. I got up slowly and felt every muscle ache with weakness and pain. My skin was red and blistered from the sun. The air was cool, but the sun had gotten me good. "What day is it?" I thought. I glanced down at my pile of three rocks and realized that it must be the afternoon of day four now. I placed another rock down so that I would remember that I could leave tomorrow morning. A surge of excitement filled me as I realized that I had only one more day and night left.

I reviewed in my head what had happened last night or at least what I could remember. I couldn't make heads or tales of it. Just thinking about it made me feel uneasy. I knew that I hadn't conquered the false spirit but I also knew that I wasn't completely consumed by the false spirit, either.

I glanced around my quest site, seeing that none of the trees were dead and charred. Everything was still alive and healthy. The air was clean and smelled like pine. I felt myself filling with so much love that I could hardly bare it. Tears easily streamed down my cheeks, as I looked at the tree that I'd had so many conversations with. I felt so much compassion for all of life and suddenly realized that I belonged there. In this moment in time, I was to be nowhere else but here. The birds chirped away in the trees, their bellies full from the worms that rose to the surface with the rains of yesterday. I could feel everything in the world within me and realized that there is no separation from one thing to the next. I felt like I was everywhere at once and everywhere was me. I knew the feelings of anything and everything if I brought my attention to it.

I spent the rest of the day experiencing the feeling of sitting in the circle of life. It is an experience that is difficult to put into words because there are no words in the English language to describe it. Perhaps there are so few people in the world that have experienced it to bother creating words to describe such an experience. I spent the rest of the fourth day and night in a state of indescribable bliss.

The next morning the sun began to rise and the sky lit up in a brilliant blue. I gathered my things together and actually felt sad to leave. I looked at the trees, birds, chipmunks, ants, and even the mosquitoes and thanked them with all of my heart. My eyes teared up with gratitude as I offered some tobacco to the four winds, mother earth, father sky, and the Creator. With reluctance I turned and began to make my journey back to camp. My heart was weightless and my feet felt like feathers. My body was weak but I felt like I had enough energy to run a marathon.

I arrived at the campsite late in the morning. A small stream of smoke swirled up from the fire pit.

Tilauth came out from the tepee and he peered at me the way he usually does when he looks through me.

I smiled at him and said, "Good morning."

"Good morning, Grandson," he said returning the smile. Tilauth extended his arm out motioning for me to sit. We sat down across from one another in a moment of silence. "Tell me about your quest, Grandson," he said smiling warmly. I told him a general overview of all that happened to me. He got particularly interested when I told him about my encounter with the false spirit and asked me to tell him every detail. When I was finished he nodded and a large smile spread across his face. "This is good, Grandson. I am pleased to see that you are discovering who you truly are. When you learn who you truly are you can then know and walk your path with purpose. You have seen the circle of life that exists within you. You have discovered the truth about many of the false spirits that have been haunting you. You now have more internal energy because you are not wasting it on dead ends. You are discovering what it means to be truly free. I still see a very powerful false spirit that lingers with you. This false spirit is going to be one of your greatest teachers;that is, if you choose to learn from him. If you choose to ignore this false spirit, he will burden you to your death and into the afterlife. Some dark days will be in your life until you've learned the truth about this false spirit," Tilauth stopped talking for a moment to allow me to absorb his words.

I was not used to hearing anyone talk. It's funny how four days of solitude can affect my ability to have a conversation. I was feeling a little socially inept.

"You are well on your path, Grandson," he said with an approving nod. "You've learned things that many don't even learn in a lifetime and only you could have taught yourself these things."

I spent the rest of the day recapitulating my quest in my mind. Tilauth said that it was a good idea if I wrote it down so that I would not forget it. I noticed that the simple act of writing down as much as I could remember brought more clarity to my quest. I also started to remember little details that I was about to forget.

Chapter 24
Spider

Tilauth and I struck camp because he said it wasn't good for the earth or the mind to stay in one place for too long.

"Humans were never meant to stay in one place all their lives," he said. Staying in one place makes a human predictable and stubborn. Predictable and stubborn human beings are just waiting to die. Life lives them, they don't live life."

So we packed up camp and I loaded up my Jeep. Tilauth made a makeshift rucksack made out of cordage and hides. He threw it over his back took one look at me and said, "Drive west, Grandson."

"Aren't you coming with me?"

"No," he said simply.

"It's no problem. I don't mind. I'll give you a ride."

"No thanks."

"How far are we going then?" I asked.

"Go until you reach the Puget Sound."

"That has to be three, maybe four hundred miles from here!" I exclaimed.

"You remember where you first saw me on the beach?" he asked.

I thought for a moment, being drawn back to the moment I fell asleep on the beach and I awoke and saw Tilauth looking at me from a distance.

"Yes...I remember," I said feeling bewildered.

"Good, I'll meet you there when you get there."

"Are you joking?"

"Well, if it was a joke I can't see how it would be very funny? You'd better get going, Grandson. I don't want to have to wait too long."

"I'm serious Tilauth...it would be easier if you just rode with me." He smiled at me and turned and walked into the trees heading down the valley.

I was completely stunned. I thought that there was nothing Tilauth could do that would surprise me anymore. The idea of Tilauth walking hundreds of miles for days on end, when it would only take me six or seven hours in my Jeep, sounded absolutely preposterous to me. I shrugged it off, knowing that there was nothing I could do to change Tilauth's mind.

I hopped in my Jeep and it glugged over. "I've got fire but no fuel," I thought. I began to pump the gas pedal like I always had to do when I hadn't started it for awhile. I then turned the key and the starter grinded away as the engine failed to fire up. As I continued to chug away at it I was getting concerned that the battery was going to die out before I could get it started. I popped the hood and primed the carburetor. It started up with a few flames shooting out of the carburetor and I held the gas down just enough to keep it from dying. I fastened the air filter back on and began to make my way through the same logging roads I came in on long ago. It took me awhile as new trees had fallen across the road and I had to cut them away so I could get by but I finally made it to the paved road. I drove up the long and squiggly highway along

Lake Coeur de' Alene. I fueled up in Coeur de'Alene and drove I-90 across the flat open pastures of eastern Washington.

Giant fast food signs like skyscrapers created oversized interruptions of life. All the signs seemed to hurt my eyes and I had to look the other way. It's strange how something so commonplace before, became this object of over stimulation. I actually felt dizzy and sick to my stomach from advertisement signs. Spending as much time in the wilderness as I did had definitely changed my perception of the world. Not only had I changed from the lessons I'd been learning from Tilauth, but I also changed from just being absent from advertisement and society.

The highway hummed under my tires as the miles passed. I stopped to get something to eat in Ritzville, Washington. The food sat in the bottom of my stomach with the weight of a bowling ball. I had to pull over shortly after eating to get sick. The vomit seeped into the dry soil as the cars flew by wafting waves of exhaust into my lungs. I gargled some water and got back on the road. "I can't eat the food restaurants serve anymore," I thought. My body had gotten used to the fresh meat and plants in northern Idaho. The food at the restaurant tasted old and created a twisted hyper sensation, similar to drinking a pot of coffee. My tongue seemed to go numb as I lightly chewed on it in hopes of regaining its sensitivity.

The Jeep whipped down the highway picking it up and slapping it down behind me. The old rig whined and sputtered as it climbed the Cascade Mountains. After passing the summit, I began to make my descent into Western Washington. The air smelled wet and I began to remember home. The forest grew thick with Mountain Hemlock, Pacific Silver Fir, and Yellow Cedars leaving the common Ponderosa Pine and Jeffrey Pine of the semi arid desert of eastern Washington behind. As I made my way down the Pass, the land began to change again from sub alpine forests to the commercial strip malls of Issaquah.

I thought for a moment, should I swing by and see my family or should I go straight to the beach where I was to meet Tilauth? I thought it would be impossible for him to already be there, so I decided to say hello to the folks and let them know I was alright.

I saw the old house set in the middle of rows of other houses just like it in suburbia Lynnwood, Washington. I pulled in the driveway and caught up with the folks. I didn't tell them much other than I'd been doing some traveling and lots of camping. They seemed to accept this and were glad to see me again. I went ahead and took the luxury of a hot shower and a home cooked meal. I slept in the spare bedroom that night and decided to go to the beach in the morning to make sure Tilauth hadn't miraculously already arrived. It took me awhile to fall asleep in a different place. I actually had gotten used to the sounds of nature at night to lull me to sleep.

The next morning I got up early before anyone else and fired up the Jeep and made my way to Picnic Point Beach. Thin flat clouds were speckled across the sky as I sped through flickers of shadow and light.

I parked in the parking lot and made my way to the beach. As I'm coming down the walkway I can see the back of Tilauth as he's sitting at picnic table facing the water. His rucksack is sitting in a plain dugout canoe with a couple of paddles.

I walked over to him absolutely astonished, "How did you get here so fast?" I asked in shock.

"What took you so long?" he shot right back at me.

"What do you mean...That's impossible...How did you..." I cut myself short, knowing that he wasn't going to tell me the answer. He looked at me plainly, knowing that I had to be dying inside with questions.

"Get your things, were going to be heading out,"

he said staring at me waiting. I shook my head and grabbed my stuff from the Jeep.

I threw my bag in the canoe and we carried it to the waters edge.

"Isn't there some kind of law we need to abide by before we take this out on the water like this?" I said pointing out into the Puget Sound.

"Probably," he said, enjoying my discomfort as he continued to pull the canoe into the water. I hopped in and we began to paddle north near the eastern shore. It took me awhile to get comfortable with sitting in the primitive canoe, being a little tipsy and the seating so hard. But I settled in and listened to the water churn with every paddle.

"Now's a good time to be heading north," Tilauth said. "We have the currents in our favor. We'll stay close to the shores as much as possible, that way we don't have to be dodging those big tankers out there," he said as he poked the air with his paddle in the direction of a large rusty barge that lumbered along full of supplies.

"Where are we going?" I asked.

"It's time for you to start learning the ways of a shaman," Tilauth said frankly.

"You mean like a healer or medicine man?"

"Yeah...something like that."

"Why me...I mean I don't know..." I felt my heart race inside me, intuitively knowing this thought felt right.

"Don't worry, Grandson, your spirit's ready and your spirit knows you better than you know yourself."

The next five days were spent paddling north in the Puget Sound, camping every night in little private areas we'd find as far away from homes as possible. The days slipped by with a mixture of sun, heavy rains, high winds, sleet, and at one time a mixture of snow and rain. This weather was a typical spring in the Puget Sound, as Salmon Berry bushes, Currants,

Indian Plum, and Daffodils were beginning to bloom.

One day, Tilauth pulled onto a beach of one of the islands strewn throughout the Sound. No houses were nearby, but the occasional kayaker or hiker would venture into this area exploring. We knew this from the old human tracks that we found here and there. Tilauth aged them to be about two weeks old.

As we walked around, I noticed that Tilauth seemed quieter than normal. He seemed to be listening to a distant voice inside his head that I could never hear. I would get dead silent to see if I could notice what it was that he was listening to. The sounds were all normal to me, waves lapping against the beach, a slight breeze from the southwest, the occasional song of a dark eyed junco, a robin, and a crow. Nothing seemed out of the ordinary, but something was deeply catching the attention of Tilauth. He stopped in his tracks and motioned with his hand for me stop. I listened hard with every ounce of awareness that I could find. Nothing came to my attention. His eyes focused on an area to the north east of us, so I looked that way and saw nothing but trees and shrubs.

After what seemed like hours, Tilauth broke the silence and said "We will set up camp further south down the beach. Promise me, Grandson, that you will never enter the area just beyond that clump of shrubs," Tilauth said, without taking his eyes from the area.

"Why?" I asked.

"You will understand why in time, but for now I ask that you stay away from there until I see that you are ready." His eyes were still fixed on the spot to the north of us.

"I promise," I said, feeling my curiosity surge. But I knew that by the tone of Tilauth's voice that I'd better listen to him. A chill ran up and down my spine and I felt it difficult to look away from the spot. I turned to see Tilauth staring back down at me curiously.

"Let's go set up camp, Grandson," he said as we turned back down the beach tromping through the Salal, Oregon Grape, and Sword Fern. Large Hemlock towered over head as we walked through the forest sprinkled with the unusual tree called the Pacific Madrone. This tree became one of my favorites. It seemed so out of place. It almost seemed to better fit the rocky cliffs in Japan with its bonsai features.

We set up camp in a small clearing just off the beach. Tilauth set out to build a slightly more permanent shelter while I made us some temporary debris huts for the time being. The next few days we worked on the shelter made primarily from cedar. It was elevated off the ground a couple of feet, with wood planks for floors and a cedar bark thatched roof.

We ate like kings, fresh steamed mussels, salmon, oysters, clams, Dungeness crab, grebe and deer jerky left over from Idaho in case we grew tired of the seafood. I made Tilauth and me cedar hats to wick away the drizzle on the gloomy days. Several weeks passed and I learned nothing that seemed to pertain to the world of the shaman. I didn't ask why since we were so busy with things around the camp.

It wasn't until one day Tilauth took me away from my usual chores that we hiked up to this high bluff overlooking the water. He had me close my eyes and he would take me on these wild adventures in my imagination. I would go to this world that I made up in my head. I was free to do and be whatever I wanted. In this world there was no rules; I could change into a marsh hawk and soar through the forests or I could change into a porpoise and skim through the water seamlessly. I could control the weather, the day, the night, or the tides. Tilauth had me create a few places in my world that were specific for doing shaman work he said. He also designated some areas where he said that I will do specific things like the act of remembering or a place where I could do healing work on myself.

In these specific places I began to notice that my perception point would move around to certain areas in my body and sometimes just outside my body. I spent every day in amongst my chores going on these adventures in my mind. I started to feel loopy and a little bit on the crazy side from all these spiritual trips in my mind.

I also found myself consistently hearing voices and seeing things move around in the corner of my eyes. When I'd turn to see what it was I saw or heard, there would be nothing there.

Early one morning I was sleeping out in the open when the weather was good. I dreamt I saw some deer pop out in front of me. I quickly awoke with a feeling that the deer would be popping out of the bushes any moment. I looked at the patch of Indian Plum where I saw the deer in my dream. I sat quietly for a moment before I saw those same deer that I saw in my dream stroll out from the bushes. The deer walked right by me as I sat there motionless watching them. They acted as if I didn't even exist or like I was just some boulder on the landscape. My heart began to soar when I realized that I'd actually knew they would appear before they appeared. I told Tilauth of my premonition of the deer and he nodded in approval, saying nothing. His nod seemed to say all that he needed to say and I knew that no words were needed.

Tilauth asked about my dreams and I said that I hadn't been dreaming much that I know of. But then I remembered I dreamt the other day that I was in a pile of wood and spiders were swarming all over me.

"That is a good dream to have," he said, smiling in approval. "The spider is the spirit between this world and that. He lives in the physical world and has full awareness of the world of spirit at the same time. The spider knows which world is the illusion and which world is the reality. The world you know as common is the illusion created through the world of spirit. You have begun to delve into both worlds and they are beginning to blur together. This is the path of the shaman. The shaman learns how to manipulate the physical world through the world of spirit. This is the essence of the shaman. The spider is a territorial creature and your energy is similar to that of the spider. So the spider is attracted to you when you come physically into his territory.

The spider also holds the energy of trickster. The lessons from spider are potent yet sometimes stressful. Listen to spider carefully and learn from her, but do not be tricked by her. You may have also noticed that the spirit of the raven has been around here a lot. The raven holds the spirit of creating. Deep in the black feathers of the raven you will see a rainbow of colors reflect back at you when the light hits it. The blackness symbolizes emptiness and the rainbow is the light of its creation. You are holding this energy within you also. It is time for you to start creating from nothing. You found some of your desires on your quest, now it's time to create those desires as a reality in this world of illusion." Tilauth quietly gets up and walks away from me.

Just then a raven swoops down onto a branch in front of me and I nod at it, feeling somehow that it understands my greeting. I did suddenly realize that my days were spent constantly swooshing spiders off me. They would hang down from tree limbs as I walked through the forest and I'd have to dodge them at the last minute before running directly into them. I remembered Tilauth telling me that people have the power to attract any animal they wish. But shamans were more aware of the different energies a particular animal exudes and can attract specific animals by simply intending it. He also warned me that some animals are not as friendly as others and can be life threatening.

Chapter 25
Old Memories

The next few months I focused everyday on my adventures of the mind, sometimes with and sometimes without Tilauth. The days warmed to summer and the rain subsided. I would swim in the ocean to cool off from the hot days. We also started to get more human visitors straying closer and closer to us. Kayakers avoided us as they assumed we had already taken that section of the beach to camp.

I watched as a couple of hikers came through the woods and nearly stepped on me as they walked by, completely unaware of my presence. They walked up to the shelter Tilauth and I built, curious no doubt, as to how long it had been there. The shelter looked like something prehistoric. I stood a ways behind them quietly as they peered in through the door.

They looked as if they were about to go in when I finally decided to say something.

"Can I help you folks?" I said. The guy slammed his head on the low door jamb and the girl spun around quickly with a scream. "Sorry I didn't mean to scare you." I said.

"Sorry to intrude, I didn't realize that anyone was

staying here," he said explaining himself to me. I stood there motionless and still as a shock of horror streaked through my entire body. I did not recognize this man's face but I recognized his voice. It reminded me of the voice I heard whispering to me as Elly got raped. I stood there motionless in front of the couple. At first I thought that he recognized me but I remembered that my hair had grown long and I had a shaggy beard now.

"You ok sir?" the girl asked as I stood there motionless, having a flash back from that dreadful night. She took a step closer as her boyfriend stared at me, confused but still not recognizing me. "Are you alright?" she asked again.

I finally snapped out of it and said, "I'm fine."

"You sure?" she asked.

"The guy's fine babe, sorry to intrude on your camp site sir," the familiar voice said.

"Do you live here?" the girl asked, snapping me away from the guys' voice.

"No...I'm just...I'm just camping here for a little while."

"Oh, well I'm sorry for our intrusion, you have a nice camp."

"Thanks," I mumbled as they walked away.

My heart pounded with adrenaline and my hands began to tingle. My stomach twisted up and squeezed until a sour taste filled my mouth. The last thing I expected was to hear that voice again, especially way out here on an island in the middle of the woods. I suddenly got the strange feeling that Tilauth was standing behind me. I turned around quickly to see him watching the whole thing from a distance.

"Did you see them?" I asked Tilauth.

"Yes, I saw them", he answered as he walked quietly towards me.

"Did they see you?" I asked as I swelled up with a mixture of grief and anger.

"I highly doubt it," Tilauth said as he studied me quizzically. "Are you alright, Grandson?" he asked.

"I'm fine!" I snapped back at him.

Tilauth studied me softly, "You are upset."

"I'm sorry," I said, catching my temper. "It's just that...well that kid's voice reminded me of someone... but I'm sure it wasn't the same person."

"You're sure?" Tilauth cocked his head at me.

"No...no I'm not sure," I hesitantly said listening to my gut. "In fact I'm positive that that kid was one of the kids that raped and killed Elly."

We were silent for a long moment before Tilauth broke the silence, "What are you going to do?"

"I don't know what to do." I said, feeling helpless and seriously confused.

"There isn't a day that goes by that that boy isn't haunted by what he's done. Your soul will not let him forget and his guilt will not let him forget," Tilauth said quickly. His words shook me down to the marrow of my bones. I stared at Tilauth with a menacing look that felt like it wasn't my own.

"I have to stop him," I said not realizing my words.

Tilauth stepped away from me quickly and he stared at me sternly without a word. Something inside me sprung free like a wild beast and I spun around and quickly headed in the direction the couple went. I stalked quickly up to them as they tromped through the woods like bumbling fools. I slinked behind old stumps and trees dancing through the shadows following them closely. They talked about me, slightly frightened from my sudden appearance to them. I heard them speculating as to whether or not they thought I was a hermit or a just a hairy kayaker on a month long trip or something. The girl found it fascinating because she saw some of the primitive looking things hanging in the shelter like furs and my handmade bow.

The voice, as I've come to call him said, "He's probably wanted by the law and is living off the fat of the land dodging the authorities. We ought to call the cops and tell them there's an illegal squatter out here. He's probably raped and murdered some girl and is now hiding out."

These words shocked me so much that I slipped up and a twig snapped beneath my feet. I hit the ground quickly as they both went silent and I could tell they were looking my way.

"Let's get out of here John," the girl said, feeling uneasy. I heard them turn and begin to jog down the trail. This was good as it was going to make it easier to stalk someone who is running and not paying attention to their surroundings. I let them get a good lead because the bird's alarm calls around them revealed their presence to me at all times.

I finally arrived at a parking lot where I watched them hastily get into a red Honda Civic. The car fired up and I decided to put the fear of God into them by stepping out of the bushes to be seen in their rearview mirror as the gravel sprung out from under their tires and they sputtered out of the parking lot. I memorized the license plate as they turned down the highway in the direction of the ferry terminal.

Without a second thought I walked out to the highway and began to head in the same direction. My vision became tunneled and I walked with purpose. My mind kept replaying his voice over and over in my head. I went through a whole series of what if I had done this or done that. "What if I'd walked right up to him and told him who I was?" I thought. Would he have remembered me? Would he have tried to kill me? I visualized in my head what a fight with him may have looked like. I pictured myself snapping his neck or slowly torturing him into apologizing for what he'd done.

Every bone of my body ached with an unstoppable

rage. The scenery blurred by me unnoticed eliciting a state of beastliness.

After a few hours I finally arrived at the ferry terminal. There were cars lined up waiting for the ferry to arrive. I quickly scanned the lot for the red Honda Civic but there wasn't one. "They must've gotten on an earlier ferry," I thought.

I passed by a drinking fountain and quickly lapped up the water like a crazed-looking dog keeping my eyes on the meandering people. I walked down to where the foot traffic usually loads and suddenly realized that I hadn't any money. I'd left the little amount of money I had back at camp. The sign said $7 to board by foot. It was a measly seven dollars that I didn't have. I turned back to the rows of cars and trucks waiting in rows and thought about walking all the way back to camp. That idea didn't seem like an option to me, so I began to rack my brain for an alternative. Begging crossed my mind but that intimidated me. I'd never begged for money before, and the whole idea seemed embarrassing.

I walked through the sea of cars and trucks pretending to be just another passenger waiting for the ferry. People watched me as I walked by, a spectacle no doubt with my long hair and hairy beard. Walking along a large semi truck on one of the far outside lanes I noticed that it had a lock box on each side that truckers put tools and tire chains in. "This box was large enough to hold a person," I thought. I bent over casually and walked under the trailer and tapped the lock box on the other side to see if it was full as I passed by it. The box made a real hollow noise and sounded empty. I popped out on the other side and I pretended to be looking at the view. There were no cars on the other side of the truck; however, I knew that that wouldn't last long as more trucks were sure to file in soon.

I glanced up to see if the trucker was sitting in the

driver seat by looking at his rearview mirror. All I could see was the leather of his seat shining in the late afternoon sun. Pulling the latch on the box, it sprung free. It was unlocked and empty, what luck. I took a quick glance around to make sure no one could see me crawling into it. There was an elderly couple looking over the fence at something in the opposite direction. I quickly slipped into it and almost completely shut the door behind me before I realized that there was no way to open it from the inside. Holding the door almost completely shut, I hoped the trucker wouldn't notice when he got back in his cab.

I sat in there for what seemed like almost an hour before I heard several car doors slamming shut and people began to start up there cars. "The ferry must have arrived," I thought and the semi truck fired up with a loud diesel grumble. It wasn't long before I heard the screech of the air brakes release and the truck began to move.

The truck bounced over the landing deck and I lost my grip on the door. It swung downward and I saw the side of a Mercedes Benz as the truck slowly passed by. I reached down quickly struggling to pull the door closed. I saw the profiles of a middle-aged couple sitting in the Benz as I quickly whipped the door closed. I don't think they saw me, but I couldn't be positive. The truck slowly came to a stop and I could hear people walking by leaving their cars to go to the upper decks.

I had no way of knowing when a person was going to walk by but I needed to get out in case those people did see me in here and told the trucker or ferry crew. So I just decided to pop out and hope for the best. Letting the door swing down I jumped out quickly. A woman let out a shriek, and I ignored her completely, shutting the door behind me. I walked in the opposite direction of her, but I could hear people whispering behind me. I swiftly found a stair case and shimmied up it, making my way through the labyrinth of heavy doors, hallways, stairs, and different levels distancing myself from the incident.

I found an open bench and sat down to relax. I remembered the look on Tilauth's face when I left and knew that something was wrong. I'm sure he didn't approve of my decision but I didn't care. I wasn't about to let this guy get away without at least reporting him to the police. But deep down inside of me I knew that I wasn't going to report him, because every inch of me ached for revenge.

"Maybe this is what Tilauth saw," I thought. But something inside me felt forever inadequate or incomplete until I managed to somehow avenge Elly. I had no idea what it was that I would do when I finally confronted this guy, but I'm sure it wouldn't be pleasant.

After a couple hours of riding the slow rocking ferry we pulled into Anacortes. From there I hitched a ride, surprisingly from the same trucker that I had stowed a ride with earlier in his lockbox. I don't think he knew that I rode in his lockbox earlier, at least, he didn't say anything. He was heading to Portland, Oregon, and said he'd drop me off at the park and ride just off the freeway. The driver didn't say a word the whole trip, which was fine with me. I wasn't in the mode for forced conversation. Besides, I was fixated on finding that familiar voice again.

Once in Lynnwood, I made the two hour walk home along the roads filled with busy weekend traffic sucking in the petrol fumes. I sidetracked into one of the small islands of natural habitat along the way and foraged for some food, nibbling on some dandelion leaves and salal berries. I hadn't eaten hardly anything all day, and this was the first time I realized it.

When I got home I showered, shaved, trimmed my hair, filled my belly with some leftover chicken, and left a note for my folks before walking to the beach where

I left my Jeep about five months ago. Surprisingly, it was still there, but it had been marked to be towed away. It was dated along time ago so the tow company must have forgotten the notice. I hopped in and fired up the old Jeep as it came to a hesitant purr.

I needed to figure out the address to the license plate number. This was going to be a task because I'm sure authorities don't just hand out that information to anyone. I drove back home and got on the internet. After about an hour of searching I managed to find his address by pretending to renew his tabs online. The website spit out his address and name for a confirmation. It was that simple.

Now that I had his address, my body surged with anticipation. Without hesitation I drove to the apartment complex and drove around looking for the Honda Civic. I couldn't find it anywhere, in fact, the parking area was practically empty. His name kept running through my head: John Covington. The more I said his name the more I despised it. I could hear his voice whispering to me as the guys raped one after the other. I remembered his breath was thick with the stench of beer. I headed out of the parking lot and drove without direction or purpose.

The sky was dark but I couldn't see the stars with all the city lights. As I meandered down random streets I could see Tilauth back at camp with a fire lit. I hadn't been gone long but I already missed the quiet nights by the fire listening to the cedar pop and crack and the distant sound of the loon echoing over the water, my favorite sound. I longed to be back at camp and for the first time since I left I asked myself, 'Why did I leave?' I knew why but I didn't give myself a second thought to letting what happened to Elly just drift into the past. I tried to imagine myself forgiving the guys that raped and killed her but couldn't even pretend to say the words.

I suddenly found myself driving past the bar where

Elly was killed. The sight of where it happened made my stomach cringe and my eyes swell up with a tear. I pulled over as a lump in my throat grew and I began hitting the steering wheel with frustration. Why couldn't I shake this horrible event? Why couldn't I just let myself forget? My chest tightened and the tears rushed down my face in streams. The street lights blurred in my tear-soaked eyes. I wiped them from my face in aggravation and took off back to the apartment building. This time the parking lot was nearly full. I carefully scanned the lot for his car but found it nowhere. I wondered if the address I had was old.

Just as I was backing up into an empty space to turn around, headlights whipped around the corner. The Civic drove by quickly as the head lights flashed into my eye's briefly before the tail lights disappeared around another corner. I shut off the Jeep and my heart pounded. I got out and quickly, shot across and parking lot, and darted through the network of apartment buildings in the direction the Civic went. At the last moment I caught him strutting up the sidewalk before climbing up one of the stairs to his apartment. It was the same guy I saw earlier that day. He must've just gotten home after spending the day with his girlfriend. At least I assumed it was his girlfriend since she wasn't with him and he didn't wear a ring.

I stood in the shadows for a while taking deep breaths. My hands trembled with nervous anticipation. I gave him a moment to get in and settled down before my legs started up the stairs without me controlling them. They just started walking as if they knew that thinking about this would only create more apprehension and fear. I walked right up to his door which had an old coffee can next to it filled with cigarette butts.

My hand knocked three times but by the third knock he opened the door quickly saying "Look I'm sorry alright?"

I pulled back in confusion wondering if he really knew that it was me that was at the door. But he looked just as startled as I did. We stared at each other for a moment in silence as I tried to get my grounds. I don't think he was expecting me but he must have been expecting someone else. "Perhaps his girlfriend was coming over," I thought.

"I thought you were someone else," he said sounding irritated. "What do you want?" he asked. I looked at him for a moment longer to see if he recognized me now that my hair was short and I had no beard. But he made no signs of recognition. "Look it's late, why are you at my door?" he said, looking as if he was ready to slam it shut at any second.

"Do you know who I am?" I asked.

"No! What the hell do you want? Are you selling cookies or some shit?"

"No...I'm not selling anything."

"Fine, then go the fuck away," he said as he swung the door closed. But I stuck my foot in to stop it just before it shut completely. He pushed on it a few times but it didn't budge. He quickly pulled it back again revealing his face, red with anger. "Do you want to fuckin' die?" he asked me as he began to ready himself for a fight.

"I used to," I replied plainly. All my hesitation was now stamped out by adrenaline and I eyed him intently to let him know that I wasn't afraid of him.

"So what the hell do you want?" he asked, and I could feel his fear. A flash of dim light moved in the corner of my eye, and I looked there but saw nothing.

He stood in the middle of his door and I asked him again, "Are you sure you don't recognize me?" He looked at me closely now. His face slowly changed from anger and irritation to complete fear. It looked as if he was looking at a ghost and I knew he recognized me.

"Look...you get the fuck out of here!" he said again

only this time his voice trembled. He looked down the stairs quickly.

"Don't worry; there are no cops behind me," I said reading his thoughts.

"What do you want?" he asked. I stepped into his apartment and he backed up quickly.

"Look, I'm sorry man. We were drunk. We..." he said pleading. "You were drunk?" I repeated him.

"Yeah..."

"So it's ok to rape and kill a woman because...you were drunk?" I said quickly.

"Well...what the hell do you want me to do?" he said, with a shaky voice. Another flash of light whipped by in the corner of my eye and again I turned to see what it was but there was nothing there. He looked at me confused at what I kept looking at.

"So John, did you enjoy your time in the San Juan Islands?" I asked. He did not answer but appeared more shaken that I knew his name and where he'd been that day.

There was more movement out of the corner of my left eye, irritated, I turned to see Elly looking at me. She wore the same clothes she wore the night she died but they weren't tattered and dirty. It took me a second to realize that she was an apparition and not really her. My heart sank like a rock in a pond as she just looked at me motionless without a word. I lost my breath and couldn't speak. Unexpectedly, John grabbed my shirt and pulled me towards his fist headed directly for my left eye. I turned my head downwards at the last second and it slammed into my skull. I heard a loud pop reverberate through my head and looked to see him cringing as he clutched his broken hand. Without hesitation I grabbed his forearm with his broken hand and twisted it into his face like Tilauth had taught me out in Idaho. I pinned him to the ground in a flash of a second and pinned his broken hand to the floor. He let out a yelp as I heard the bones crackle free.

With him face down I turned to see Elly still standing there. I could hear her speaking through her heart rather than her mouth. Her face softly gazed at me in compassion as if she knew everything that I'd been going through since she died. Her gaze startled something deep inside me and my gut felt as if it were breaking free. A shadowy figure lurched out just over my other shoulder. I turned to see the same false spirit that confronted me on my quest. He moved like an insect even though he was human in form. The false spirit seethed and lurched back and forth and I could feel him pulling me to kill John below me. I looked down at John to see him pleading for his life but I could hardly hear him. "He has no right to live," the false spirit hissed.

In the far off distance of my heart I could hear a song that Tilauth would sing when emotional healing was needed. Deep in my heart, I could see Tilauth singing next to the camp fire. To my surprise as I looked at him, he looked up to see me looking back at him but he did not stop singing. I could tell he was singing the song for me. He was crying as he looked directly into my eyes. He kept singing the song over and over again and I felt my heart lighten with a surge of peace. I turned to the left of Tilauth and I could see Elly sitting there looking at me. My eyes quickly pulled away from hers and I saw myself sitting at the fire only I didn't look like me. I was the shifty looking false spirit that was encouraging me to kill John.

I quickly realized what I'd become or rather had been for sometime. I felt sick, and began to vomit only the vomit didn't look like normal vomit but it looked black as night. I threw up all over John's carpet. I let out a cough just before something slammed into my rib cage knocking me into the side of his couch. I struggled to regain my breath when John pounced on top of me. His hands quickly clasped my neck and I couldn't breathe.

"It was your fault, not mine. You did it to yourself. You raped and killed her...not me! It was your fault." John yelled at my face that was no doubt turning different shades of color. Slobber drooled from his mouth as he manically continued to say, "It was your fault. It was your fault."

With a strange feeling of compassion, I reached up and touched his face gently as he continued to choke me. I even managed to smile at him before pushing his face sideways throwing him off balance just enough for me to slither out from under him. I quickly pinned him again by twisting his hand around to the point I had full control of his actions. I struggled to regain my breath. After I regained my composure I began to speak but only coughed hoarsely. He choked me so much that I could only manage to whisper.

"John," I whispered. "I'm not going to kill you. Killing you would be far too easy for me and for you. The only way you're going to find peace in this is if you admit to what you've done," I said calmly.

"Go fuck yourself!" he retorted quickly.

I ignored his comment, "I'm going to give you two days to turn yourself in. If you haven't turned yourself over to the police in two days, I will call the detective myself and tell him where you live, your name, your car, your license plate number, and the names of the other guys that were there," I said, bluffing about knowing the other guys' names. "So you have a choice; you can turn yourself in and spend some time in prison or you can run and be constantly looking over your shoulder to see if the cops are closing in on you, or wondering if it is me lurking in the shadows. And believe me, I will be in the shadows. And trust me...you will not be able to trust anyone, including your girlfriend you took out for a walk on the island today." He stopped struggling against me and I knew he wanted to know how I knew so much but hadn't turned them in already.

I quickly slipped out of his apartment before he

could turn around and see me leave.

"You go to hell..." I heard him yell. "You better watch your back!" he called out trying to appease himself. I quickly slid down the stairs without a sound and disappeared around the corner blending into the shrubs and shadows. I saw his girlfriend walking through the parking lot from her car. I slipped away knowing that he would now have to explain to her what happened and why.

Chapter 26
Internal Wars

The next two days I spent at home visiting with my folks. I didn't tell them much of what I had been up to because I knew that some things were better left unsaid. Explaining what I'd been doing with Tilauth would only raise questions I would have difficulty explaining since I barely understood it myself. Telling them that I'd found one of the guys who raped and killed Elly would only make my mother worry. So I kept quiet about my double lifestyle and talked about simple things.

The morning of the third day I drove to the police station. The sky was overcast and chilly. Rain was threatening to down pour but things remained dry. I went up to the counter and asked if Detective Wittenberg was in. The young man asked who I was and what it was about. I told him and he paged him over the phone. "He'll be out in a bit, you can have a seat over there," he motioned to the aluminum framed chairs against the wall. The vinyl tile floor was in dire need of replacement. Chunks had cracked off to expose the concrete beneath it.

It wasn't long before I saw Detective Wittenberg

appear in the room with his same big curly hair and his pudgy belly. His button up shirt appeared to fit a little tighter as if the buttons were about to burst off, creating a pucker in the cloth between each button.

"Well, look what the cat dragged in," he said smiling down at me. I quickly stood up,

"Hello Detective, how are you?" I asked.

"I'm doing alright, yourself?"

"I'm hanging in there."

"It's been awhile since I've seen you. Last time I tried to get a hold of you, your parents told me you were traveling around the country."

"Yeah...I didn't feel like sticking around much after what happened."

"Well, come on back to my office," Wittenberg said as we started down the hall. "So what brings you in?" he asked.

"Well...I found one of the guys that killed Elly." Wittenberg glanced over his shoulder but continued to keep walking. He was quiet until we reached his desk.

"So," he said as he grunted into the same rickety chair he'd been sitting in the last time we talked at his desk. "This guy you found...you know his name?"

"Yeah...his name is John Covington," I looked at Wittenberg to see if he recognized the name or to see if John turned himself in.

"Covington," Wittenberg repeated searching his mind. "Oh yes, John Covington," he exclaimed as if remembering the name.

"You know the name?"

"Yes, we questioned him when one of the bar patrons mentioned that he was there at the bar. The bartender said he was sitting at the bar the whole time the incident occurred. The detective looked at me quizzically. I didn't show any signs to him to reveal any questioning on my mind. Realizing that I wasn't dissuaded by his statement, he continued. "I wasn't satisfied with the bartender as an alibi because I think they were personal friends. However, I had nothing on John so I couldn't hassle him anymore than I already had. There were a lot of people at that bar that night. John was just one of the hundred or so there drinking and he had the bartender adamantly state that he was there the whole time," Wittenberg's eyes studied me carefully. "So what makes you think that he was one of the guys that participated in the occurrence?"

I quickly tried to think of what it was exactly I was going to tell him. I didn't want to tell him that it was my intuition that brought me to him because I knew the detective was a hard facts only kind of guy. I also wasn't sure if I wanted to tell him about my run in with him at his apartment. I'm sure no doubt that that was illegal in some way.

"Well...I saw him out hiking in the woods with his girlfriend. He didn't recognize me because I had a beard at the time but I recognized him. His voice is what gave it away to me. I got his license plate number before he left," I said as Wittenberg studied me carefully.

"It's kind of strange that he ran into you out in the woods don't you think?" he asked.

"Well, if anybody was going to run into me lately, it would be out in the woods since that's where I've been for the past couple of years."

"What've you been doing out in the woods?"

"Well...let's just say that after getting lost in the woods I decided to make it my goal to be able to survive and live out there comfortably on my own."

"And how has that been going for you?"

"I've been enjoying it," I said affirmatively.

"I see..." Wittenberg said with a whistle.

"So you think this John Covington played a part in Elly's murder because of his voice?" he asked.

"Well..." I said starting to see where the detective was going with this. "Not just his voice but his mannerisms too; the way he walks and holds himself. There is not doubt in my mind that he was there that night," I said assuredly.

"So what was John's role in Elly's death that night?"

I told him everything that I could remember between my conscious moments. Wittenberg listened to me carefully until I finished. He sat up in his chair and slid his finger tips across the desk edge as he thought about what I was telling him. This would be so much easier if I could tell him that John confessed to me that he was there. But, there was no way I could tell the detective without getting into trouble. So I had Wittenberg dangling with the idea that I knew John was involved simply from his voice and mannerisms. Wittenberg seemed to want to believe me. Here was a crime committed by several people in a public place and he had one witness; me and no other leads. Perhaps he was feeling humbled from a case that should have been solved in a few days after it happened. His mind seemed to churn as some internal dilemma appeared to be working itself out in his mind.

He sat back in his chair with a long slow creak that echoed through the room. "Neal...I can't hassle someone about a crime years ago simply because his voice and mannerisms seem familiar to you. Why don't you go home or...out to the woods for that matter and if you think of anything else that might better incriminate this person you let me know." His beady little eyes stared back at me from his fat head encompassed in a helmet of tightly curled hair. My heart began to race and I hesitated for a moment debating the thought of telling him everything that I knew. I decided to hold back and say nothing until I figured out something better to tell him. I didn't want to reveal anything that might end up backfiring on me.

So I got up from the chair, turned around and left

without a word. He said nothing as I left, and I began to feel absolutely helpless. Here, I had found one of the people that raped and killed Elly, handed the information over to the detective, and he was going to do nothing. I took some deep breaths as I fired up my Jeep, to calm myself. This didn't seem right to me. I got back to my folks' place and walked out onto the deck. The grey skies had cleared, and the sun beamed down for some much needed warmth. The drone of lawnmowers filled the air as they coughed and hacked while the driver went over an area that must have had limbs and rocks. They were so loud that I couldn't hear any song birds. I looked out across the fenced cubicles of perfectly manicured backyards, and realized that man has no idea where he is living. Man trims and tames the alien plants, saturating the soil with poison so he can pick and choose which plants stay and which must go. I could see one woman with a blow torch burning the weeds in her gravel driveway. "There is a war and it is happening in man's own backyard," I thought. Every spring man declares a war on the weeds in his small plot he calls his own. He will poison, torch, gas out the moles, and fertilize his little fenced in prison every weekend to receive compliments from his neighbors and friends when they come over for the backyard BBQ. They will eat their potato chips, patties of greasy ground beef, drink their beer, all the while standing atop their conquest of a poisoned prison cell. Human beings somewhere along the way got the idea that nature must be manicured and controlled; otherwise it is wild and useless. After living with Tilauth I tend to look at weeds as medicine or food rather than a nuisance that brings a homeowner to arms.

I was getting worked up about nothing, and decided to walk down to Meadowdale Beach; a small chunk of land that hasn't been too stricken with the war man has declared on nature. The walk calmed me and I munched on some salmon berry flowers that were in full bloom along the way. I allowed myself to get distracted by the coyote tracks that crossed the trail and I followed them through the woods. They went all the way to the parks boundary and went straight through someone's backyard. I decided not to trek through the manicured yard and went back down the gorge to the trail again.

When I popped out onto the trail from the bushes a tall attractive jogger lurched away from me with a small yelp. She picked up her pace from a jog to a run, thinking that I was some sort of park pervert no doubt. I chuckled to myself and hoped she wouldn't report me, because I don't think authorities would believe that I was tracking a coyote. I walked all the way down to the beach where I saw the attractive jogger stretching her hamstrings over a picnic table. I sat down against a piece of driftwood in the sand and soaked up the sun. The jogger paid no attention to me and I ignored her in hopes to not frighten her anymore. I watched the small waves lap up against the beach and breathed in the sea air. I bet Tilauth's view was probably pretty similar. I longed to get back to him and continue my learning. Suburbia was beginning to get to me and I longed for the peace I would have while sitting with Tilauth in the middle of nowhere.

After calming myself from the state Wittenberg put me in, I headed back up the trail. There was nothing I could tell Wittenberg without getting myself in trouble, so I decided to tell him nothing more and hopefully John will continue to go about his life always looking over his shoulder. This hardly seemed like a fitting punishment but I was running out of options.

As I walked a strange thought crossed my mind. I began to imagine what Tilauth might do or say if he was in my predicament. He would probably say that John and the rest of the guys that night live with their own guilt. And if they have no guilt it would make no difference anyways because they are living their lives the way they want to experience it. 'Life is about experiences' he would say 'and it isn't my place to judge another person's experiences.' I could see myself then asking, 'even if that experience comes in contact with my experiences?' And he would probably reply, 'your experiences and another's experiences are still the individual's experience even if they are at the same event. You have the choice, Grandson, you can waste your time and choose to judge and punish the other person for their choices of experience which will never remedy the pain you experienced, or you can allow the person to experience their life the way they choose, which is what they are going to do no matter what you do. You fight the natural flow and rhythms of life. People are born and die all the time. Sometimes the birth is unexpected, and sometimes the death is unexpected. This is the natural flow of the spirits on Earth experiencing life as they have chosen. Until you can embrace this, you will always live in discomfort with yourself because you haven't opened your heart to the beauty of life's natural rhythms. Embrace John and the others, and see that they are learning from their experiences the same as you. Elly agreed before she was born to offer you and the others this opportunity for the experience you experienced. Regardless of how horrible it may seem, there is a beauty in it. And if you don't believe me, ask Elly.'

I stopped in the trail and realized that I was no longer imagining what Tilauth might say, but I felt he was actually saying these words in my mind. I could feel him around me and knew that he was there, even though I couldn't see him. His words filtered through me and I noticed that he used words that I normally used. The feeling was strange, but what Tilauth said shook me up a bit. Deep down, I knew that if I avenged Elly's death I would still feel the pain and hurt of losing her. I knew that this whole experience had taught me leaps and bounds about life and death. I understood the natural flow that Tilauth mentioned, and I had the choice to embrace it or to resist it. If I resist it, it will only continue to haunt my thoughts because there is no way of winning. If I embrace this thing, I can see the beauty of Elly's death and understand that my experience has brought me many positive things. Besides, I know that Elly's spirit continues on, and she is not actually dead, but has just changed forms. I will miss Elly as I knew her, and that's ok. She did this for me, for herself, and for everyone else. My seeking vengeance is actually a selfish act to bring myself some sort of empty peace. It has nothing to do with Elly, it's all about me. I stood there dumbfounded, staring down the ravine from the perch of the trail. I walked all the way back up the trail and walked back to my folk's house.

I came home and had dinner with the family. I felt liberated from myself. I no longer needed to do anything. I was now free to live my life with the experiences that I chose to. I no longer felt like I was walking around in the prison cell I'd created for myself. I could now look at John and the other guys of that night with love and compassion for them. I actually felt a little sorry for them. I could look out at the neighbors spraying their weed kill and felt not angry and frustrated with them but I could love them for who they are. They just choose to walk through life with a limited awareness of themselves and the world that surrounds them. They resist nature the way I was resisting my experience of that night. I have the choice to resist or to embrace. And I now realize that I can't accomplish anything by resisting the natural flow of life, spirit, and nature.

I talked with my folks about simple things like the weather and enjoyed it. I no longer had this internal war going on inside of me, resisting the natural flow of my life.

I went to bed early and decided that I would go back
to islands first thing the next morning. I fell asleep
feeling light and peaceful. This was a feeling I couldn't
remember ever experiencing my whole life.

Chapter 27
Indifferent

I was awakened to the phone ringing. I peeled my eyes open in a groggy state to see the clock come into focus. It was 1:15 in the morning and the phone rang again. I picked it up and said 'hello' but it came out garbled in my sleepy voice.

The voice on the other line said with a whistle, "Sorry to wake you Neal, but I need you down at the police station immediately."

"Detective?" I asked.

"Sorry, Neal...Yes, this is Detective Wittenberg," he said, forgetting to introduce himself. "I think we may have found all of the guys who attacked you and Elly that night," he said calmly. It took me a moment to process what he was saying. "Neal...you there?" Wittenberg asked.

"I'm here..." I said, not sure I was hearing him correctly. "Did you say you have all of the guys from that night?" I asked.

"Well, I need you to come down and confirm it, but yes, I think we have all of them."

I sat there in silence trying to decipher what is real and what is a dream. I felt like I was still asleep.

"Uh...alright...I'll be right down."

I got dressed, threw some cold water on my face and headed out the front door when my mom caught me. "Everything ok?" she asked.

"Yes, everything's fine. I'll tell you about it in the morning...go back to sleep," I whispered and headed down the front stairs.

I drove to the police station to see a news crew standing around near the front door. I parked around the corner so I wouldn't draw any attention to me. I didn't know if they were there because of the new developments in my case or they were there for some other reason. Needless to say, I don't have the fondest memories of the press so I wanted to avoid them no matter what their purpose.

I briskly walked along the building in the shadows to the front door to keep a low profile. As I rounded the corner to the front door the camera light blew up in my face with the man squeezing out his one question in the brief moment he knew that I would give him. "Neal, how do you feel about the fact that your attackers and the murders of your girlfriend may finally be brought to justice?" I hadn't planned on saying anything to the reporter but for some reason I was stopped in my tracks. I turned and looked at the reporter. "I feel..." then I looked at the camera, "indifferent." And I turned and went through the front door of the police station.

I knew that the comment would make very little sense to anyone watching but I didn't care. Perhaps there was someone out there who would understand or it would make some one think what it means to forgive and forget without repentance from the attackers. 'Forgiveness without repentance' I said to myself, 'now there's an absolutely foreign idea to our world.'

I was met by an officer whom I'd never met before but somehow he knew who I was. "Follow me, Neal," he said as he headed down the long hallway of fluorescent lights. He led me to a room with a privacy window. The room next door was empty and had the height measurements on the back wall for viewing a line up. I sat down in a chair when detective Wittenberg came into the room. "Neal...thank you for coming down so late at night."

"Sure...so what's going on?" I asked.

"Well, I looked up that license plate number you gave me and found that John had a minor traffic violation on his record that was still outstanding. So I went to his house to ask him about the traffic violation as a front. Now...when I got there and showed him my badge, he got very nervous. The strange thing was, the first words out of John's mouth was, 'That guy's full of shit'. Dumbfounded, I asked him, 'What guy?' And do you know what he might have said?" Wittenberg asked. I said nothing but shrugged my shoulders, playing stupid. "He said it was you. You were the one who was full of shit." Wittenberg looked at me closely but I said nothing. "Why would he say that you're full of shit Neal, not unless you've already talked to him?" I hesitated for a moment before saying too much.

"Ok...I confronted John a few days ago and told him that I would be getting in touch with you - which I did."

"I see. Well, I don't want to know the details of what exactly happened when you spoke to John. You obviously must have shaken him up because I never got a confession so easily in my life. I'm going to forget whatever happened with you and John. But I need you to be fully honest with me if you want me to help you. Am I understood?"

"Yes," I replied, breathing a little easier.

"Anyways, not only did I get a confession from John, but he told me who everyone else was that was involved that night. I just need you to help identify them for me." Wittenberg turned to the officer who showed me in, and nodded at him to signify that we were ready. The officer left the room and a couple of minutes later five guys came walking into the other room. They all looked tired, as if they'd been rudely woken up. I scanned the faces as they stared plainly back at me.

A real hefty guy stood second from the right. I knew he was there that night without a question in my mind. I could see that he was haunted by a false spirit. The false spirit taunted him with guilt and rage. I watched the man as he let the false spirit feed off him like he was lunch. I could see that his soul had been enduring a long life of horrible torment. I felt sorry for him, but I understood that he was choosing all these things as his experience. In a moment he could change everything, but it wasn't this moment. In this moment I could see the man's soul was longing for relief but was scared of what that relief may result as. I knew my role in this man's life and decided to follow that path because there is no other choice ultimately.

"The hefty guy, second from the right," I said confidently.

"Are you sure?" Wittenberg asked.

"There's no doubt in my mind," I said without hesitation.

"How about the other guys?" he asked.

"No. None of the other guys were there," I said.

"Good. Bring in the next set of guys," he told the officer. The officer disappeared once again and a new set of five guys came forward.

This time John came in with the other four. I looked at them all quickly and recognized another one of the guys. He was slender and scrawny. I could see that he was the timid follower lacking any confidence. Both John and the slender kid had similar false spirits that lingered about them. The false spirits would hide behind their victim and peek out to see me staring back. The spirits could see me but the row of guys could see nothing. I watched the false spirits cower behind the row of guys, afraid to show themselves to me. They obviously find me a threat to their existence, which is a change from me usually trembling at their looks. Some of the other guys had false spirits of their own, but I recognized the truth that sits within the ones that were there that night.

I named the two and they brought in another row of guys. I kept pointing them out row after row, recognizing their spirits instead of their physical appearance or the way they talked.

There was twelve in all that I picked out from the line ups. Each one had their experiences written on their souls.

After the last row left Wittenberg stared at me curiously, "You're confident with all your choices?"

"Yes," I said quickly.

"Well..." he said, scratching his head through his large patch of curly hair. "This is highly unusual, but you picked out every guy that John had told us about. To be quite honest with you, Neal, I didn't think you would be able to pick out most of them because it was so dark and there were quite a few of them," Wittenberg said pausing to study my reactions. "Are you sure you're telling me everything you know?" he asked.

I smiled at him and said, "Honest, you know what I know. I'm not hiding anything." Knowing full well that if I told him how I identified each one he would no doubt think that I'm crazy.

Wittenberg nodded, took a deep breath and sighed, "Well, that's everything. You can go home now."

I stood up from my chair and yawned, feeling the need for sleep. "Sorry about the reporters out there, Neal. I don't know how they found out about this. You can leave out the side door so you don't have to deal with them." The officer showed me to the side door where he punched a code into the key pad and opened the door for me.

"Thanks," I said to the officer.

"No problem," he said as I walked by him.

"Say..." the officer said as I was walking away. I turned around to see him. The building side light shined down on his face, and I noticed for the first time that he was an American Indian. He looked at me closely for a moment, then I felt him look through me the way Tilauth usually did. We said nothing to each other but understood one another. I nodded at him and got in my Jeep.

I saw through the window of my Jeep that Detective Wittenberg was outside talking to the reporters. I fired up the old Jeep and pulled out of the parking lot. Wittenberg was in the center of the bright TV light answering the reporter's questions. I drove home and went straight to bed, feeling indifferent about the whole ordeal. If I had feelings towards anything it was the feelings I had about being indifferent. It was a sensation I that was completely new to me. I enjoyed the new found freedom of not feeling responsible for everyone else except for me. My desire to direct and control my surroundings and the people around me lost all importance. Things are the way they are because that is the flow of life and I have finally chosen to embrace it instead of resist it.

Chapter 28
Peace

I slept in the next morning to make up for the lost sleep from the night before. When I finally peeled myself out of bed and wiped the sleep from my eyes it was ten o-clock. I left a note for my folks to tell them what happened last night and that I would be gone again for awhile to do some more traveling.

My funds were getting low, but living off the land with Tilauth didn't require much, so I wasn't too worried. I climbed into my Jeep and drove back to the islands parking exactly where I saw John Covington and his girlfriend parked about a week ago. I found a nice place to drive my Jeep further into the woods and cover it with debris to hide it from authorities who may be tempted to tow it away, thinking it was abandoned. I began to make the trek back down to our camp. I could smell the ocean air as I walked under the looming madrona trees.

I walked into camp to see Tilauth brewing up some tea. His face rose to see me making my way through the sword ferns. He smiled at me with a grin that stretched from ear to ear.

"I'm happy your back, Grandson," he said with a calming tone.

"It's good to be back." I quickly replied. "What are you brewing there?"

"I've got some Pineapple Weed tea for you. It will help balance your energy out."

"Can't say I've ever had Pineapple Weed tea before? Does it taste good?" I asked.

"Try it," Tilauth said as he handed me a cup. I smelled the steam coming from the cup. My nose filled with the scent of Pineapple. It tasted pleasant, like a mixture of Pineapple and Chamomile. I immediately started to feel calm and relaxed. All of the exciting events from the past few days had me reeling.

We sat there in silence, drinking our tea, and listening to the wind whisper through the trees above. Today was exceptionally warm with maybe a speck of a cloud off in the distance. I breathed deeply, letting my bones rest back into the wilderness. It's funny how easily uptight I would get without even noticing it when I was back in civilization.

"Civilization…now there's a word," I thought. "The wilderness seems far more civilized than the human world. Perhaps, I thought, those two words 'civilization' and 'wilderness' should exchange meanings. The wilderness seems more civil-ized to me and civil-ization seems more wild to me in all reality."

"It's good to see that you've learned from the false spirit that has possessed you for so long, Grandson," Tilauth said, breaking the silence. I looked up from my cup of tea and smiled peacefully. He nodded at me in approval saying, "False spirits are some of the most powerful teachers in the spirit world. You should be proud of yourself, Grandson. Most people would have struggled with a false spirit of that magnitude for a lifetime, maybe even more. Come to think of it, I know of a few people that have struggled with a false spirit like that for several lifetimes," he said, sipping his tea.

My ears perked up, "What do you mean several lifetimes? You mean...being reincarnated?"

This made him chuckle a little. "Yes," he said simply.

"Well...to be honest with you, I'm still struggling with this. I know you've taken me to the moment when I supposedly was killed by a bear in a past life, but for some reason that just feels like I imagined it. Christianity, Judaism, and Islam all say there is only one life that is lived. So...are you Buddhist or Hindu or something?" I asked.

Tilauth was quiet for a moment as he chose his words carefully. His careful words always set me back for a moment and I tended to listen to him more carefully knowing that what he was saying was never whimsical.

"I don't follow or subscribe to any of these religions you speak of. These religions are fine and provide a good attempt at answering many of the questions a human may ask themselves about life, love, God, and the reasons or purpose for living. But as many people walk their path following the doctrine of their chosen religion, they'll begin to find some holes, unanswerable questions, contradictions, and restrictions to the growth and progress in one's life. In my path, I've discovered that when I come across a person who is ill and they've asked me to do some work on them, sometimes their illness can stem from a life they've lived previously. So I go back to that moment in their previous life with the person so they can understand and heal themselves. This is where most healing work begins." Tilauth stopped talking for a moment and he studied me briefly. "I could take you, Grandson, back to the moment when you were killed by a lion in Africa defending your family. This might help you understand why you are so obsessed with courage and rescuing someone. The situation is similar to your night with Elly and those boys." He paused to let me think about what he was saying.

"You mean to tell me that I was an African once and I was killed by a lion?" I asked, feeling a little awkward.

"Don't take my word for it, Grandson, go and see for yourself." Tilauth motioned for me to close my eyes. I hesitantly closed them and Tilauth picked up his drum and began drumming it softly. "In the world of spirit there is no time or place, just now. What we are going to do is look at the reflection of your past. Tilauth said some words to get me to calm my body and quiet my mind by taking me through an imaginative walk through a natural setting.

I imagined myself walking down well-trodden path in the middle of the desert. The soil was compacted tight on the trail, yet cracked everywhere else creating a mosaic design like the scaly skin of an alligator. The trail came to an abrupt halt, "to the right is the future" he said "and to the left is the past." I turned left and went through a series of flashes leaving my eyes blinded from the light so I could barely see anything. The last flash erupted and when my sight came to I was walking with my wife and son in a semi arid part of Africa. My skin was black and the sun beat down upon us with intensity. Behind me was my tribe. They had banished me because I had cowered and hid when the lion came into the village one night. It was the duty of all grown men to help the tribe defend itself when a lion came looking for something to eat. But because of my cowardice I was banished from the tribe for an unknown amount of time. My wife loved me dearly, but she was ashamed of her husband. My son was too young to fully understand the situation we were in, and the shamefulness he would no doubt have for his father. Friends and relatives mourned our leaving but they could do nothing. The council of the tribe had decided and they had to respect the decision or suffer the same banishment.

With all our possessions on our backs we walked for four days before finding a place to live in solitude. Life was difficult for me and my family, but we tried to make the best of things. I hunted and provided for them, but I could still feel my wife blaming me for our problems. We didn't talk about it, but we thought about it all the time, especially me. I reviewed in my head what I would do if I were to ever confront a lion. I would face it with a fierceness and ferociousness that superseded the lions and attack it with a maniacal fearlessness.

It wasn't long before I got my opportunity. I awoke one hot night to the sound of a faint crunch in the soil around our home. I quickly grabbed my largest spear and crept up to the doorway. I could feel the tribe welcoming us back now as my wife wears the pelt of this lion over her back and I, adorned with a necklace of its teeth around my neck. My son could carry a bag of the lion's claws as we were praised and welcomed. My wife would look at me with pride again and my son could grow with other children feeling proud of his father.

I could hear the lion sniffing the air with quick breaths in and out with a loud final exhale. I felt the surge of adrenaline rush through my body and a strength rose from the center of my bones. I was ready to hunt the hunter. I slipped out of the doorway just in time to see the lions' rear slip behind the corner of the hut. The moon shone down with a silvery glow. I crept silently yet briskly after the lion, figuring that I could have the advantage of killing it without it being aware of me. But when I rounded the corner I came eye to eye with the powerful animal.

Its eyes glistened in the moonlight, and I thought it was better this way. I was fearless and mad, with a power that came from the depths of my soul that I didn't even want the lion to think I was a coward by stabbing him in the back. A deep grumble slowly gurgled from the farthest depths of its chest. The growl was something that I could feel more than hear. But I was not afraid and I even growled back. I raised my spear to shoulder height and waited for an opening for attack. The lion sunk back on its haunches preparing to lurch. I gripped my spear tightly waiting for the lion to reveal its chest as he came in for the kill.

The lion lurched forward, but I was too close, and the back of the lions' front paws just pushed the tip of the spear upward and clearing the way for the lions attack. The spear snapped as I struggled to get it under the lion. I tried to slide out from underneath his pounce but couldn't get out in time. The lions' mouth enveloped most of my head and I heard a loud pop as its fangs punctured my skull. My body fell to the ground, crushed under the enormous weight of the animal. I could see out into the brush as the silver moonlight shone brightly down. There was a moment of peace before I died, despite the crunching sound of my bones deep in my head. Blood pooled out from my head into my view that glistened like black oil under the moon.

My last thought was how I disappointed my wife before returning to the spirit world. I then watched as my spirit followed my wife and son around, haunting them. In spirit I still desperately wanted to prove to them my fearlessness and courage. My wife and son went back to the tribe and continued with their lives. Without my burden of cowardice, the tribe welcomed them back without hesitation.

Some flashes over came me, and I found myself sitting with the tribe pretending to be a part of them again. That was when a shaman of the tribe saw me, which was strange because nobody else seemed to notice me except for this shaman. His eyes looked at me sternly and I could feel him unwelcoming me without saying or doing anything. He nodded his head at something behind me. When I turned around there was a bright light blinding me.

Suddenly, Tilauth's voice broke through, "Grandson. Grandson!" My eyes opened up slowly to see him hovering over me. He looked at my eyes carefully, "You in there?" he said with a grin.

"Yeah…I'm here. Are you here?" I said feeling a little disoriented. Tilauth started to laugh

"You've got be careful wondering around in the past, Grandson, you could get lost and want to stay, thinking it's a reality. I had to go back and find your spirit. It had started to meander around aimlessly. Meandering in the spirit world is never a good idea. It makes you vulnerable and one could easily get lost in that open sea."

Somewhere along the line I had gotten on the ground and was now lying on my side. Tilauth helped me up and I sat on a log and came back to the now. Tilauth studied me as I assimilated what I had just experienced.

"You see, Grandson?" I looked at him and nodded realizing that there was no possible way I made that story up. I felt it deep in my bones. The truth resonated through my body and I new there was no way of denying that I had lived through that experience before. "You see, Grandson, I cannot subscribe to say the Baptist religion because I would have to deny something I know to be true. I would have to lie to myself. So, my religion doesn't require me to believe or have faith in something I don't' know to be true.

Most religions require that there is a faith in the unknown. Like Christians and Muslims believe that there is a place in heaven for them when they die, provided they meet the requirements of course. They don't know for sure that there is a heaven because they haven't been there so they have a faith in that uncertainty. This is fine and great for those who find what they are looking for. But for a person like me, I would be forced to deny certain things Christians say are true, because I've experienced something otherwise.

Now anybody could come along and say to me that I'm making reincarnation up or that it all falls under the power of suggestion and my experiences are just my imagination going wild. But, I'm looking at you, Grandson, and I know that you would have a difficult time telling yourself that you didn't experience what happened to you in Africa, and that that was your imagination getting the best of you." I looked up at Tilauth as he waited for my thoughts. Every moment that I relived in Africa was just that; an experience I knew down to the marrow of my bones that I had experienced it all before. I had been on other spirit adventures before since I met Tilauth and none felt like I was reliving it except for when I was killed by the bear. But somewhere along the line I reasoned that I had to have made it up. But there was no doubt in me that I was once an African struggling with the issues of courage. This left me with the question of reincarnation. Obviously, there is something to it otherwise I couldn't have gone back in time and experienced something that resonated so true with me.

Now at this point in my life I had already diverged away from the religions I'd been raised with but I still hung on to many of the things put forth by Christianity as common truth. But now I'm struggling with a new unanswerable question that Christianity couldn't answer, other than to tell me to deny what is true within me.

"Am I lying to myself? Is Tilauth lying to me? Is he manipulating me?" I thought. But as I thought about it I realized that it makes no difference to Tilauth what I believe. He doesn't benefit from my donations of money in an offering plate. The man doesn't need money. He lives off the land and that's all he needs. He could disappear tomorrow and never speak to me again and he would see it as the path of our spirits. My beliefs don't change or affect him, he will still be Tilauth which is what I admire about him. He is fearless in who he is. He needs nothing and desires nothing he doesn't have.

"You're right...I wouldn't be able to deny what happened to me in order to be a true Christian." I said feeling a little like I was dangling now from the far limb of Christianity. "So what does that make me...a Hindu?"

Tilauth began to laugh real hard, "Try not claiming any religion as yours. Religion will only claim and limit you with doctrine, guidelines, and rules. These things are fine, but can and will stand in the way as your understanding grows. How about you don't have any title?" he suggested.

"Well that sounds a little unnerving. So I should just run around without any morals, without any concerns with the salvation of my soul?" Tilauth laughed again. "I'm glad you're finding the lack of salvation of my soul entertaining," I said, seriously concerned. This only made him laugh harder.

When he finally gained his composure back and calmed himself down he said, "You're not going to run around without any morals. It's not like you are going go on a killing rampage because you have no religion. In fact, some of the most religious people go on killing rampages. Take the Christian Crusades, for example, or any holy war, for that matter.

The fact is, you can choose the morals based on the experience you want, it makes no difference to me. But you are the one who has to live with yourself. With that given, you will make the decisions based on what you want to experience. If you want to experience a living hell...than go ahead, and one could say you are in hell. But you could also choose something different if you wish."

"Well what does God want from me then?" I asked feeling a little uncomfortable hanging out in the middle with nothing to grab onto. "Perhaps you should ask God yourself," he quickly replied.

"Yeah..." I said smiling uncomfortably. "Why don't I just give God a call and ask myself?"

"Grandson, I know that you're trying to fill a hole in your life where religion sat so comfortably for you for so long. It has been the temporary answer for the unanswerable questions you've had about life. Now that you are finding the true answers within yourself, religion has lost it stature in your life. I'm not going to fill that void with just another religion. This would only put you back to where you started from. So if you want something to believe, believe this. Believe that anything is possible. Believe that your understanding of God will and can change from day to day or minute to minute. Believe that truth resides within you, and that that is where God speaks to you. Believe that your understanding of God can speak to you from within. Believe that even what I just told you to believe can be completely different and your understanding can be far greater and the truth can resonate beyond your wildest imagination." I looked down at my empty cup of tea feeling like my mind was swirling out of control.

"Well what do I say to someone if they ask me what's my religion?" I asked feeling completely ungrounded.

Tilauth chuckled, "You're still striving to fill that void. You want a word that defines the indefinable. There is no word in any language that defines the indefinable religion."

Tilauth studied me while I struggled with my discomfort. The white man's anthropologist tried to give a word for this type of beliefs a long time ago for the convenience of simple conversation. They called it Animism. But even this word has a definition that lacks the truth of what it is when someone believes in such an open-ended belief. Aside from that, scientists refer to all living cultures that predate mainstream religion today as cultures that believed in Animism. Without any written doctrine and a set of rules, or commandments guiding ones soul to some sort of salvation in the afterlife, scientists find it difficult to describe just what it was that ancient peoples believed in. So if you want to call yourself an Animist for sake of telling someone what it is that you believe in, then go ahead. But be aware that those people will then define you and limit you to that limited definition of an Animist."

"I understand what you're saying," I said feeling myself sink into my new understanding of myself. "It's just different thinking that God doesn't want something from me and want me to do something."

"Perhaps, God doesn't need anything from you because God is everything?" Tilauth said knowing that he was only going to spark more questions in me.

"Well...doesn't God want and need my love?"

"Don't ask me, ask God," Tilauth said quickly.

"Right...so I look within to find out what God needs?"

"Yes, ask God and God will tell you. Don't ask me because then you will be left with a choice of whether or not to believe me. I might venture to say that God will provide you with the answer that requires no belief. It will simply be truth and you will know it because you went within."

I stood up and nodded at Tilauth and walked to the beach silently. I hadn't been back for more than hour and Tilauth had already shaken my world up so much that I was now questioning my religion. I walked out to the beach with the sun in my face and the wind was whipping around me like a loud monster. I sat on a log and listened to the waves slap up against the sand. I breathed slowly and began to relax my body and quiet my mind. This took awhile since my mind was reeling with questions.

When I finally relaxed I asked with my heart, "God, are you there?" I waited for a moment and heard nothing but the waves and the wind. Then I heard a voice come from within me that sounded a little different than my own voice but it spoke to me with the sensation of feeling with words. I could feel the intentions behind the words so there was an unusual clarity.

"I'm here Neal. I'm always here," God said.

"So...are you really God?" I asked feeling that this was the most necessary question to get answered before I ask any other questions.

"I am God as you understand me. I am the collective spirit of all that is, ever was, and ever will be," the voice resonated within me.

"Prove it to me that you are God," I said putting this voice to the test.

"Very well...here is a glimpse of...everything," the voice said simply. Suddenly in a flash, one of the most inexplicable things happened to me. All at once my awareness was everywhere, everything, in every time, and in every place all at once. I laughed, cried, smiled, hated, loved, pushed, pulled, rose, sank, spun, flew, dug, sat, etc... I was the tree in Australia, the fly in Paraguay, the snowflake in Canada, the cloud over the ocean, the weed on a lawn in Denmark, the baby in Fiji, the star person in outer space, the fish in the river, the scrambled eggs on someone's plate in Israel, the duck on the pond, the mother, the father, the grandparent, the child, the air, the moon, the rock, the worm... I felt and saw this all at once and tears streamed down my face because I saw the reality of everything. My spirit spun to depths I couldn't put into words and couldn't even imagine. And it all came to a sudden halt leaving my head buzzing.

"So...what is your question Neal?" God asked. I slowly tried to get my bearings again. "Sorry, Neal. You asked for proof so I gave you just a glimpse. Had I let you experience anything more I fear that I would be intervening in your life more than your soul can handle."

Feeling the truth well up inside me I asked with confidence, "What do you want from me?"

"Nothing."

"Nothing?" I said confused.

"Nothing." God replied.

"If you want nothing, then what am I supposed to do?" I asked.

"I need nothing from you. I don't need you to do anything for me. I am everything, why would I need something from you?"

"I see your point. But what am I supposed to do if you don't want me to do anything?"

"You do what you want to experience. In your heart you have desires to experience different things. Do those things. But do them for the sheer joy of experience. Don't do them because you think I want you to do them, because it makes no difference to me whether you seek out your desires or not. But if you want something to do, I think you should consider seeking out those desires and...experience them."

"That's it. Nothing more," I said feeling stupefied.

"Wait a minute, Neal. I'm not asking you to do this. I don't need or want you to do this. You just asked for something to do and I provided you with a suggestion. Take it or leave it, it makes no difference to me."

"Well that's just a little different than what I expected is all."

"What, you were expecting this big elaborate complex request?"

"Well, yes I guess."

"A common misconception of me. I'm actually quite simple. Humans have been making me out to be quite the complex needy God for sometime now. Do whatever you want or don't, it makes no difference to me."

"I see...so God needs nothing?"

"That's correct."

"Well...then how...why does just about every religion in the world paint you out to be the almighty creator that needs to be pleased and is easily angered by the disobedient human being?" I said feeling, like I was being blasphemous by just asking the question.

"Well Neal, that's an excellent question. Let me give you a brief history lesson that is in your history books, but isn't spelled out so simply. I'm going to take you back to a time before the well known religions of today came into place. Long before mass agriculture was invented. Back to when human beings lived off the land, just like the rest of Earth's creatures, subject to the natural ebb and flow of the circle of life.

Human beings used to live in tribes scattered across the earth. Their base beliefs were all things animate and inanimate contained a spirit. This is true. Now there were a few that believed that things were a little different but that's beside the point. The fact was, the majority believed in these different entities that had some sort of energetic tie to a thing, whatever that thing may be. Humans lived with this understanding for a long time.

To give you an example of how long, let's take Hinduism, one of the oldest main stream religions on earth. Let's say that Hinduism has been on earth for one year. Then the tribal religion I mentioned earlier has been around for ten thousand years. This is a substantial difference in age. So why did humans suddenly change their beliefs so dramatically and all these new religions sprouted from what seems to be out of nowhere you ask? Sprouts!"

"Sprouts?" I asked.

"Yes, sprouts! Well not sprouts, specifically, but food. You see, humans lived just like the animals. They were subject to ebbs of flows of nature. Take for instance, the mountain lion. The mountain lion loves to eat deer. It is its most favored food above all else. But sometimes there is a drought and the plants that the deer eat are not as plentiful. Then winter comes and the winter is exceptionally colder than most and the snowfall was heavy. The deer population drops out the bottom along with several other animals the mountain lion likes to eat. Then the mountain lion has a hard time feeding not only himself, but his family. Many of the lions starve to death the next year because there is no food. So the mountain lion population drops because it takes awhile for nature to regain its bounty of food for the lions. But in five years a spring comes with heavy rains. The summer is warm but not too dry. The winter is mild and the deer population explodes because of the abundance of edible plants. The following year the mountain lion population explodes because their bellies are full and they are healthy.

You see, human beings used to be part of the same times of abundance and lack. This natural ebb and flow kept nature in balance. These ebb's and flows weren't seen as good or bad, just the natural flow of things.

Then one day a tribe discovered a way, or rather decided to mass produce, their favorite foods all the time, despite the ebb and flow of nature. They started to cultivate the land and grow huge fields of their favorite food. They also started to breed the many animals they liked to eat and keep them locked up in a pen so they could kill and eat them at any time. The crops were watered regularly and the animals fed from the new abundance of food to create even more abundance. Now nature still went through its natural ebbs and flows, but it didn't affect this tribe as much as it did the other tribes.

As time passed, the tribe found new ways to create and preserve their food. The tribe grew rapidly because there was more food available and they were no longer kept in check by nature's cycles.

The tribe grew cocky, feeling that they had the best way to live and the rest of the tribes were primitive and less than them. So this tribe started to do something that no other tribe had done before. They invaded, conquered, and took over other tribes. They forced the conquered tribe to adopt their new ways of living and the tribe quickly doubled in population.

The tribe's lifestyle also changed dramatically. People worked twice as hard to keep the abundance of food growing. Other creatures that ate the same food as the tribe also became an issue because their populations began to grow also. Certain insects and birds that normally fed on certain crops grew to massive swarms so the farmers had to invent new ways to preserve their crops. Today farmers use pesticides that kill the insects, but it also poisons the food. It is not so poisonous that humans would die right away, humans could go on living just fine, but not as healthy. The large abundance of sheep that the humans liked to eat also caused a surge in the wolf population. So humans started to kill the wolves and all the other creatures that competed for the same food. This would ensure an abundant food supply for the human. To the outside tribe's point of view, it appeared that this new way of living was like playing God by creating an environment that didn't need God. But to the tribe on the inside they felt differently. You see, their lifestyle was changing in complexity. New elaborate laws and legal systems came into place along with an elaborate government to manage the large population that was not only growing from an abundance of food but because they continually conquered neighboring tribes. The new laws kept people from just walking out into the field and eating to their hearts content, even though they offered no help in cultivating that crop or tending the herd. So food which was once free for the taking as one walked through the woods now had to work for it. The laws imprisoned those that stole the food without working or paying for it. The new elaborate government was emplaced to manage the inner workings of the society, ensuring its continued growth and people paid taxes for the first time.

The other surrounding tribes that still lived by the natural laws of nature were helpless from invasion of this enormous society. The society had invented new weapons to kill their enemies more efficiently.

The people began to see their beliefs differently also. They went from believing that spirits simply existed in all things to some of these spirits needed things from humans. These spirits that needed things became gods and these gods needed appeasing or they would make life difficult for the human. Churches were built to do a number of things in a society. The churches helped define the religion and the needs of the gods. This kept the society on the path of continual growth by creating certain moral laws. And some of these godly laws would offend a god if broken. Some of these early religions are known to you as Hinduism and Greek Mythology.

One tribe went as far as to say that they were chosen by the God of all gods. And in fact there was only one God and all other gods where simply myth, hence the title Greek Mythology. The chosen people are known as the Israelites and Judaism was born. According to Judaism, God gave them a particular way to live with certain do's and don'ts. If the Jewish abide by these God-given laws, they will prosper.

From Judaism, Christianity and Islam were born. Jesus Christ was the prophesized Messiah or Savior that existed in Judaism. Some Jewish people did not believe that Christ was the direct descendant of God and they continue to wait for the messiah. Those that believed that Christ was the son of God became Christians and the human soul was in need of salvation from the God that humans had angered with their disobediences. If they believed that Christ was the son of God then God would forgive their trespasses if they asked for forgiveness through Christ. Islam stemming from Judaism and Christianity was born from the prophet Muhammad who also preached of the one God, with the emphasis of no other idols or other worldly things exist before the one God. Those that follow the teachings of Muhammad, who became one of many prophets in Islam, were known as Muslims.

There is minor yet distinct differences between these three religions. Islam sees Jesus Christ as a prophet but not the son of God. Islam's only difference is the teaching from the prophet Muhammad which lacks from the Judeo-Christian religions. These three religions have grown in complexity in the way they see and interpret this one needy God. Different interpretations have led to different sects of the religions like Greek Orthodox, Catholic, Orthodox Judaism, Modern Judaism, Sunni, Baptist, Protestant, Methodist, Episcopalian, Mormonism, Lutheran, Methodist, Seventh Day Adventists, and on and on and on. Each sect quarrels with each other, claiming that they hold the truth and others are inaccurate. The quarreling and bickering often leads to what we know of today as holy wars. Sometimes the minor differences lead to wars that seek to eliminate an entire race or religion. Like Adolph Hitler exterminating Jewish people and non-white races by the truck loads.

Hinduism gave birth to Buddhism, Shintoism, Confucianism, Taoism, and a number of other eastern religions. Hinduism believed that God was one or many depending on what aspect of God you were looking at. In other words, God was one with many parts that could be distinguished as different entities. Hinduism holds a strong importance on living a life with good karma and pleasing the gods or God. This will ensure the person will be reincarnated into more evolved life the next time around. Ultimately a Hindu seeks to reach the state of Nirvana where their spirit has reached what could be described as a heavenly state in the Judeo-Christian understanding.

Buddhism stemmed from the teachings of Lord Buddha. His teachings provided minor yet distinct differences from Hinduism being that there is no God or gods that govern or need appeasing. Yet reincarnation, karma, and nirvana are still a distinct basis to the religion. Several religions have branched from Hinduism and Buddhism adding the different interpretations and dogmas.

Now there are also many other religions and movements on earth that I didn't mention like Rastafarianism, Scientology, or the New Age movement. The fact is, theology has grown extremely complex on earth and a person can spend an entire lifetime just studying one religion and not fully understanding it.

To make a long story short, all these religions stem from a needy God or gods or a salvation or ultimate place of peace for the human soul. This idea stems from a distortion that is traced back to the base belief of all things animate and inanimate having its own entity or spirit. The distortion comes from the imbalance that humans have created in their new way of living. The new way of living has created a pyramid of a few extremely wealthy people that live at the top which is supported by the masses of poorer laborers at the bottom. The poorer people work a hundred times harder than when they lived the old primitive lifestyle. But they dare not turn back and return to the life subject to the whims of nature and the slow drive to improve technology. They've come to enjoy their comforts and are blinded to the suffocating civil laws of the legal system and the moral laws of the many complex religions.

So the complex religions of today were born to fill a hole that seemed to appear in everyone's life with the new way of living. But few seem to be putting these things together. It's all spelled out in front of them but they've blinded themselves to these connections.

I'm sorry it has taken me so long to answer your question, but in order to answer it with some sort of understanding, I needed to give you a clear picture of human history. Your understanding of God needing something from you, stems from a distortion that starts with sprouts. Humans' imbalance with nature has led to an imbalance with God and ultimately with themselves. So I need nothing from you. You live your life as you choose to experience it. That is my gift to you. Complete love unconditionally with complete freedom. I am everything, therefore I need nothing. My spirit runs through all things animate and inanimate. Everything exists within you, because my spirit runs through you.

Your soul doesn't need salvation or to live a life a certain way to achieve salvation or reach a state of nirvana. You have a choice right here and right now. You simply choose to live in a state of heaven on earth or nirvana however you want to see it. In the world of spirit there is no time or place so heaven is not a destination but rather a state of mind. You can choose to live in resistance to the natural ebb and flow of the circle of life or you can embrace the natural ebb and flow of the circle of life. Resistance leads to the lack and imbalance the general society is feeling today. Embrace the natural flow and it will lead you to the wise sage that seems to lack the burdens of the modern world and has found a heaven on earth.

So you may choose to live your life the new way and you can abide by a religion of your choice like Christianity or Buddhism. It will make no difference to me. In your complete freedom that I have gifted to you, it is your choice to live your life as you choose to experience it. But I have heard your heart, Neal, and I know that you desire to experience life with a clearer understanding and a life that doesn't lack the ordinary holes that exist in most people's lives today. This is what you sought when you would hike out into the woods by yourself. With nature surrounding you, you could feel that natural flow of the circle of life and you intuitively knew that somehow that would fill the hole you were feeling inside. Now you know that the wisdom and guidance and understanding you're looking for exists within you because your spirit is tied to all things and is lacking nothing.

So hopefully I've answered your question, Neal."

"I'd say so," I said feeling absolutely bewildered. "I'm glad you didn't hold anything back, God." Suddenly I felt God laughing, and it made me laugh out loud until tears rolled down my face. My laugh went from a deep belly laugh to a cry of joy and astonishment. I'd never felt so ignorant in my life. The awakening made me cry in a shamefulness of my idiocy.

"Don't be too hard on yourself, Neal. Now you know where the wisdom lies and it is yours for the taking anytime and anywhere, I am always with you," God said to comfort me. "I think we will talk like this again soon," I said. "I'm going to go back and visit with my friend some more."

"Good, I like talking with you, too. And tell your friend I said hi."

"Oh...sure. Uh...goodbye, God."

"There is no goodbye to me. If you leave me, you'd leave yourself. Which might be a difficult thing to do, leave yourself that is."

"So...are you saying...that you are me?"

"I am everything, remember."

"I see, so you were making a joke just then."

"Well, I was...but the joke I think, was more so

funnier to me."

"No, it's funny to me too. I just needed a little clarification is all."

"Fine, fine."

"Well this is me signing off then, for now."

"However, you want to look at it, is fine with me," God said.

I got up and felt the sun on my face. My eyes looked at the world a little differently and I felt strangely excited. I whispered a thank you into the wind and headed back up to Tilauth.

Tilauth was sitting on a log doing some repairs to his fire starting tools. His eyes raised up to meet mine as I languidly sat down across from him. A smile spread across his face and he nodded at me knowing what it was that I was going through.

He continued back to refining some cordage on his bow drill and said, "If Christianity is the religion you choose to follow, than you should follow it. I'm not here to sway you one way or the other but I will offer you a word of warning. If you wish to continue learning from me, your ideas about religion, God, the world, what's possible, and what's not possible will be turned upside down."

"You're warning me now?" I said sarcastically. "My world has already been turned upside down!" I exclaimed.

Tilauth laughed, "Trust me, Grandson, this is only the beginning. You've scratched the surface of the spirit world. All that you've done so far is become eligible to begin to learn about the world of being a shaman. So far you've managed to learn and understand the false spirits in your life. I wasn't sure if you were going to face the false spirit when you left the other day, but you did. That false spirit was the driving force in your life and we would have run into a wall soon if you hadn't faced it. I thought you would have faced it on your vision quest but you weren't ready yet. So the spirits guided us out here on the island so that you would come face to face with the false spirit again. Now, you still will and do struggle with different false spirits, but we at least can move forward with these teachings. You will also find that the false spirits you encounter will get stronger and more powerful the more you learn. This is because you are growing stronger in spirit and you become more of a threat to the false spirit. They will begin to target you and challenge you even more than the false spirit you just faced. You will also find other false spirits that will try and hide from you because they know that you can wreak havoc in their lives."

"So all that I've done so far has just scratched the surface of what there is to learn?" I asked.

"Yes…you've learned how to heal yourself, now it is time to learn how to heal others."

"I see."

"People, animals, plants, spirits, and the unknown will start knocking on your door needing help. It is a busy job and requires you to be extremely efficient with your energy, otherwise you will burn yourself out and become useless."

"So when do I start?" I said as matter-of-factly. Tilauth laughed at my eagerness.

"There is nothing easy about the path of a shaman. But it is a very freeing path too. But…before we begin, I will be leaving you," Tilauth said.

"Leaving…leaving where?"

"That is the first lesson."

"I will be waiting for you and you will need to find me. If you cannot find me, then our relationship ends here."

"You mean we're going to play hide-n-seek?"

"Sort of, only I'm not going to be hiding behind a bush in these woods, although it is possible. We're going to play hide-n-seek, only you have the entire world to search for me."

"Sure right," I said, hoping he was joking.

"I'm serious, Grandson," he replied sternly.

After realizing he wasn't joking I said, "Well that would be impossible."

"Nothing's impossible," he quickly replied.

"Well...that could take me years or a lifetime before I could find you...that's if I find you."

"Yes...but you have only ten days, which begins tomorrow."

"Tomorrow! You're leaving tomorrow?"

"Yes."

"How...I don't...There is no way I can track you around the world."

"Oh, I won't leave tracks in the dirt. You will have to follow your heart; your heart will guide you directly to me if you listen to it."

"I can't do it."

"You've done it before. Every time you've found me it has been because your heart led you there. This time you are going to make a conscious effort to listen to your heart. This will be the guide you need to find me."

I looked at Tilauth hoping he was joking, but he alluded to nothing of the sort. My head filled with doubt and I was certain that this was going to be the last time I would probably ever see Tilauth. He pissed me off so much. These stupid lessons were always hard, but this one was impossible.

"So that's it, you'll leave tomorrow morning?" I said, feeling stressed.

"I'll disappear sometime during the night," he said dryly.

"I just got back, can't we just relax for a bit?" I said, almost pleading with him.

"When the time comes, the time comes. Sometimes we have to be patient and wait years and years, and sometimes we have to act right now. Right now I'm being guided to bring this lesson to you without delay.

If it were up to the spirits I should have done this the moment you got back, but that wouldn't be practical. If I just disappeared you wouldn't have any idea as to why, so I will stay and answer any questions you may have to get you prepared." Tilauth looked at me and he had to have seen the anguish I was going through in my head. "Tonight we will feast on mussels, clams, and some crab I caught earlier. We will fill our bellies and relax."

Tilauth got up and walked down to the beach where he had the crab still in the water inside his primitive trap to keep it fresh. We cooked up the food and added some seaweed for vegetables. We ate as the sun set in our eyes and mingled about small things. I enjoyed Tilauth's company so much. He had become one of the single most important persons in my life these past few years. He was like my best friend but he pushed me harder than any other person ever had.

The pebbles rustled as the waves receded back into the ocean. The golden light of the sunset danced off the waves in the ocean and I could hear a varied thrush singing to its hearts content behind me. A loon called softly down the beach and I sank down into the sand relaxing my bones.

"Tilauth..." I said, breaking through the sound of the waves.

"Yes?" he said softly.

"I'm running out of money. I can't afford to fly across the ocean or travel anywhere far."

"That's what you're worried about...money? Money should be the last of your worries. If you want money, ask for it."

"What do you mean...ask you for money?" I asked confused.

"Me!?! Nooooo...do I look like I have any money?" he said, chuckling. "I don't have money because I don't need money. The land provides me with all the wealth I need. If you want money, you've got to send it out to the wind. The money will show up whenever or wherever it's needed."

"What do you mean send it out to the wind?"

"Money has a spirit like everything has a spirit. All these spirits are connected like the way you are connected. If you ask for money with a clear heart, money will be provided with the desire of what you want to experience. If you want to experience wealth, then all you have to do is ask and become it. You have come to understand the false spirits that have run your life for so long. Your heart is now clear so your intentions of what you want to experience are also clear to you. So now you may send out to the wind what it is you want to experience with a clear heart and you can be certain that the experience will come to you. If it comes differently than you expected, then check your true desires and you will find you've gotten what you truly desired to experience. So money should be the least of your concerns at this point."

We lit a fire and relaxed on the beach breathing in the salty air. The stars were twinkling overhead with clarity. The new moon set shortly after the sun with just a sliver of light. We slipped into our shelter to bed down. I wanted to somehow prolong my time with Tilauth but knew there was no way around it. It wasn't long before my worries began to blur and I passed out and slipped into a sea of dreams.

Chapter 29
What Bob Wants

I awoke the next morning to a chorus of birds singing to their hearts content. A brief rain came through late the night before bringing the worms and bugs close to the surface.

I suddenly remembered Tilauth's next challenge for me and spun around to see that he was gone and his things left with him. I felt a sudden surge of loneliness fill me and my heart filled with doubt. I scampered out of the shelter vigorously searching for a track to get me pointed in the right direction. But the recent rains had washed away any signs of tracks. But I knew that Tilauth wouldn't have been as careless as to leave me even one track that I could easily identify. He no doubt would have covered every revealing track so that I would have to rely completely on my intuition.

I looked around the forest to see the birds happily hopping around the ground and fluttering from one branch to the next. A family of flickers pecked away at the ground while the adolescent waited patiently for its next meal. Their chirp sounded otherworldly and didn't seem to be bothered in the slightest by my plight.

I walked down to the beach underneath the slate gray skies above. The skies seemed to sink down upon me with astounding pressure, pushing me into the gloom that encompassed my heart. I stood in the water letting the cold salt water chill my feet. A mist lingered along the shore hanging like ghost in a world of silence. The forest seemed dark and mysterious behind me and I felt a strange twisting inside me.

I remembered one of my many dreams that swam through my mind last night. I was walking through a bed of dried, golden, oak leaves. The short oak trees hovered above me, leafless, yet strangely making me feel protected. A river meandered trough the sea of oaks lipping over large slate rocks. I stood on a rocky outcropping along the river and could hear distant voices from a sacred past singing. I couldn't make out the words of the song, but I could feel the urgency. The singing beckoned me from every part of my body and I felt a longing and a need for something I couldn't explain.

I tried to interpret this languid dream but couldn't get a clear understanding. I grabbed my things and began to make my way back to my Jeep. I hadn't a clue as to where I was going yet but I figured if I just started going, I would figure it out. My breath whispered through my mouth and nose as I silently made my way down the trail. I felt outside myself as if my body was its own separate entity and I was watching myself walk along the trail lost from within.

I drove onto the ferry hoping for a sign or a direction to give me some guidance but none came to my awareness. The ferry rocked in the waves and it crossed my mind, what if Tilauth never left the island. But in argument, my gut felt certain that the island felt alone. This was going to be my dilemma every step of this task. So this narrowed my search by an infinitesimal amount and I had the rest of the world to look.

By the time the ferry docked, I had no better idea as to where Tilauth may have gone but I decided to head to my folks place to gather some provisions for my travels. I picked up my passport, whatever money I could find, changes of clothes, and whatever else I could imagine myself possibly needing. I filled my tank full of gas and drove to the main road and asked myself, 'Which way do I turn? Do I turn right, left, do I go straight, or do I turn around and head the direction I came from?' I got nothing and I felt nothing. Or at least I thought I felt nothing. I slammed my hands down on the steering wheel saying aloud, "Damn it Tilauth!"

A car honked behind me so I turned left feeling like I wasn't being pulled in any direction. I drove to the freeway and headed south on Interstate 5 towards Seattle. 'Why?' I asked myself. I hadn't a clue. It just felt like somewhere to begin. I weaved in and out of traffic sputtering along.

The Jeep rose to an apex in the bridge and I could see all of downtown Seattle. The high rises, the space needle, Queen Ann Hill, Capitol Hill, and Mt. Rainer in the distance.

Caught up in the scenery my Jeep suddenly began to gasp and spit, coughing along the road. I pulled it to the side of the bridge flipping on my hazards.

"What the hell am I supposed to do now?" I thought. "I've got nine and a half days to search the entire world for Tilauth and my Jeep sputters out of existence." I check the inner workings of my rig as cars whip by sucking and pushing the air in a whirl of exhaust fumes. "It isn't getting fuel," I thought. So I checked the fuel filter, which was fine and the fuel pump seemed to be fine. "A line must be plugged or the carburetor finally kicked the bucket. Nothing I can do about that along side a major freeway, on a bridge, two hundred feet up in the air. Is this a sign?" I thought. "I don't know. What do I know about signs and omens?" If I wasn't supposed to be going this way than I didn't know what way I was supposed to go. Nothing seemed to be guiding me other than what seemed practical and nothing seemed practical at this point.

I pulled my rucksack from inside the Jeep and walked out in front of the broken down Jeep and stuck out my thumb. I felt bad about leaving my Jeep behind since it had been so good to me over the years, but I hadn't a choice. I figured, once I got near a pay phone I'd call my folks and let them know where it was. I half doubted anyone would pick me up hitchhiking but I had to try.

People whipped by, their eyes carefully averting to appear to have not noticed me. I decided not to walk away from my Jeep so passerbys would understand what had happened.

Surprisingly, it didn't take long before a small tan pick up pulled over. A woman in her forties reached over to open the door to let me in. Her eyes were kind and I felt at ease.

"Car trouble, huh?" she said as I slid onto the seat. "Unfortunately, yes," I said feeling frustrated. She pulled out onto the freeway again saying, "Once, when I bought a car my instincts told me that this was a bad car to buy but my logic said it was a good deal and I really like the look of it. But oh man, let me tell you; that car lived in the repair shop. I never got to drive the damn thing. I dumped that car and ever since then I've only bought cars that my instincts gave me the go ahead. That's why I got this beaut'. It's not much to look at but I've never had a problem with him," she said as she caressed the top of the dashboard gently.

"So where are you headed?" she asked as she peered out to the traffic.

"Uh...you can take me to the airport, I guess," I

said quickly thinking of the first thing that popped in my head.

"The airport!?! You don't sound very sure of yourself. Don't you know where you're going?" she said, seeming genuinely concerned.

"Well, it's a long story but I'm kind of guessing where I should go." She looked at me with a tender smile.

"Want some advice?" she asked.

"Sure," feeling like I could use any advice that I could get.

"Listen to your instincts, they've never failed me," she said with a wink. I nodded pressing my lips together tightly.

We passed through downtown Seattle going in and out of tunnels. Skyscrapers loomed high above and I watched the reflections dance across the glass buildings.

"So…not many people pick up hitchhikers nowadays, especially a female picking up a strange man given the crime we have," I said.

She looked at me and smiled, "Why, are you up to no good?" she asked.

"No, no, no!" I quickly said. "No, I didn't mean that, I was just saying is all."

She laughed, "Instincts! It's all about the instincts. I've been on a few adventures of my own and I know when I see someone on an adventure. You have a lot more on your mind than committing some ridiculous crime. At least this is what my instincts are telling me."

"Well your instincts seem pretty perceptive." I was silent for a moment listening to the drone of the tires. "I wish I had as sharp as instincts as you," I said.

"Oh, you do. I can tell these things. You just got to pay attention to them closely. My grandmother taught me when I was a child how to listen to my instincts and I've never stopped listening. Well…except when

I bought that car way back. You just gotta listen to that voice inside your heart. That voice can be trusted because if it's lying you'll know it." I looked at this woman carefully. It seemed too coincidental that the first person I meet on my search for Tilauth would talk about instincts and inner voices.

"I think I have a pretty good idea what you're talking about," I said.

"I'm sure you do. Sometimes we just need somebody to paint it out simply for us," she said as she weaved around an elderly man who looked as if he could barely see over the steering wheel.

I quickly remembered the conversation I had with God last evening and was taken back again by the thoughts of religion. The whole idea of abandoning Christianity frightened me to no end. It was so ingrained in my head that my soul's salvation was completely dependant on my beliefs and if I changed them around than I risked being sent to the bowels of hell. What if I was wrong? What if the voice I was listening to last night was the voice of the devil trying to lead me astray? The devil was supposed to be this devious fallen angel bound and determined to lead god's children from the flock.

"You seem bothered by something," she said interrupting my thoughts. "Do you mind if I ask what?" I turned to see her eyes filled with compassion. "Well...you don't have to answer this if you don't want to but, out of curiosity; do you believe in a particular religion?" I asked.

"That's a deep question." Her face turned from compassionate to concern. "You aren't trying to save my soul are you?" she asked.

"No!" I laughed uncomfortably. "I didn't think that was why you were asking but I had to make sure. There is nothing more tiring than dealing with religious recruiters. I'd rather shove a needle in my eye than deal with another poor Mormon kid with a back pack, tie, peddling around on his mountain bike," she chuckled. Her smile seemed to slowly disappear as she thought about my question. "Well, I personally have gone back and forth with religion. I was raised in a Christian home that went to church every once in a long while. I think my parents wanted everyone to think that they were good Christians but deep down they weren't very religious, or at least not very Christian. My family had some unique beliefs that didn't necessarily follow the typical Christian way of life, but if you asked them they were good God-fearing Christians. I myself would probably call myself a Christian but there are many things in the Bible that doesn't agree with me.

There are a lot of crazy cults out there, and one could easily consider some Christian sects a cult.

Explain Christianity to someone who knows nothing today of the world's religions and that person would think Christianity is a cult." She looked at me to see my reaction but I made no gesture in response. "Yeah…I'm serious. The orthodox has been proclaiming anything less than orthodox as a cult. From an outsider's point of view, orthodox is a cult.

Let's say a scientist discovers a new tribe deep in the rainforests of Brazil. As the scientist examines this new culture, he is introduced to this tribe's religious beliefs.

The tribe up until recently has been killing cows, goats, sheep, panthers, snakes, fish, monkeys, birds, and even their own children for a god they called Bob. They have been killing these animals and laying them on an altar for Bob because Bob requires this of them to appease their offenses against him. You see, Bob told a couple of the tribe's men a long time ago that he had a certain set of rules that he would like followed. The rules were extensive and very difficult to follow.

These rules were applicable to the very thoughts, which the tribe's people would have. And Bob knew all their thoughts without question. So the tribe's people broke these rules often no matter how hard they tried and Bob would be hurt and sometimes get angry. So in order to allow the tribe's people to return to good standing with Bob they had to kill something of value to them and offer it to Bob. Sometimes the offerings included the offender's own child. After the sacrifice was made the tribe's person could go about there daily lives until they offended Bob again, which was usually the next day because of the extensive rules Bob had put forth.

All the sacrificing was posing a problem for the tribe and Bob saw that it was doing no good because they just kept breaking the rules. So one day Bob decided to live with the tribe as they did. Bob lived a perfect life, without breaking any of the rules. Bob lived his life teaching the tribe's people how to live a life within the rules. Bob cured sicknesses and raised people from the dead. A neighboring tribe heard about how Bob had come to this tribe and they were jealous and felt threatened by Bob. So the neighboring tribe came over and killed Bob. Then the tribe was sad because Bob was dead. That was until one day some of the tribe's people saw Bob leave his death bed and rise up into the sky. This was the ultimate defeat Bob did because the tribe felt death was the biggest enemy.

So now the tribe no longer sacrifices animals and babies. They still break all of Bob's rules all the time but they ask Bob to excuse them because they didn't mean to do it. But Bob told the tribe's people that they were the only ones that were going to join him in the sky where it is paradise after they die. Any other people that don't believe that Bob used to live with these tribe's people and that Bob was god, will not be allowed into Bob's paradise. So this tribe began killing neighboring tribes because other tribes didn't agree with Bob or they could possibly deny Bob's people the freedom to worship Bob.

Bob sometimes gets angry and hurt with people

because they haven't asked to be excused or they don't believe in Bob. So Bob punishes the people with big storms, floods, fires, famine, disease, and other forms of punishment. Sometimes Bob will even ask his people to kill others in his name. The people don't always understand why Bob wants certain things done but they do them without question. It is a matter of faith in Bob and realizing that Bob works in mysterious ways. Sometimes the tribe's people will do things they personally want done and proclaim that Bob asked them to do it. These fraudulent excuses cannot be proven and are often abused. But Bob knows who's doing good and whose doing bad and Bob will punish those for doing bad. But the tribe's people do not fully trust Bob to punish the bad doers so the tribe's people have often killed the bad doers if a majority agree that they have done something bad.

So do you get what I'm saying?" she asked looking at me.

"I understand what you're saying. Bob seems to be far from perfect and he is making things worse down here. If Bob is all perfect, all powerful, and all knowing, than why does he create a people that he knows will betray him before he creates them, then get hurt and upset when they do? He knew before he created them that they were going to offend him. Granted Bob's people have free will but Bob already knows what decisions they will make. In fact one could argue that it seems like his people are making more mistakes since his visit."

She interrupts me, "Well Bob's people would blame it on everyone who doesn't believe in Bob. They are the reason the world has so many problems."

I interrupt her, "But if it is Bob's people that are doing most of the killing or are at least supporting it..."

She interrupts me again, "Not only are they just killing, but they are jealous and angry and they are learning it from Bob.”

I cut her off before she can say anything else, “Yes Bob gets hurt and upset because someone doesn't love him or believe in him. You know what? If Bob were a husband on earth and his wife didn't love or believe in his ways, he would threaten to send her to the depths of eternal damnation if she didn't change her mind. On earth we would say that Bob needs some therapy because one cannot force someone to love them. And using threats is just not healthy. Bob seems pretty needy and that is probably why his wife no longer loves him,” I said feeling a little surprised. We both looked at each other and started to laugh.

“Thanks for that,” I said smiling at her.

“Hey, no problem, I was just saying it, like I see it,” she said smiling back at me.

“Well that's what's been bothering me lately,” I said. I've been struggling lately with the teachings of Bob.”

“Yeah…you and the rest of the world - even those that don't believe in Bob. Bob's got a lot of good things to offer and teach but when Bob doesn't help you further down your path, it might be a good idea to thank Bob and move on.”

I looked out the window to see a parking lot of idling cars and trucks dropping off passengers as they pulled out there luggage. “Sea-Tac Airport at your service,” she said squeezing her truck between some cars.

“Say I never got your name,” I said leaning back into the car before shutting the door.

“It's Janice.”

“Nice to meet you, Janice. I'm Neal.” I reached out and shook her hand. Her hand was strong and dry. “Thanks so much for the ride and the conversation. I think it will help.”

“Good, glad I could help. You remind me of myself when I was younger.”

“Yeah?” I said.

"Yeah, my grandmother taught me a lot and sent me on crazy adventures. You look like you are going through some of the crazy stuff I went through. Well, anyways…you take care of yourself and may Bob be with you," she said grinning from ear to ear.

I laughed, "may Bob be with you too," and I shut the door still laughing.

I walked into the airport feeling at ease and confident that I could find Tilauth anywhere. I walked over to the screens displaying the outgoing flights and scanned the different cities.

I quieted my mind and said, "God, are you there?"

Surprisingly he answered back, "of course I'm here, I'm everywhere."

"Oh…right, sorry I forgot."

"Not a problem, happens all the time," god said.

"Say God, so you know I'm looking for Tilauth, right?"

"Yes, I know."

"So, where am I supposed to go to find him?" I asked.

"Do you want to find him?"

"Yes…that's why I'm asking."

"Well your heart isn't very sure."

"It isn't!?!"

"No, your heart knows that if you find Tilauth your life will change and you will find commitments you're not sure you want to take on. Are you sure you are ready for that change?" God asked.

"Well, my life has already changed so much I don't think I could go on knowing that there is more and I chose not to learn it. But I don't know what commitments I will be facing."

"Tilauth will train you to be a healer of anyone or anything that comes to you. You already know that. Being a healer is not a life of riches, fame or success necessarily and it requires you to work at anytime of the day, night, week, month, year, or lifetime. The obligations can be very demanding and strenuous. In a world that could use so much healing there is very little down time. You're constantly bombarded by people, animals, plants, waters, rocks, spirits, or whatever it may be, that will be asking your for help. Your personal life will have a tendency to fall in second place. This path will also lead you to being a teacher and you will have students. These students will also demand your time and energy. This is what your heart knows and as I say these words I can tell that you intuitively already know this. In a sense, by becoming a shaman you will lose the humanness that you've come accustomed to."

"Yes you're right. I do feel like I already know this and I guess I just wasn't verbalizing it to myself," I replied.

"Well then, are you ready for this path?" God asked again.

"Uh...so I'm going to be a teacher as well?" I asked.

"If you choose to."

"So will I be a great healer and teacher?"

God laughs, "I will not tell you anything more about your future that you don't need to know. If I told you everything you wouldn't try hard and your life would be boring and predictable. There would be no adventure in that. Besides that would defeat the purpose of why you have chosen to live this life. Much of why your spirit has chosen this life is to face certain fears and obstacles along your path back to your complete self."

"My complete self? What is that?" I asked.

"Your complete self is a reunion of all that you are, which is a piece of everything. Any atomic scientist on your planet can tell you that you are made completely up from energy. Atoms are made up from subatomic particles which are positive, negative, and neutral charges of energy and this energy is not confined to a specific individual or thing. In other words, you are tied to everything. When you completely reunite with your whole self, your awareness will expand through time and space. Your spirit passed through the veil of the great, forgetting when you were born and when you reunite with your whole self the veil will be lifted. This is the path that all spirits on planet earth are on. Some paths are slower than others, and some may even seem to be going backwards. But never the less, your complete self is the union of all that is and ever was."

"So by you just now telling me that, doesn't that make me aware of my whole self and I'm then already reunited with all that I am?"

"No, your awareness is still far from your whole self. My words are just words. They've only given you a basic understanding of who you are. It is up to you to discover on your own who you truly are."

"I see, so now I have a choice on moving forward or moving backward," I said trying to clarify my predicament.

"No. No matter what you choose to do with your life, it will always be moving forward. Sometimes, you choose to be what you're not, to discover what you are."

"I hear what you're saying."

"So you may choose to do whatever you want to do, it makes no difference to me. It's all good to me," God said.

"Well this path that Tilauth can teach me intimidates me and I'm quite honestly afraid."

"Nothing wrong with being afraid. Usually a spirit will choose for an option, a particular path that is challenging for them prior to being born. This path will be frightening because it means jumping out into the unknown and letting go of the things that comfort them."

"So this path is the challenging road that my spirit

has chosen prior to my birth?" I asked.

"This is part of it, along with many other paths yet to come."

"I see. Well with that in mind, I don't feel like I'd be very happy if I backed down from this challenge. The regrets and the 'what if's' seem too great when I'm looking back on my life and I don't want that. Give me adventure, give me challenge, and most importantly, let my fears be faced."

"Very well, take a flight to Salt Lake City and catch a bus to the town of Moab, Utah. There you will need to find a place called Mesa Arch. Go there and you will be on your way."

"Ok...Salt Lake City...then Moab...find Mesa Arch, got it."

"Great,"God said.

"Hey, thanks God," I replied.

"No problem."

I scanned the screens to see that a flight was leaving for Salt Lake City in a couple of hours. I went up to the counter and purchased a ticket for Salt Lake City.

Chapter 30
Chinese Food

The ticket was expensive and I nearly emptied my wallet completely of cash. I still needed to buy a bus ticket, and perhaps a little food to sustain me.

The stewardess came by with a packet of pretzels and I asked for a second helping, thinking that this might be the only food I could afford for awhile. I needed money and knew that I wasn't going to make it there if I didn't get some cash soon.

I remembered what Tilauth told me about money so I decided to send out to the four winds that I would like some cash to get me to where I needed to go. My prayer sounded something like this, 'To the winds of the West, where the sun sets, the season of fall, the time of adulthood, and a time of inner thinking. I invite you to hear my words. To the winds of the North, the season of winter and old age, the home of the white hairs, a time of rest, and place of wisdom. I invite you to hear my prayer. To the winds of the East, a time of birth, adolescence, fresh starts, great learning, spring time, home of the rising eagle, and the mystery of decisions. I invite you to listen to my words. To the winds of the South, a time of the young adult, hard work, hot summers, and endurance. I invite you to hear my words. Mother Earth; the provider to all living things, the slow heart beat of life, and the heart of the female, I invite you to hear my prayer. To Father Sky; the mystery of the wind, the openness of freedom, bringer of rains, the depths of the unknown, and the heart of the male, I invite you to hear my prayers. Creator, Great Mystery, Grandfather of all, the Spirit that breaths through all things, all that is and ever was, and all that is known and unknown, I invite you here to hear my prayers. From the winds from within, I pray; provide me with the money I need to accomplish my journey. From the depths of my heart I wish to experience this without a doubt in my soul. Spirit of money hear my request and know that I seek you not from a place of greed but from the desire to learn and help heal the spirit of life. I release this desire for this experience to the different winds to be carried out in all directions to the ends of time swift like an arrow. Hear my words and know that they are true.'

I opened my eyes to see a woman and her child were reluctant in disturbing me so they could get into their seats next to me.

I quickly jumped up to allow them in, "I'm sorry, I didn't know you guys needed in," I said, feeling stupid.

"That's ok, you looked so peaceful sitting there I didn't want to disturb you," the mother said as they squeezed into their seats.

"Oh...well I hope you weren't standing there long," I said.

"No, no, we had just walked up. No big deal. My little guy has got an overactive bladder so this probably won't be the last time we have to squeeze by you," she said. The young boy flipped through a Dr. Suess book, completely ignoring his mother talking about him.

"Well, don't hesitate to disturb me next time, I don't mind."

It didn't take long before I fell asleep with the drone of the jet plane and the gentle bobbing of the occasional turbulence. I awoke to the pilot blaring over the intercom saying that we were about to land in the next fifteen minutes. I looked over to see the child passed out with his head cocked in a position that had to hurt, but he obviously didn't seem to mind. The mom thumbed through her Sky Mall magazine which rested on top of a book titled 'The Book of Latter Day Saints'. I smiled as I thought to myself; the book should be called 'The Book of Latter Day Bobs'. I let a little laugh out under my breath and the woman turn slightly to look at me.

"You're awake. Did you sleep well?" she asked.

"Yes I did...thanks."

"You were snoring."

"Was I? I'm so sorry. I've been told that I can be pretty bad," I said feeling my face flush with embarrassment.

"No, you weren't too bad. In fact I thought it was kind of cute," she said, grinning at me. I then realized that this woman was flirting with me. I smiled back, feeling embarrassed and noticed that she wasn't wearing a wedding ring. She was a single mom looking for a man, a husband, a father to her son no doubt.

I felt ridiculously shy all of a sudden. I hadn't been hit on or even had any kind of love interest since Elly. She was attractive and no doubt a conservative Mormon, given the bible she carried and the old fashioned, conservative clothes. "She would think of me a heathen no doubt when she got to know me, a true enemy of Bob," I thought.

We were quiet awhile as the pilot gave the weather

conditions and the time on the ground in Salt Lake City.

"So, do you live in Salt Lake City?" she asked.

"Uh – no. I've been living a number of places lately but my home base is in Lynnwood, Washington."

"Oh, so you're a bit of a wanderer," she said digging for a background.

"Sort of...well I guess you could say I'm doing a little wandering lately."

"Well...there nothing wrong with doing a little wandering. Perhaps a little soul searching?" she inquired.

"Perhaps," I said trying to be as vague as possible.

"Well does your wandering plan on having dinner tonight?"

"Uh...well..." I fumbled my words, feeling like I wanted to disappear. "I suppose I will probably eat sometime tonight." I didn't want her to ask because I knew what she was looking for and what she wanted I wasn't going to provide. She was quiet for a bit. "You're going to make me ask you aren't you?"

"Ask me what?" I said playing stupid.

"You are going to make me," she said sighing with discomfort. I said nothing, desperately searching for a way to remedy this situation. "Well I was trying to open the court up to you since the man is really the one to do the...asking, but maybe I'm just not good at this whole...thing. I'm old-fashioned I guess but, anyways here goes nothing, would you like to have dinner with me tonight? Well, that is if you aren't already with someone?"

"Uh...no...I'm not with someone. I guess I'm...well I on a limited time schedule and..."

"Well you're still are going to eat aren't you?" she replied giving me a strenuous smile.

"Yes, well I'm on a..." I stopped myself short, thinking that I was being rude.

"You know what, yes; I'd love to have dinner with

you," I said throwing all caution to the wind. I had no money to feed myself let alone this woman and her child. But I figured that people come into my life for some reason so she must have some reason. "It'll all work out," I thought, or at least I hoped.

"Good, I'm glad you said yes. I know a pretty good restaurant in Salt Lake that serves up some great Chinese food. Do you like Chinese food?" she asked smiling.

"Yes, I love Chinese food."

The plane landed with a couple screeches and bumps and we rolled up to our gate. We walked down the terminal making small talk as she pushed her son in a stroller. She was sweet, and deep inside me I knew she just wanted to find a good man to marry and have a family. There was something about her that seemed to be off. My intuition told me that her husband must have died unexpectedly. I then quickly noticed in the corner of my eye his spirit walking next to her. His spirit was obviously annoyed with me, and I felt that he was protective over her and his son.

I tried to express to him through my thoughts that I meant no harm to his son or his wife. He appreciated that but still seemed agitated with why we were going out to dinner together.

"Do you have someone who planned on picking you up here?" she asked.

"No, I was planning on going straight to the bus station."

"Oh, well did you have a bus that you needed to catch?"

"No, I haven't gotten the ticket yet. I was planning on getting it whenever I got there."

"You are truly wandering!" she said smiling. "You're a bit of a free spirit aren't you?" she asked.

"Well I didn't used to be, but for the past few years I have been."

"Why the change?" she asked.

"Uh... well..." I struggled to figure out an answer for her.

"I'm sorry, I'm being too nosy. You don't have to answer."

"No, you're fine. I guess I just haven't ever answered this question before. Let's just say I felt my life was getting a little ordinary and that disturbed me so...I changed."

"Well that's a good enough answer. My car's in the parking lot, you don't mind if I drive do you?"

"Of course not," I replied.

We hopped into her car. It was a simple car with no frills or luxuries. She drove to the restaurant while we sat in an uncomfortable silence. The spirit of her husband came and went expressing his upset with the whole situation. I breathed slowly, feeling unsure of what to do about him. He was trying to talk to his wife. He kept yelling at her, saying 'Nadine, what are you doing. Stop the car. Let him out! You are with me! Nadine! Nadine!' he yelled. She reached up and scratched the corner of her head where her husband was yelling. She stretched her shoulders as an indefinable response to the yelling of her husband's spirit. I could tell that she wasn't listening to his words but she could feel a discomfort.

"So, have you lived in Salt Lake all your life Nadine?" I asked to fill the silence and push away her late husband's frenzied anger. She quickly looked at me with her eyes full of confusion, pain, which quickly led to a stern anger. She turned her blinker on and quickly made lane changes over and over and pulled onto the shoulder of the freeway. For a second there I thought she must have heard her husband ask her to stop the car and let me out.

When we came to a full stop she put the car in park and looked at me carefully, "Why did you call me Nadine?" she said with a shaken voice.

"Uh..." I struggled with words. I forgot that we

had never introduced each other.

"Tell me now? Why did you call me that?"

"I'm sorry...is that your name?"

"Why did you call me Nadine?" she said sternly, pressing me for an answer.

"I guess I thought you looked like a Nadine is all. I'm sorry I didn't mean to upset you," I said feeling a little stupid for my slip up. She looked at me for what seemed like an eternity. She then turned to her steering wheel and began to sob uncontrollably.

"Look, maybe you should just take me to the bus station. I..."

"It's ok," she managed to get out in-between her sobs. I looked back to see her son still sleeping comfortably in his car seat. "I'm sorry," she said trying to pull back her tears.

"It's alright." I tried to ease her discomfort.

"It's just that you caught me by surprise. You must have some sort of gift or something. There is no possible way that you could have known that. It's just that...well...my husband passed away last year. He used to drive heavy construction equipment, and well, he died in an accident. He was driving a dump truck at the time. It was a really old truck and there was no wall protecting him from the load in back except for a window. The guy operating the tractor was new and he was filling the truck with hot blacktop to make a driveway. The guys accidentally went forward instead of reverse while he was filling his truck and it broke through the back window and filled the cab up with my husband in it. They were unable to get him out..." she sobbed. "...in time before he was burned to death. The thing of it is...he was the only person that called me Nadine. Everyone else calls me Nancy. He called me Nadine because when he first asked me out he was so nervous that he fumbled my name and called me Nadine. I was so smitten by him that I just let him continue to call me Nadine the entire date. He of course figured out his error by the next date but he thought it so funny that he just continued to call me Nadine. So you see you remind me a little of him. And when you called me Nadine it shocked me. I don't know how you know that name other than god must work in mysterious ways," she said still appearing to be shaken up.

"I'm sorry I didn't mean to..."

"It's okay. You didn't know," she said, wiping her tears with a tissue from her purse. "I'm sure you're thinking, 'Why would I want to go out to dinner with this hysterical woman?" she said laughing uncomfortably.

"It's okay. I'd still like to have dinner with you."

She smiled at me saying, "You're sweet. My husband, well he wasn't always so sweet but he loved me and I understood he just wasn't going to be the sweetest of guys. That's just who he was." She tried to regain her composure. "So you're sure you still would like to have dinner with me?" she asked.

"I'd love to," I said honestly.

She began to merge back into traffic.

"I'm Neal, by the way," I said trying to lighten the mood. She grinned at me looking like she was embarrassed.

"It's nice to meet you, Neal."

We drove to the restaurant, chit-chatting about Salt Lake City and her life growing up in the suburbs of Salt Lake. We got to the restaurant and sat down. Her son sat in a high chair and colored on some paper the waitress had given him. I ordered the lemongrass chicken and Nancy got the Mongolian Beef. We talked about small things as we ate our dinners and her son had some of hers. I made her laugh a lot because that seemed to be what she needed. I think we both knew we weren't meant to be together but we enjoyed each other's company.

I excused myself to use the restroom and made my

way through the busy restaurant. I walked into the men's restroom to see a wallet sitting on the counter. Looking around to see if the owner was near by but the restroom was empty. I grabbed the wallet and opened it up to see whose it was. Craig Murdock, 248 Terrace Heights Ogden, Utah. The wallet had to have close to a thousand dollars in it, credit cards, and receipts. I put it in my back pocket and used one of the urinals. "This could be the way money is given to me," I thought. I'd completely forgotten that I didn't have any money to even pay for dinner. She would think I was such a chump, going out to dinner with her and expecting her to pay for everything. I walked up to the sink to wash my hands. I looked up into the mirror to see my face staring back at me. "I can't take this wallet," I thought. The man wouldn't have left it behind not caring. If it were my wallet I would hope that an honest person found it and returned it. But I needed the money pretty badly.

I walked back to my table. Half way there I ran into our waitress, "Excuse me mam," I stopped in mid stride. "Yes?" she said appearing to be really busy.

"I found this wallet in the men's restroom. Could you make sure it gets back to the rightful owner?," and I handed her the wallet.

"Sure," she said looking at me briefly.

I sat down at the table and noticed that she was nearly finished eating and I only had a few more bites left. I told Nancy about the wallet I found in the restroom and how I gave it to the waitress. She said that that was probably a good thing because the guy could accuse me of stealing something from it because someone previously found it and took some money but left the wallet behind.

I got dessert to prolong the bill but of course that just made the bill more expensive. Her son was getting grumpy from the long flight and was ready for bed. I ate my dessert and began to wonder how I was going to do break it to her that I had no money. I had a total of four dollars and seventy eight cents in my pocket. This meal had to be over thirty dollars without the tip. My palms began to sweat with nervous anticipation. I could see the waitress coming across the room to no doubt give us our bill. When she got to our table my heart began to pound.

"Excuse me sir," she said looking at me. "This gentleman would like to talk to you if you don't mind." A tall gentleman in a suit with salt and pepper hair looked at me over her shoulder.

"You are the one who found my wallet?" he said as his steely blue eyes pierced through me.

"Great," I thought. 'Now this guy is going to accuse me of stealing his money. I should've just left the wallet on the counter and let somebody else deal with it. But I had to answer and the waitress knew who I was and there was no way around this.

"Yes, I found your wallet."

"Mr. Murdock is one of our most regular patrons," the waitress inserted. She stood by us as if to make sure we didn't make Mr. Murdock's dining experience an unpleasant one.

"My father told me that if anyone tries to steal from me and I catch them, then I should give them whatever it is they were trying to steal," he said, studying me carefully. "He said that I should do this because the thief must need it more than I do. I think my father felt that it was better to show the thief how to be kind and giving because a thief has most likely had a life that is otherwise," Mr. Murdock said while hovering over me.

"But sir, I didn't steal..." I interrupted.

"I know you didn't steal anything. I checked and it was all there. My father thought it was good to reward a thief in hopes of rehabilitating them. This may be true. But I think it is also a good idea to reward someone who is honest. So..." he opens his wallet and hands me all the cash that was in it.

"Sir, I couldn't possibly take..." I said.

"No, no I insist. I won't take no for an answer. You just have to promise me that you will do the same for the thief or the honest person when the tables are turned," he said setting the money on the table.

"Well, thank you sir."

"No, no, thank you for being honest," he said as he walked away. The waitress grinned at me as she set the bill on the table and walked away.

"Wow," Nancy said.

"Wow is right. Well, dinner is on me," I said, feeling relieved from my financial noose.

We packed up and headed out the door. I went in with four dollars and came out with eight hundred and sixty two dollars. She drove me to the bus station and I thanked her for the company. She leaned over the consol and kissed me gently on the cheek,

"Thank you Neal; if your wanderings bring you back to Salt Lake please look me up," as she handed me her phone number.

"I'll be sure to do that," I said and shut the car door.

We both knew that that would be the last time we'd see each other, but it made no difference. The night was perfect, and that was all either one of us needed.

Chapter 31
Raven's Call

I walked up and purchased the first bus going to Moab. Fifty three dollars later I was laying down on the bench to wait for four hours before it left. I wrapped the straps of my bag around my leg and stuffed my wallet down the front of my pants. A thief would surely wake me if they tried to take off with either item.

The station was for the most part empty except for a couple of older Hispanic men sitting a few benches away and a janitor mopping the floors. The buzz of the fluorescent lights hummed above shining down a greenish light on the stale tiles that covered the walls and floors. I pulled my hat over my face and no doubt appeared to fit in quite perfectly at the station.

I awoke several hours later to an old woman's flatulence at the other end of the bench I slept on. She sat there with her hand firmly grasping the handles of her purse resting in her lap. She made no attempt to excuse herself as she let out another long one that reverberated loudly through the wooden bench. I got up slowly, ready to move at the first whiff of stench. But I either was up wind of her or was at a safe enough distance. Her eyes stared straight forward unflinching like a stone statue.

The clock showed I had twenty minutes before my bus left. I asked the attendant if my bus was loading yet and she pointed at it without a word. The bus's front door was open and a few passengers had already loaded and were seated inside. I went to the bathroom before loading and did a quick wash of my face and hands. I sat down on the nice soft seats and fell back asleep almost instantly. Anything felt better than the hard reverberating wooden bench of the bus station.

I awoke to the air brakes squelching. The bus driver came through and collected our tickets. It wasn't long before the bus pulled out of the garage and into the brilliant blue skies that peaked around the buildings. The bus was nearly empty and I had two seats to myself. I spaced out watching the scenery as the bus worked its way out of Salt Lake and climbed its way into the mountains. The landscape was arid and full of colors of mid-summer. Golden grasses carpeted the rolling topography speckled with brown and green ponderosa pines. The clear blue skies seemed to come down and hug the land.

After a couple of bathroom stops we were getting close to Moab. The sign said nineteen more miles. The land was rocky and barren like what I'd imagine the moon might be like. It wasn't long before I started to see massive canyon like rock formations in the distance. My eyes glued to the brilliant red rocks that seemed to defy gravity by reaching up and scratching the sky. The bus rolled into the small town of Moab. It was a trendy adrenaline junky town geared for the college kid. Mountain biking, rock climbing, river rafting, jeep tours, hiking tours, and four wheel drive rock climbing machines loudly clambered down the streets. This was quite the difference from the wet topography of the north western state of Washington.

The heat was hot and hit me like a wall after stepping off the air-conditioned bus. I stretched my bones before walking over to the information center in the middle of town. I asked the guy where Mesa Arch was and how I would get there. He said it would be a long walk to the park and it would be night by the time I got there. If I planned on staying the night I would need a backcountry pass because the park closes and I could only camp in the lower half below the rim. He recommended a company a few blocks down that did tours of the park. I wasn't looking for a tour but I wanted to get up there quickly. I didn't know how long it would take me to find Tilauth but I didn't want to waste any time just in case this whole ordeal takes along time.

I paid twenty three dollars for the tour plus a ten dollar park pass. I planned on ditching the tour once I found Mesa Arch. Hopefully they don't end up sending out a search party for me because I disappeared.

The tour consisted of a small bus filled with the elderly touring the states fresh into retirement. A college student guided us over an intercom system as he drove the bus through the winding canyons. I was the youngest on the bus except for a couple of grandkids. With the sun directly overhead, giant canyons began to emerge from the depths of the earth. I had never seen anything so breathtaking. The canyons stood like giant monuments of the earth's past. We got out a couple of times to photograph the sites and walk out onto ledges that somehow manage to not fall into the valley below.

To my relief, Mesa Arch was one of the first places we stopped. I got out, seeing two ravens cawing overhead. We meandered down the trail and came down to a massive arch of rock that hung over nothing.

I looked around to see if I could find Tilauth anywhere but all I saw was tourists. They wandered all over the place photographing the rocks, themselves in front of the rocks, their grandkids in front of the rocks, and themselves with their grandkids in front of the rocks.

The place felt strangely familiar to me but I knew that I had never been there before. In fact I'd never even been to Utah before. I walked over to a ledge away from the crowds and sat down. The moment I sat down two ravens flew in and landed no more than two feet away from me. I was startled at first. The birds seemed much larger up close. Their jet black feather framed their black eyes. They let out some deep guttural clucks as they hopped around eyeballing me. I hadn't any food for them but something told me they weren't interested in food. I took a deep breath and began to quiet my mind. I decided that I was going to try and talk to these birds. Perhaps they know where I can find Tilauth.

In my mind I said, "Hi guys." At first I heard nothing except for the wind whispering up the canyon.

"Hi back," the raven said. Its voice sounded a little like a raven yet with an accent that reminded me of Tilauth's subtle accent.

"So what brings you two here?" I asked making small talk.

"We once went on a vision quest here just like you," they both said in unison.

"What do you mean just like me?" I asked.

"You don't remember us?" one asked. They seemed familiar to me like the place seemed familiar. "You seem familiar to me but I've never known any ravens until today," I said feeling a little strange talking to birds.

"Well, we weren't ravens when we knew each other," one said.

"If we weren't ravens that what were we?" I asked.

"Why we were friends," they said in unison.

"Friends?"

"Yes, friends. We were young boys when we each quested up here in different places."

"So we were humans."

"No we weren't humans we were more than humans, we were Tabequache of the Ute nation," one raven cried out hoping around excitedly.

"So now you're both ravens?" I asked.

"No were not ravens. We have just come to visit you and decided to show ourselves to you as a raven. Do you like the way I look?" one raven asked.

"You look pretty good," I said. I could feel that our friendship had a history of playing tricks on each other. We were best of friends.

"We thought this would be a good place for us to reunite since this place meant so much to all of us," the raven said.

"It's a beautiful place," I said, looking out across the view. I noticed that all the old folks from my tour were already heading back to the bus. "So, we were friends in a past life?" I asked to get clarification.

"Yes," they both said.

"Well I was sent here in search of my mentor, Tilauth."

"Tilauth is your mentor?" one of the ravens asked.

"You know him?" I asked.

"Yeah we know him. The Osage holy man stopped by here a couple of days ago."

"He stopped? Well did he say where he was going?" I asked.

"He said something about going back to his people."

"His people...you mean the Osage peoples?"

"Yeah...the Osage peoples."

"Where do the Osage live today?"

"They used to live in the Missouri area but the

reservation is in Oklahoma now."

"Oklahoma?" I asked.

"Yeah, Oklahoma. Hey you know our people the Ute were once jammed onto a reservation in Oklahoma," one of the ravens said hoping from rock to rock.

"Yeah?"

"Yeah. Now our peoples reservation is what they now call south western Colorado or some such."

"Well it looks like I'm going to Oklahoma guys," I said.

"Oklahoma, eh?"

"Yep Oklahoma."

"Well I hope you find your mentor there my brother," a raven said.

"Me, too."

"Don't you forget about your Ute brothers, alright?" the ravens said as they began to fly away.

"Don't worry; I don't think I can forget. You two were the first couple of ravens that I've ever talked to."

I looked out to see that all the tour folks had left. I hurried down the trail wondering if they left without me. I ran into the tour guide half way down the trail.

"Hey, I was just coming to look for you. My head count was one short," the guide said as he turned back towards the bus.

"Sorry about that, I got a little distracted."

"Yeah well, I know these views are pretty magnificent, but we've got a schedule to keep."

"Sorry, it won't happen again."

I got back to the bus to see a bunch of scowls as I passed by to my seat. "My life has already changed drastically. I'm talking to ravens and to God none the less. Is this what it means to be insane?" I thought. I knew that I wasn't insane, but I'd probably appear to be an average person but a little eccentric.

I impatiently finished the tour all though I did enjoy

the park. The earth is truly an aw-inspiring place. On my ride back down to Moab I couldn't help but wonder how Tilauth got here so quick and managed leave already. I was at the tail end of two days into my search and the ravens said Tilauth was at Mesa Arch two days ago. That means Tilauth was at Mesa Arch the same day he left me in the San Juan Islands of Washington state. It was an impossible feat but anything I've learned is possible with Tilauth. 'In the spirit world there is no time and space,' I remembered Tilauth telling me. He must've figured out a way to meld the physical world with the spiritual world and travel to far off places without actually traversing the land. He could be sitting in a bar in China drinking beers for all I know.

Chapter 32
Texas

After I got back to Moab, I quickly purchased a bus ticket to Albuquerque, New Mexico, where I would then board a train to Oklahoma City. From Oklahoma City, I would then get back on a bus to Ponca City, Oklahoma, where I would switch buses to Pawhuska, Oklahoma. Pawhuska was the heart of the Osage Indian Reservation. From there, I was hoping to find some more guidance.

I caught the bus early the next morning to Albuquerque. A hot meal the night before, a shower, and a solid night sleep at one of the lodges left me fresh and ready in the morning. The drive across New Mexico's high elevation desert scattered with prickly pear cacti, sage, and antelope was long, yet beautiful. The sky always shone a brilliant blue with the occasional lonely high cloud. Adobe-styled houses with sun-bleached branches tied together to form a fence were built around the houses that were often overlooking valleys from the canyon ridges. The small towns were filled with dusty individuals wearing dirty cowboy hats with tanned, dried-out faces that peeked out from under the brims of their hats. Time slipped by here, unnoticed. New Mexico was like its own country, completely separate from the United States. It seemed that if I listened close enough I could hear the distant cry of an eagle bone whistle.

Albuquerque was a big, dirty city that didn't seem like it belonged. It was only there out of the necessity of having a pit stop between the east coast and the west coast. I boarded the train in Albuquerque. I have never ridden a train before, but the seating was a bit more spacious than the bus. The trained chugged along the country side, pushing its way through a much more barren flat part of the state.

I went through the flat, windy, beef hungry, part of the states known as Texas. The buckle of the bible-belt was what the locals called it.

"Beer, sweat, violence, cattle punchin', suede, dusty, flat, gun racks, boots, ropes, racist, blonde bimbos, pickup trucks, women raping, small minded, bible thumping, fire and brimstone, rednecks should sum up Texas for ya.'" a slightly annoyed passenger told me as I glanced out the window. "I fuckin' hate Texas. I think when God made the earth he ran out of ideas when he came to Texas, so he just squatted down and dropped a big turd here," the young girl said with a southern accent. I turned to see her nodding her head and pointing out the window.

"I lived in Texas for eighteen years of my twenty-two years of being alive and those were the worst eighteen years of my life. I hear Texans want to be a country apart from the United States. I say let them. The U.S. would be better off without them. Texans screw up the national IQ average and give Americans a bad name with their conservative, right-wing, bible preaching politics," she ranted on. I let her babble away, finding it all entertaining and amusing. Anything to kill the time as we passed through some of the most un-scenic country I'd ever been in. "Don't get me wrong, Texas has some beautiful parts," she continued on. "They're just few and far between. The Rio Grande is a beautiful place. And the Mexicans...they're some of the hardest working people on the planet. If people were paid by how hard they worked, the Mexicans would be some of the richest people on the planet. And the bigot, rich, white, racist, Texan slanders them every chance they get. That's fuckin' Texas for ya." I listened to her go on and on, smiling at her lack of concern for who might hear and be offended.

"Where are you from?" she asked.

"I'm from Washington," I answered, feeling a little reluctant to get into a conversation with her.

"The capital, uh."

"No, I'm from Washington State, just north of Seattle."

"Ohhhh, where it rains all the time," she said, smirking at me.

"It doesn't necessarily rain there a lot, but the skies are overcast most of fall, winter, and spring."

"So summer is when you get to see the blue skies."

"Pretty much."

"I don't know if I could handle all that grey. Sounds depressing."

"Yeah, but everything is lush and green...big trees, big mountains, the Pacific Ocean, the islands. Eastern Washington is much drier with lots of sunshine... cold winters and hot summers. There's four distinct seasons where in western Washington there is only two; grey skies and cold, and blue skies and warm. I grew up in western Washington, and the grey skies tend to get to you by spring. By June we're begging for a sunny day," I said trying to give a true feeling for the area.

"Microsoft, Starbucks, Pearl Jam, Nirvana, Jimi

Hendrix, the Seahawks, and rain; that's all I know about Seattle." she said twisting the corner of her lip.

"Well there're a few other famous things that Seattle is known for, but you named some of the bigger ones."

"You have a lot of bigot racists up there, like there are in Texas?" she asked.

"Well...every place has its share but probably not like the way you described Texas," I said, feeling awkward.

"Never been to Washington State. Been to D.C. though...once on a high school field trip," she smiled. "Sorry for goin' on earlier like I was. I guess I just needed to vent a little."

Her hair was a straight sandy blond color. She sat across from me, slender, and obviously fearless. An elderly gentleman across the aisle appeared to be a little annoyed with her, but he tried to ignore her by flipping his newspaper up between him and her. She wore sneakers, tight jeans, and a cotton hoody.

"So, where you headed?" she asked.

"I'm headed to the Osage Reservation to meet a friend."

"Osage Reservation uh, ain't much up there," she stated.

"No?"

"Nope. Did you know they are the richest tribe in the states?"

"No, I didn't know that."

"Yep, U.S. government shoved them on a reservation way back when and then later discovered oil on the reservation. The natives own the rights to the oil, so they got kick-backs. Isn't that somethin'?"

"I never heard that." I said, finding myself more amused by her personality than interested in the conversation.

"I'm headed back home to see a friend too, only he's in a coma now. Got a wife and kid. Everyone's a little worried about him."

"That's too bad."

"Don't know if he'll come out or not. It's funny. Being in a coma is like being dead when you're alive," she said shaking her head.

Just as she began to talk about her friend I noticed that his spirit was listening to her. He hovered around her listening to what she had to say. The spirit's eyes turned to me and he noticed me noticing him. His head cocked like the way a dog's does when it hears something and it doesn't understand what it is. He began to talk to me as she continued to talk about different things. I lost track of what she was saying.

He came up near me and said, "She won't listen to me."

In my heart I replied back to him, "She won't listen to you because she isn't aware of you."

"Why is that?" he asked.

"Well...because you're here in spirit and your body is elsewhere. Many people are not aware of the spirits around them."

"But you can hear me."

"Yes, I can."

"So you are aware of me, then."

"Yes," I replied simply, acting like the way Tilauth would treat me.

"Well, could you tell her something for me?" he asked.

"I can try, but...well...it's a little bit different for me. She's going to wonder why I know certain things or why I'm saying them. To be honest with you I've never done anything quite like this."

"Will you at least try?"

"Why don't you tell me what it is you want me to say and we'll go from there," I said, still giving myself an out.

"Well, we've been good friends for a long time. So, she knows me. But what I want you to tell her is; to not worry about me. Tell her I'm fine and that I just need to take a break from things."

"You need to take a break from things?" I asked to make sure I understood him.

"Yeah, well, I've been thinking lately before I slipped into a coma that I wouldn't mind dying. You see, I've got a child and a wife that need me, but I feel caught in a tight spot. I know that I'm not supposed to be living this life anymore, but I'm having difficulty leaving my family when they need me so much. I love them dearly, but I'm not sure if the responsibility is something I can handle right now, either. But I don't want anyone to worry about me though. I'm fine. You can see that. I just need some time to think this all through."

"You know if I tell her all that she's going to want to know how I know all this. She might think I've got a screw loose or something and ignore what you want me to say." I said to him, feeling uncomfortable about the whole idea.

"It's worth it. This would mean a lot to me and who knows, she may believe you," he said.

I looked at her, talking away about her home in Texas and how horrible it was. The whole thing made me shiver involuntarily with nervousness. I finally worked up the nerve and leaned forward in my chair.

"Excuse me for a second," I said, interrupting her. "My name's Neal," I said, biding my time.

"Oh...oops I forgot to introduce myself. My name's Mary. My mom calls me Mary Lou, which I can't stand. Everyone down south has to be called by there first and middle name. It's gotten so bad that people can have two first names and two middle names. It's absolutely..."

"Mary," I said cutting her short.

"Yes."

"Your friend that you're going to visit?" I said noticing that my voice was a little shaky.

"Yeah."

"Well…" I struggled to find my breath, but it wasn't there. I felt like I was going to hyperventilate.

"Are you alright?" she asked.

"I'm fine. I just…well…I've never done this before, so please bear with me."

"Done what?" I decided to ignore her question and move forward. "There is no backing out now," I thought. "Well…you know how some people can see spirits?"

"Yeah?" she said shifting in her seat uncomfortably.

"Well…"

"Don't tell me that you can see his spirit and that he's dead," she said holding her hand up to the tip of her nose getting ready to fend off the tears.

"No, no, no, no…he's not dead," I said not realizing where she was going with my words.

"Oh, thank God," she said taking a deep breath. "I thought that you were one of those gifted types and you were going to tell me that he had already passed away."

"Well, I guess you could say I'm like one of those gifted types, but I wouldn't call it necessarily a gift. Well it is, but everyone can see they just haven't learned where to look is all," I said. She looked at me without saying a word of any kind and nodded slightly.

I told her what her friend was going through, and she listened carefully. As I talked, I saw a tear streamed down her face when I told her that he was feeling a lot of pressure lately. When I finished, she wiped away her tears and was quiet for a moment.

"You know…the last time I talked to him on the phone he said he was feeling very stressed out. He said that he loved his wife and son a lot but…well, he was having a hard time is all."

"Well, he just wanted me to tell you that."

"I'm glad you did. Really I am. I already knew for

the most part, but this gives me more...clarity."

"Good...I'm glad I was able to help," I said feeling relieved.

"Thank you," she said still obviously thinking about him and their past conversations.

We talked all the way into Oklahoma City. She asked how I learned my skills and I told her a little about what I'd been learning lately. She seemed fascinated but still distracted by her friend. Her friend whispered a word of thanks into my ear, which I responded with a 'No, thank you.' This was a good learning experience for me and seemed to be helpful for Mary and her friend. Mary and I parted ways and I caught a bus going north, and she headed south.

Chapter 33
Pawhuska

I could feel a deep pulling or a longing that seemed to suck me to the reservation like a vacuum machine. The closer I got, the more I was certain that I would find Tilauth there. I scanned the entire globe trying to feel where I might feel a pull or a longing to go but I felt little to nothing like the way I was being pulled to the reservation.

Why Tilauth chose the reservation as his destination seemed too obvious. This was where his family or ancestors were supposed to be living. The place seemed too logical and I began to wonder if my intuition was clear. Perhaps the logic of the place seemed appropriate and this was why my intuition seemed to direct me there. The last thing intuition needs is doubt. 'Logic and intuition mix like fire and water' is what Tilauth used to always say. I decided to go there anyway and learn perhaps the reasons as to why my intuition would be wrong or not. Obviously the ravens told me that Tilauth was going to the Osage

Reservation, but what if I misunderstood them? What if I didn't hear the ravens properly? Tilauth did teach me that the ravens did symbolize some of the trickster spirit, and I did remember that these old friends were practical jokers. Perhaps my friends were playing another practical joke on me for old time's sake.

The bus stopped at a rest stop for a bathroom break. The evening wind was warm and dry as it whipped around my face. The picnic tables scattered around the rest stop where covered by metal tepee frames; a decorative effect that seemed to pour salt on the wound for many Native Americans I imagined.

Here are a people that were robbed of their way of life from the way they hunt to their religious beliefs. Their land was taken from them with war. Using war to own the land, control the people, and take away everything from a people was a complete foreign concept to the Natives. Now most of them have been absorbed into our modern society and have forgotten their ancestral ways of life. Today the American Native struggles to keep their customs and religion alive in a modern society that sees their old ways of life as a novelty from a long ago forgotten past.

Seeing these purposeless metal tepees that provide nothing more than a decorative effect reminds me that non-natives see the American Indian's culture as dead and lacks any significance in the modern world today. I envisioned the typical grandma and grandpa touring the United States in their RV stopping here and saying, 'Oh isn't that nice, we're in Indian Country dear. Let's eat our bologna sandwiches under one of those tepees.'

I suddenly felt a surge of gratefulness for what Tilauth has taught me. The awareness and skills that I've learned from Tilauth bore great responsibility. I knew deep inside me that these skills were not my own. "These old ways managed to be persevered all the way to me," I thought. "It was not only my responsibility to practice these old ways with the utmost respect, but to pass them on so they would continue to be preserved.

We now live in a society that has lost itself in the disharmony that has been ingrained in nearly every individual for the past ten thousand years. The old ways that existed before humans started to mass produce the foods they liked to eat is currently hanging by a thread. This thread is the thing that can help heal our society of its disharmony. It is now my responsibility along with any other people that know these old ways to help strengthen this thread so that tomorrow's people might find their way back to the harmony that existed ten thousand years ago," I thought to myself. I got back on the bus and I left the metal tepees behind.

I spent the night in Ponca City, where I would catch another bus to Pawhuska in the morning. There was nothing special about Ponca City, it was just another highway town. Oil was the primary industry for the small town. It sat on the border of the Osage Reservation just outside the wealth of dinosaur fuel that lay resting below.

The bus to Pawhuska was small and didn't have too many passengers. Three other natives were on the bus that rode along the rolling highway with me. We all kept to ourselves, watching vast rolling hills pass by out our windows as we bobbed up and down on the earth.

It didn't take long before I was dropped off in Pawhuska. Like most reservation towns, it didn't have much commerce. The town had the basics; post office, small restaurant, and a general store. The rest of the town consisted of homes scattered about the area. Small towns on the reservations seemed to struggle for economic riches. Pawhuska lacked the need or the desire to economically thrive. It just seemed to exist because it simply was what it was. It didn't want to be something else that it wasn't. This reservation town existed as a place where people with a common bond lived together and nothing more.

I glanced down the virtually empty street to see a sign that said 'museum' and it bore an arrow pointing to the left. I decided that that was as good as a place as any to start asking around for Tilauth. The occasional face I saw glanced at me, knowing that I was not from there. Everyone knew who everyone was in Pawhuska, no doubt, and I was the fresh face.

I opened the museum door with the clank of a bell that hung over it. The building was chock full of old artifacts and black and white faded photos. An elderly woman who bore a striking resemblance to my grandmother only with darker skin called out, "welcome." She was busy talking to the repair guy who was wrestling with the copy machine. I looked around the museum for awhile hoping she would finish with him soon. The shelves were covered with ancient tools used by the natives, many of which I recognized from the tools Tilauth had taught me to make and use. There were also tools used by the first white settlers. Old clothes that were worn by female mannequins from the sixties bared breasts that curiously reminded me of pointed torpedoes.

The repair guy soon left and I made my way to the front counter. "Are you enjoying your visit?" the old woman said.

"I am thank you. I was wondering if you might be able to help me."

"What is it and I'll do my best," she replied graciously.

"I'm looking for an older man that lives on the reservation. He lives here but spends a lot of his time away, however."

"Well you've come to the right place. I know everyone that lives on the rez," she said smiling.

"His name is Tilauth."

"Tilauth uh?" she said as her face squashed into

a scowl. "Tilauth," she said again as she seemed to be searching her mind. "Can't say I've ever heard of a Tilauth living on the reservation. In fact I can't say I've ever heard the name period. Does he have a Christian name that he was given or was that his name?"

"It's the only name I know. He's a very traditional man. He lives off the land a lot like the way the old ones used to," I said, hoping that that might help trigger her memory.

"So you say he's a bit of a traditional, eh. Well I'd remember someone like that. But I don't recall a Tilauth ever living on the rez. You know what? Wait a minute; let me give a call to Margie out in Barnsdall. She is like the queen of rez gossip. There isn't anything or anybody she doesn't know." She reached over to grab the phone and quickly punched in the number she had memorized. She no doubt spent a lot of her time on the phone. I don't imagine this place gets all that many visitors way out here.

"Hey Margie! - How ya doin'?" she said with a similar accent that Tilauth spoke with. "Yeah - Say how's Walt doin' with his heartburn? - No kiddin' - That's great, fixed him right up then. - Oh say, you ever heard the name Tilauth before? – Yeah. – Oh a young fella's come in askin' if I know where he might find this Tilauth. – He says he's pretty traditional. – Yeah. – Oh, yeah? – Well, that's pretty strange, eh? – Well I'll have to call ya later. Oh hey, tell Lucy that Jerry gave me her sewing machine. I'll drop it off for her this weekend. – Good talkin' to ya. – Okay." she hung up the phone. She turned to look at me, "Margie doesn't no any Tilauth, sorry." My heart sunk.

"But when you asked her, you said something about that's strange. What did Margie say?" I asked feeling a little helpless.

"I said something about something being strange?" she asked looking perplexed.

"Yeah, you told her Tilauth was pretty traditional than Margie said some things and you said, 'Well, that's pretty strange'."

"Oh yeah, that's right I did," she said remembering. "Margie said she's heard the name being brought up once or twice by the elders. She said that Tilauth was an old holy man that lived a long time ago. Long before white settlers came to the states. But he obviously died a long time ago. He couldn't possibly be the man you're looking for."

"That is strange," I said thinking aloud. "Tilauth is a holy man, but he is alive and well today. Well... thank you for your help," I said as I walked out of the museum and into the dusty heat of Oklahoma.

I headed over to the small restaurant to grab a bite to eat. I sat there eating my food wondering what I was going to do now. I couldn't just start wandering the reservation without some sort of intuitive guidance. It is strange that Tilauth did come from this reservation but the two people that knew everyone had never heard of him. The reservation was huge, not exactly something you could walk around in a day or two.

I needed some intuitive guidance, but felt no pull anywhere. All I could feel was to stay on the reservation. The greasy french-fries slid down my throat as I pondered my predicament. The locals would glance at me once realizing I wasn't from around there and then go about their business. I was so busy trying to figure things out that I didn't notice much of anything going on around me.

That night I caught a bus to the near by town of Bartlesville where I could sleep and shower at a hotel. Pawhuska was where my intuition guided me to be, but there were no hotels there and a shower was becoming very necessary.

Bartlesville was a highway town that lacked any appeal other than a pit stop between places. Early the next morning I had breakfast at a greasy spoon diner. After breakfast my belly felt like I was carrying a bowling ball around. Lugging my belly to the bus stop, I caught the bus back to Pawhuska.

The bus stopped with a squelch as the air brakes released the excess pressure. I stepped out onto the dusty sidewalk. A few parked cars, but nobody was walking around. The town grocery mart was open as I squinted under the bright rays of the sun. The bus pulled away with a loud roar and I took a seat on a sidewalk bench to listen to my gut.

'Nothing, I'm getting nothing,' I said to myself. So I just sat there under the heat of the sun. "Day five," I whispered out loud. Sweating in the heat and I'm sitting on a bench in a nowhere town in Oklahoma. I shook my head frustrated. Tilauth was no doubt having a good laugh at my expense. I tossed small pebbles out into the road watching them bounce off the pavement. "Day five," I whispered out loud again.

Before I knew it, it was one thirty in the afternoon and I was getting mildly hungry. With nothing else to do I walked over to the diner and got something to eat. As the waitress brought my food I nonchalantly asked, "You ever heard of an old man that goes by the name Tilauth?"

She put her hand on her hips and said the name aloud, "Tilauth? No can't ever say I've heard that name before. You supposed to meet him around here?" she asked.

"Umm…sort of," I said, giving her a look that said how'd you know?

"I saw you this morning waiting on the bench, figured you must be waiting for someone. Tell you what, if I see a Tilauth I'll be sure to let him know you're looking for him."

"Thanks." I said, knowing that she was just trying to be helpful.

I was in a grumpy mood and easily agitated. I was truly frustrated down to the marrow of my bones. I spent the next four days easily agitated and short–tempered, and by the evening of the fourth day of my quest for Tilauth, I was flat out angry. Every night I was catching a bus into Bartlesville to sleep and shower then catching the bus back to Pawhuska in the morning to sit and wait around for a sign. The locals got used to seeing me around hanging out in the town. Nobody really talked to me, but they all knew I was waiting for someone named Tilauth as gossip got around. Folks would just give me a simple nod as they passed me by and I returned their nods with another nod and that was that. I ate at the same diner for lunch everyday patiently waiting for some sort of direction.

Now it was the end of the ninth day and I sat waiting for the bus to catch back to Bartlesville. With the hiss of the air brakes the bus came to a stop and I boarded the bus. I dug in my pocket and pulled out some change. I counted it…a dime…two nickels…and a penny; a far cry from the $4.50 I owed for the fare. I looked up at the driver with a blank look, feeling embarrassed for boarding without enough money for the fare. The bus driver opened the door behind me again without uttering a word. I stepped off the bus, realizing that I had only twenty one cents left. I spent all my money on food, buses, and hotels.

I walked up to the brick wall of a building and stopped just short of punching it with all my anger. I would have surely shattered the bones in my hand and been in a much worse predicament. I spun around in a fit of rage I was carefully containing to avoid observing locals coming to the conclusion that I was truly crazy.

Sitting back on the bench I gripped one hand around the other in a fist slowing my breath to calm myself.

The sky had already turned a heavy blue as the sun sank behind the earth. An old dodge pickup rattled by and shined a light on a sign ten feet away from me that said, "Osage Hills State Park, 15 miles." I suddenly felt my gut unwind in relief. Here I'd been waiting for days for some sort of sign when the damn sign was right next to me the whole time. I felt like an idiot for not noticing it sooner. I'd been so caught up in my agitation that I'd lost focus of my clear intuition. My intuition guided me to the next sign every day, again and again and I had the clouded awareness of an addicted, video-game-playing teenager. Now I knew if Tilauth had seen me he would be surely laughing one of his full body laughs.

I quickly got up and began walking down the road, setting in for the fifteen mile walk. The crickets came out in full force, singing in one of the largest choruses on earth. I listened to the cricket songs and the crunch of my shoes as I walked along the side of the road. I must've walked seven miles when I realized that I could use a little water right now.

A car came down the road behind me casting rays of light and shadow that danced mysteriously around me like spirits crawling through the bushes. The car slowed, and I saw the flash of red and blue lights blink behind me. It was a tribal police car that pulled up alongside of me. The officer rolled down his passenger window and he said something in his native tongue that I couldn't understand. I peered down into the patrol car to see a kind-faced officer who nodded at me.

Without hesitation, he said whatever he said before in English, "You need a ride, friend?" I looked down the road again to guesstimate how much further I needed to go. "You know, you don't want to walk too far on these roads at night...rattlesnakes come up on the road at dusk to warm themselves and it would be a long walk to find a pay phone for help if you get bitten." I glanced back at him to see him nodding at me and lifting his brows, knowing that I hadn't thought about rattlesnakes.

I got in the front seat and he turned off his emergency lights and we pulled away.

"I'm headed to the State Park," I told him.

"Yeah...goin' to do some fishin'?" he asked.

"Uh...no...I missed my bus back to Bartlesville, so I thought I'd camp in the park tonight instead of staying at a hotel." The officer said nothing to this for awhile, then said, "You know, if you want, I could give you a ride out to Bartlesville if you'd like?"

"Thanks, but I think I'd actually rather camp in the park," I said not wanting to tell him that I had no money to even pay for a hotel. He looked down at my small pack.

"You don't have much gear for camping, you sure you wouldn't rather stay at a hotel?"

"Naw...I'm good...I like to camp simply anyways," I said.

"Sounds like my kind of camping," he said smiling. "Say you're that kid I heard about, aren't you. You waiting for some guy named Tilauth?" he asked.

"Yeah...I guess news travels in Pawhuska."

"Yep...small town gossip...news travels faster than words on the internet," he said with a grin. "Can't say I've ever heard of a Tilauth," he said pulling his mouth to the side with a click of his tongue. "Nobody out here has ever heard of a Tilauth ...You say he's supposed to meet you in Pawhuska?"

"Well not exactly...I'm supposed to find him...You see...well it's a long story but to make a long story short, he's a medicine man or a shaman. Well...he's been teaching me for some time now and this is one of his... well, I guess you could call it a test of determination and ability. I've got to find him in ten days using only my intuition, and there are no boundaries as to where he might be."

The officer took his eyes off the road and looked at me several times before pulling to the side of the road.

He stopped the car and turned to focus his attention on me, "You mean to tell me that a holy man is teaching you." His eyes squinted, "and one of his lessons is playing hide n' seek and the boundaries are limitless?" I nodded at him without a word. He sat back into his seat with a squeak of vinyl. His eyes peered out over the hood into the beams of the head lights. "Well he could be anywhere," he said throwing up a hand. "What day are you on?" He quickly asked turning to me.

"I'm on day nine."

"So you have only one more day?"

"Yup."

"And so far your search has brought you to Pawhuska?"

"Yup."

"Where did you start?"

"I was up in the San Juan Islands of Washington State. That was the last time I saw Tilauth. At first the journey seemed simple. I just started going and I seemed to be right on his tracks. But when I got to Pawhuska it just stopped. It wasn't until a couple of hours ago that I figured out that I'm supposed to go to the Osage Hills State Park."

"No, shit," the officer said, shaking his head back in forth. "I'm sorry, but that just amazes me. So you're actually going somewhere based fully on your intuition?"

"Yup."

"That's...that's crazy. I've met some holy men, and women, for that matter, who have done some pretty wild stuff but this..." he lifts his brows, shakes his head back in forth, and turns his hands up off the steering wheel, "this guy takes the cake." He put the car in drive and the far wheel spits gravel as we get back on to the road. "I'm dying to know if he's there at the park," he said looking back at me.

I shrugged my shoulders, "I don't know if he's there

or not...I just know that I need to go to the park."

"Well it's your journey...so I'll drop you off and get out of your way. If you're still around when you find him...stop by at the office and let me know. It sounds like you're on a true adventure that belongs in a book or something." I just grinned at this. I'm glad he was excited about this whole thing because I on the other hand was little stressed out.

"So what do you do if you can't find him?" he asked.

"Well...he stops teaching me and I never see him again."

"That is some crazy...so you got one more day to find him or that's it?"

"That's it," I stated.

"Well...if there is something that I can do...call me." He hands me his card. I slipped the card in my pocket with a nod, "Thank you."

"Forget that...you call me and let me know how it turns out."

We pull into the park and he drives me in to the park office.

"I think you fill out the envelope and put your money in it. There's a metal lock box next to the door where you put the envelope in," the officer said.

"Thanks for the ride, sir," I said as I got out of the patrol car. "I'll give you a call one way or the other."

"You better," he said pointing at me with a smile. "All right, you have a good night and good luck to you." And he pulled away.

I watched him pull away until he was out of sight. I didn't want him to know that I couldn't even pay for the camping. But since I wasn't going to be using a traditional campsite or any of their facilities, I didn't feel guilty about it.

I turned around and walked directly into the woods, leaving the dim amber glow of the parking lot lamp behind me. Dried leaves from last year's fall lay scattered across the ground. It was difficult to walk quietly with the constant crunch, crunch with every step. I walked deep into the woods, up hills, around small rocky ledges, and down hills until I felt I was far enough away from people. My intuition felt like I was going the right way. The night air was growing colder by the minute and I decided to stuff my clothes with the dried leaf litter from the ground to add insulation to my clothes. I found a nice rocky overhang to shelter me from any winds or possible rains through out the night. I built a small fire between me and the open air and leaned up against the rock at my back. There was a small boulder on the other side of the fire to deflect the heat towards me. I placed some rocks around the fire to heat them up. Once I got them good and hot, I buried them a few inches under ground in a line where I was going to sleep. This was going to be a luxurious heated bed as I slept through the cold night.

I could feel my gut still pulling me deeper through the woods, but knew that walking at night without any moonlight was dangerous. The night was pitch-black and I could hardly make out my hand in front of my face. I could hear the occasional mouse scampering through the leaves on their nightly runs.

It felt good to be back in the woods and out of the prison like cell of a dingy hotel room. Before sunrise I decided, I would set out to wherever my intuition guided me.

Chapter 34
The Ends of the Earth

I awoke to a chorus of birds singing. I spun around abruptly looking at the sky, hoping that I hadn't wasted too much time sleeping. It was still dark with a faint glow rising in the east. I got up quickly and stood up, waiting for a pull. The pull was still the same as just before I fell asleep and I began walking. The hint of light made the going much easier. Instead of doing the blind man toe tap in a semi circle every time I made a step, I was able to walk normally without fear of falling off a cliff.

The birds were singing like mad. Their songs were different songs from the birds in the Pacific Northwest. I enjoyed the different tunes and learning the different birds as I walked along. Lots of oak trees grew everywhere. The walk was easy with little underbrush but plenty of killer rocks that would have no doubt offered a challenge while wandering in the dark of the night. I stopped periodically to listen and check my gut, walking like a deer but I tried to keep a fast pace. Without even thinking about it my awareness was expanding across the woods listening to the nuances in nature and listening to my intuition. The only animals I saw were little chipmunks that chattered and scampered through the dried leaves as I passed by.

My intuition pulled me left then right and I just followed it wherever it led me. I passed the skeleton of an old pickup truck and wondered how it had gotten way out here.

It was noon and I must have walked ten maybe twelve miles in a half a dozen different directions. I was hungry, but I didn't care. I managed to gather some water from the morning dew that settled on rocks which appeased my thirst for the time being. I sat resting on a rock looking at my surroundings. I didn't rest long, as the pull inside me grew stronger and I kept pushing on.

I made my way along ravines and over ridges and winding through the trees. My feet were sore and my legs were fatigued. I saw an occasional deer, but kept pushing forward trying not to let myself get distracted.

Another twelve or thirteen miles had passed under my feet, and still no Tilauth. The sun was getting ready to set, and in a panic I began to run. Every joint in my body ached and my legs wobbled under me as they struggled to hold me up. I kept running, feeling the pull more than ever. It felt like a yearning that needed to be filled and I would die without filling the void. My chest heaved and my face dripped with sweat. I desperately needed water, and I had dribbled the last drop of water from my water container hours ago.

The sky was growing dark, and I had to stop and rest or I would collapse. Through my heavy breath I could hear way off in the distance a stream or river. With a new surge of energy, I pushed toward the sound, which was the same direction my intuition pulled me.

My feet scrambled as quickly as they could down a hill where a small river flowed. I hurriedly dunked my water bottle under the water and dribbled some drops of grapefruit seed extract in it to purify it. I shook the bottle vigorously and set it down to wait about ten or fifteen minutes. I looked around to see flat rocks that the water traveled over which created little waterfalls everywhere the rock abruptly sank. This place felt strange to me. This must have been the Sand Creek Waterfalls that I remembered seeing on one of the signs when I was dropped off by the officer. I also remembered that the falls were supposed to be only a short mile from the campground. I suddenly realized that I must have gone in a huge circle looping back to almost where I'd started from. I looked around and saw a few people down river hopping from rock to rock. There was no way that campers would be nonchalantly walking out into the woods twenty four plus miles to see some small water falls. I had to be near the campsites.

My shoulders sank and tears began to well up in my eyes. I'd gone nowhere fast. The sky was turning colors as the sun set further and further in the west. The tears began to flow uncontrollably and I felt the sting of defeat deep in my heart. My chest tightened and my knees began to buckle. I sat on a log along the river side to wallow in my loss. But when I sat the log felt exceptionally soft.

I heard a strange noise cry from inside the log. "Heeeeey!" I heard as the log began to collapse under me.

I jolted up again as fast as my legs would move me and spun around to see Tilauth appearing from the log. In fact the log was no log at all. It was Tilauth cleverly disguised as a log.

"Tilauth!" I squelched from my parched throat. "I

found you!" I grabbed him and hugged him tightly before he could get a word out.

He laughed whole-heartedly, "Take it easy...you're going to squeeze all the air out of me."

I felt like a kid on Christmas morning. I completely forgot all my aches, pains, and even my thirst. I tried to speak again but nothing came out. I drank some water to re-hydrate my throat, nearly choking on it. Tilauth brushed the dirt off himself and washed his face in the river. I was so ecstatic I could hardly sit still. This was hardly the way one carried themself around Tilauth, but I couldn't help it. I managed to calm my childlike behavior down to a smile, at which Tilauth responded with a smile.

"I'm happy to see you too, Grandson," he said. "Your search was a challenging one," he said nodding with grin.

"Not exactly easy."

"Good. You learned a lot about intuition and a lot about yourself then."

"To say the least."

"Good. We have a good place to move forward from, then," he said grinning.

Tilauth took me back to where he had set up camp in the park a good distance from exploring campers. Even if a camper came by his campsite, I don't think they'd even realize it, given how camouflaged it was. We sat back with a small fire and ate some dinner. I told him some of the highlights of my search and I relived the trials and tribulations with the only person who could truly understand them.

"So, how come nobody has ever heard of you on the reservation?" I asked the gnawing question. Tilauth glances at me briefly before tilting his head up to the canopy of the trees and let out a quiet chuckle.

"Let's just say that I'm not around much anymore so most folks have forgotten me."

"Well don't you have family here?" I asked.

"Yes, I have family here, but my family is mostly spread all over. I even have family in the Pacific Northwest. I visit family members here and there and I guess I haven't visited my family on the reservation in a long time. It's been so long I suppose they have forgotten about me. Maybe the ones that would remember me have passed away now, and all that is left is their children." Tilauth smiled at me, "I wasn't about to make it easy on you so you didn't have to rely on your intuition."

"Well, you sure didn't make it easy," I stated.

Tilauth let out a chuckle, "I went through the same thing you did. I struggled just as much as you when I was learning."

We reminisced and laughed through the night until I couldn't keep my eyes open any longer. I fell into a deep dreamless sleep. I didn't awake until Tilauth woke me. He had let me sleep in knowing that my search the day before had taken a lot out of me.

The next seven years I spent learning from Tilauth. We traveled all over while Tilauth introduced me into the infinite world of spirit. He taught the ancient ways of being a seer, healer, and a shaman. I learned the vast world of healing plants. I spent so much time in the other worlds that I was having difficulty distinguishing the world of spirit and the physical world. The dynamic of my life had changed so drastically from the ordinary nine to five, five days a week, relax on weekends, get married, have kids, retire and die lifestyle that it is difficult to put into words that the ordinary person could understand. Every event in my life was experienced with an awareness of both the physical and spiritual worlds. This awareness forced me to function on multiple levels unimaginable to myself before I met Tilauth. I discovered who I was and I healed myself. I took charge of my life and pursued it without the common worries, fears, and doubts I would normally have. I was free in my heart, spirit, head, soul, and body. I now know who I am and I am pieces of everything. I know this because I've brought my awareness to the world of spirit and this is the way things are. Our physical reality of being separate is an illusion we've pulled over ourselves. Knowing the reality and the illusion I'm able to heal, create, and experience life the way I desire because I am a piece of the great circle of life.

It is difficult for me to put into words the things that I learned from Tilauth in those later years. Most of what I learned can only be expressed through an emotion or an experience. Some of it I'm still coming to grips with myself. The depth of the spirit is infinite and sometimes the experiences of the spirit are difficult to remember like the way one tries to remember their dreams from the night before.

Tilauth and I still visit from time to time. I just have to think of him and call him through the world of spirit and we meet sooner or later. I don't question how, it just happens. I've learned the basics. In other words Tilauth has given me the foundation that all shamans would be given on this path. The learning never stops for there is always more to learn and more of life to experience. Once I've experienced all that I'm to experience, my life will come to an end. So I will continue to experience, learn, teach, and seek out the truth until I die. Then I will reunite with my full self in the world of spirit and all that there is and I will remember who I am completely. That is until I decide to return to the illusion and experience something new for the shear joy of the adventure.

Chapter 35
Relatives

It has now been about thirteen years since I first met Tilauth. It is January and I'm visiting my Grandmother on one of my sporadic visits. We talk of the usual things of what I've been up to and what she's been up to lately. We talk about the weather and the latest things on the news. The snow has been falling for the past couple of days but has been having difficulty sticking. By late afternoon the temperatures rise above freezing and everything turns to slush. After the sun sets the temperatures drop dramatically and everything turns to ice, making the driving conditions extremely dangerous. In the Pacific Northwest, driving in the snow is rare so there are a lot of amateurs on the street. Driving becomes more like a game of dodge ball.

Somewhere in my conversation with my grandma, I'm not sure how it came up, but I mentioned the name of Tilauth. My grandmother fell silent and her eyes pierced through me. It took me a moment to try and figure out what it was that she seemed so taken back from, but I suddenly realized my slip up. I have never mentioned the name Tilauth to my family or my friends for the most part. Everyone assumed that when I was gone with Tilauth, that I was just on another one of my adventures in the wilderness by myself. But now I slipped up and mentioned his name.

The strange thing was, my grandmother wasn't responding at all to his name. She fell silent and her mind appeared to be somewhere else. I sat there silently while she appeared to be in a daze.

Finally she seemed to come back to the present moment with look of confusion that spread across her face.

"Is Tilauth a friend of yours?" she asked. I suddenly felt like I was cornered. What do I say? If I say too much she will get curious and I will be forced to explain. Not only would I have to explain but I wouldn't even know where to begin. All set aside, it was Tilauth's wish that I didn't mention him to anybody. Now I'm being asked about him because I somehow slipped up and mentioned his name. My grandmother must have noticed that I was reluctant to say anything so she decided to say something.

Little did I know that what she was about to say was going to send shivers up and down my spine. Nothing in the world could have prepared me for what I was about to hear.

"Tilauth isn't a very common name. The reason why I'm asking is because Tilauth is your great, great, great, great, in fact I'm not sure how many great's, but a lot, grandfather. I remember my grandmother speaking of him on occasion. She said he was a very powerful holy man for our people long ago. I remember her telling me of great things he did. She always told me that it was Tilauth's blood that runs through our veins, and he put some energy in that blood so that his relatives would have the desire and talent to seek out the 'medicine,' as she put it." My grandmother continued to look at me as I no doubt had a look of shock on my face.

She kept talking, but her voice fell to the background, being secondstaged by my own thoughts. This would explain why Tilauth didn't want me to tell anyone about him. He knew that I would discover who he was and I probably would have thought that I was crazy. If I hadn't already been knowledgeable of the world of spirit, I would probably think I was crazy now.

No one else ever saw Tilauth but me. He said he had relatives everywhere and the Pacific Northwest was one of them. Most of his relatives had forgotten him. I had a desire or a strange pull for the knowledge Tilauth knew. Tilauth was my great, great, great, etc... grandfather and I his grandson.

I felt a strong urge to suddenly see Tilauth and tell him that I knew. But he no doubt, already knew. He was in the world of spirit and has been manifesting himself on Earth to teach me. I suddenly realized that Tilauth took on some of the same characteristics that a spirit would take on when they walked on the Earth. I hadn't realized it before because I just thought Tilauth was always a bit unusual.

"Are you alright, Neal?" My grandmother asked seeming very concerned.

"I'm fine... I think... I think I'd better get going. I just remembered that I have somewhere I need to be," I said as I stood up and began heading for the door.

"You forgot your jacket Neal," my grandmother called after me.

"Oh right, oops," I said grabbing the jacket from her. I hugged her goodbye and began heading for the door. "You sure you're all right," she asked appearing very concerned.

"I'm fine. I'm just a little confused right now."

"You know I used to have dreams about Tilauth

when I was a little girl. That's why when you said his name, it caught me off guard. I hadn't heard the name in so long," she said with a smile.

I paused for a moment, realizing that Tilauth has probably been visiting all my family in one way or another.

"I need to get going. It was nice to visit with you grams."

"You drive safely, that black ice out there is dangerous."

"I will," I said as I walked down the driveway to my car.

Chapter 36
Retracing

I drove straight to my home on Camano Island and packed a bag. Tilauth wasn't revealing himself to me no matter how I asked him. I went deep into the spirit world to call for him but he seemed to disappear the moment I got close. So I packed my bags and drove straight to the airport and caught the first flight to Oklahoma City. As soon as I got on my feet, I rented a car and drove all the way to Pawhuska.

It was noon when I arrived in Pawhuska and the area had a cold nip in the air. All the trees where bare and the sky was a brilliant blue. This was a sweeping change from when I first visited Pawhuska in late summer. I drove straight to the town museum where I had been so many years before. The town hadn't changed at all. Still the same businesses, houses, etc... No new developments. The only thing that has changed is the people have gotten older. As I opened the same door I did long ago with the same creek the same women stood behind the counter that I'd spoken to many years ago.

"Welcome to Pawhuska. Let me know if there is anything I can help you with," she said with a warm smile.

I walked straight up to the counter, "Yes, I was wondering if you could look up a name for me in your records of Tribal Members?"

"Sure, do you know when this person was alive or when they may have died?," she asked?

"I don't know, other than it was a long time ago."

"Well if it's too long ago we won't have the name. I'll pull out our oldest records and go from there."

"Sounds good."

"Do you know the name?"

"Tilauth," I answered.

She stopped everything and took a long look at me. "Wait a minute. You've been here before. You were that young guy here, years back looking for a man named Tilauth, weren't you?"

"Yeah, that was me."

"Now you're here again lookin' for that same name, only it's in our archives. You've been looking for that man ever since?"

"No." I said realizing I probably was appearing to be pretty crazy sounding. "I was looking for someone who was named after Tilauth back then," I said thinking quickly.

"I see. So this Tilauth...is he a relative of yours?" she asked setting the books on the counter.

"Uh...yeah I suppose he is," I said, feeling strange saying it for the first time.

"Well, I'll look in this book if you want to look in that one," she said as she scanned the pages.

"I appreciate your help."

"Oh, I don't mind. I've got nothing to do here all day so you're just keeping me busy."

We went through several books going through name

after name until it felt like our eyeballs were going to fall out. It's a little more difficult because some people have two names, their tribal name and their Christian name.

"Here he is," she said, pushing the book over to me. There it was, 'Tilauth.' Nothing more of his name was present, except for a squiggle mark to represent his signature. She told me of the clan he came from and a little about the clan. I thanked her for her help and headed out the door into the cold air. I got into my car and sat in utter astonishment. I couldn't believe that not only was Tilauth my grandfather, but he was a spirit that had been teaching me all these years.

I drove to the local café and got something to eat. After filling my belly I drove to the Osage Hills State Park. Like usual, I have a tendency to speed and not even realize it. I had way too many speeding tickets and my license was going to be suspended if I got another one.

Well needless to say, I saw the usual lights and heard the familiar blare of a siren behind me. I pulled over, cursing myself, knowing that I should've used the cruise control. This invention has saved me from getting tickets thousands of times. I set the speed for the legal limit and forget about it. It isn't until I see a trooper hiding around some bushes that I quickly check my speed and realize I've got it on cruise control. But this time I didn't have the pleasure of realizing I set it. My speed checked at about seventeen over the limit. I was screwed and I knew it. I never get a warning. The cop takes one look at me and for some reason thinks that I need a ticket, not a warning.

"Perhaps this time I should squeeze my pecks together to increase the cleavage," I thought. "Or maybe I should just cry." All these things seem to work well for women.

But to my surprise, when I glanced in the side mirror I saw that this cop had hips. I rolled down the window to see a very attractive woman looking back at me.

"I got you speeding back there," she said in a soft tone.

"I'm sorry; I have a really bad habit of not paying attention to my speed. It wasn't intentional, I can assure you." I said, flashing my green eyes at her with a desperate look on my face.

She seemed undeterred by my looks, "I'm going to need to see your license and registration." I pulled out my license and dug in the glove box for the registration. "The car's a rental. I rented at the airport"

"What you doin' up here?"

"Uh…well I was just trying to figure out some of my heritage."

"I see…so you part Osage are you?"

"Well…it appears so," I said.

She smiled at me, "I'll be right back".

"Look officer, you're going to go back there and run my record and you're going to find that I have…well a lot of speeding tickets. I've been trying real hard to watch my speed. You will notice that it's been a year since my last ticket…and well, I'd like to continue the good momentum if you know what I mean." She just smiled at me and went back to her car without a word.

She had dark black hair that was tied up in a knot behind her hat. Dark skin and her dark brown eyes made my heart squirm every time she looked at me. I looked in the mirror to see her walking away from me and my pulse quickened and my face felt flush.

Just then another officer pulled in behind her. "Great," I thought, "now I'm going to probably get two tickets." I sank down in my seat, let my head rest on the headrest, and closed my eyes. My license was going to be suspended for sure after this ticket. I sat in pity over my predicament and waited for her to return.

I was startled to suddenly hear her voice when I

didn't hear her walk up. "Soft soled shoes," I thought. "Mr. Neal Forester" she said peaking down into the car. I quickly propped my head up realizing that I must've look like I'd been sleeping.

"Yes." I quickly replied with my best smile. "One of the things you should know about being Osage, now that you've figured out your heritage, is we look out for one another. You're part of the tribe now, so you need to look out for your people and help them when in need. I can see that you've been trying to watch your speed and I can see you've been doing much better. You went from getting tickets just about every month to going a whole year without one. Now being Osage myself, I should give you a ticket to make sure you keep your speed down. I don't want to see you gettin' hurt or hurtin' someone else. But I'm going to let you go this time", she said with a beautiful smile.

"Hey Neal, you givin' my sister a hard time?" I heard a voice call from behind the car. I poked my head out to see the officer I had met thirteen years ago on this same road.

"Hey...it's good to see you officer. This is your sister?" I asked. He nodded with a smile. "I wouldn't say I'm giving her a hard time, but she is giving me a lesson on what it means to be Osage," I said.

"Oh yeah," he said as he walked up to the car. "Say, I never did hear back from you. Did you ever find that holy man?" he asked.

"Oh shoot, that's right I promised I'd call you. I'm sorry. I'd..."

"It's alright. I figured you were going through a lot," he said.

"This is the Neal," she said turning to her brother.

"Yeah, this is the Neal" he said. "Well..." he said motioning back to me to signal he was waiting for an answer. She turned at me and gave me a new look that no longer held a certain professionalism but rather a burning curiosity.

"Well...I went out into the woods of the park and searched for him all day following my intuition. I must have walked about 25 miles before the sun began to set on the last day and I was losing hope. I stopped to rest at the water falls, you know to rest and recoup when I realized that I was sitting on him."

"You were sitting on him?" she said in astonishment.

"Yeah...he was camouflaged and I took him for a half rotten log."

"Get out," he said laughing.

"Yeah...so I found him, and we continued our teaching for the past thirteen years. Now I just see him every once in awhile and he teaches me a few things here and there."

"That is great. So you found him. Impressive. I don't think I could've ever done it myself," he said. "So you headed back out to the park?"

"Yeah, believe it or not I'm looking for Tilauth again," I said.

"Can I meet him?" she asked.

"Uh..." I now realized the difficulty in this. "Well... Tilauth is a private man, but if he wants to meet someone he will seek you out. That's kind of the way he works."

"I understand," she said. "Well you tell him I wouldn't mind meeting him someday."

"I'd be happy to tell him."

"Well...I suppose we should let you go. You don't be a stranger. You're Osage now, and we need our people to keep in touch with us. Look me up at the patrol office," she said, smiling at me.

"I will," I said, caught in her eyes.

We said our goodbyes and I pulled away towards the park. That had to be one of the most pleasant experiences I have ever had, being pulled over for speeding. I don't know if I would ever stop by at the patrol office and ask the officer out, but I was definitely having a hard time getting her out of my mind and focusing on finding Tilauth.

He usually seems to just appear almost out of nowhere when I simply want him to. But for some reason this wasn't working no matter what I did. I parked the car and walked all the way to the falls. The sun was sinking into the horizon and the sky was streaked with a rainbow of crisp colors. I zipped up my jacket to ward off the ever penetrating nip in the air. The ground was covered in a thick bed of fallen leaves that made it impossible to walk quietly. Every step felt like it could be heard around the world and back.

Standing at the edge of the water falls where I had found Tilauth so many years back, the mist rose like a magician in the fading sun light. This time nobody was at the falls, no visitors, and most importantly, no Tilauth. As I stood there resting and listening to my heart, I heard singing. I turned my head in the direction of the songs and across the river on the flat stone I could see spirits dancing. It was the old ones singing and dancing through the mist. I watched them trying to understand what this meant. 'Why was I seeing the old ones, I asked myself? They sang a song I had never heard before. Their voices cried out with such a passion that it sent chills down my spine. Then just as mysteriously as they appeared they disappeared. The mist still rose from the falls but the spirits were no longer there. I searched my gut for the reasons for such a vision but I couldn't find the answer. Either I wasn't supposed to know yet or I wasn't clearing my head enough.

I sat there for another hour as the sun set and listened and waited for some sort of sign but to no avail. I walked back to my car and drove. I drove all the way back to the Oklahoma City airport. I caught a flight to Spokane, Washington after sitting in the airport overnight. Sleeping in a chair with my back pack strap wrapped around my leg so nobody would take off with it or they would yank me out of my chair first.

When I arrived in Spokane it was about eleven in the morning. I rented a four wheel drive vehicle, for I knew the trip was going to require nothing less. They gave me a Ford Explorer with highway tires. I had a feeling that that was about all the grip a rental agency could muster. They did offer me some chains, which I had a feeling would come in handy on those logging roads. I drove out onto I-90 and headed towards Coeur d'Alene, Idaho. The roads were clear, but obviously plowed first thing this morning for the morning commute. It wasn't long that I realized that the roads were sprayed with a de-icing agent; "No doubt it does wonders for the environment", I thought.

When I started heading down the highway along Lake Coeur d'Alene I noticed that the snow was piled about three feet along side the road. This was going to make it difficult once I got up on those old logging roads.

I don't know why I thought I should go to Tilauth's and my old camp but I didn't have any other answers. "Why wasn't Tilauth talking to me anymore?" I thought.

"Was he finished with me now that I knew that he was my grandfather?" It took me some remembering to figure out which roads I turned down last time but I managed to figure it out. The pavement disappeared and was replaced by gravel, mud, and slush. The Ford swished down the road as the flakes began to fall. I turned on the wipers and saw that this was going to be a tough haul. At least the dirt roads were plowed but I wasn't sure how long that would last.

It wasn't long before I found my turn and realized that the road I needed to take wasn't plowed and a large berm of snow blocked the way from repeated snow plowing. I got out into the falling snow and silence. All I could hear was the annoying squeak of the fan belt. I strapped the chains on the tires without a glitch. The tamaracks and pine trees drooped with the weight of the heavy snow. A loud squelch echoed across the ridge from two fighting horses at a nearby ranch.

I got back into the Explorer and cranked the heat, placing my fingers in front of the vents to thaw. When my hands retained their mobility, I backed the rig up for a momentous puncture into the snow berm. The engine groaned and the wheels spun, sending the rig flying forward in a rough vibration of chains. As the berm grew larger and larger, I peered over the hood of the rig and it slammed into the snow. To my surprise, the rig did not puncture the wall of snow but rather went over it. The wall was solid ice and I heard the suspension slap with a loud smacking noise. The Explorer went into the air for a brief moment before slamming down into the soft blanket of untouched snow. I spun around like a ride at the fair a few times before sliding sideways to a halt. This was all fine and dandy, but my heart was pounding because on one side of the road the ground dropped steeply down hill that I would have surely toppled down bumper over bumper smacking into a few trees and stumps before resting in an inescapable ravine. Luckily this wasn't the scenario and I managed to keep the rig on the road.

I spun the Explorer around pointing it in the right direction. The suspension was still intact, but no doubt had a few new squeaks for the next sorry soul that rents the piece of crap.

I pushed down the road carving some new tracks in the snow. I drove for miles without a hitch until I came across some down trees. Without any kind of saw, I wasn't about to make an axe and start hacking at the large trees, I decided to head out on foot.

Snow shoes would've been a nice idea to pack along

but I didn't think I would need them in Oklahoma. So I trudged along in my water proof boots and the little gear I had on my back. I left the Explorer locked and shoved it as close to the hillside as I could. Hopefully if somebody came along they could squeeze by without slipping down the hillside on the other side of the road. I left a note saying "Be back in a day or two." Hopefully someone will understand that that means don't tow the vehicle.

The forest was eerily silent with the snow everywhere. I saw deer, coyote, mice, elk, rabbit, and turkey tracks as I crunched through the snow. I stuffed some dry debris I found in the thick of some trees, in my clothes for extra insulation. It took me the better half of the day to hike all the way to Tilauth's and my old camp. When I got there I wasn't surprised not to see any sign of Tilauth.

I knew about an old fallen tree that was not far that I could build a shelter in and hunker down for the night. I cleared some snow away and built a fire with a rock wall on one side to reflect the heat into my shelter.

Aside from the cracking of my fire I heard nothing. The forest was silent and seemed to be well settled in for a long winter sleep. I decided to do the same and letting myself fall into a deep sleep. My dreams were vibrant and very active but I couldn't remember a one when I awoke. Tilauth told me this is common. When a person dreams they are in the spirit world and when you awake you often abruptly switch to the physical world. This abrupt change makes it difficult to remember what was happening in the spirit world.

I awoke early, before sunrise. I gathered up my things and walked back to camp in some hopes of a sign or a feeling to give me understanding as to why Tilauth was avoiding me but I came up with nothing. I looked around at the trees silently reminiscing those first few lessons that Tilauth had taught me. I missed the camp.

It was like I had a second home here. Tilauth and I spent so much time here and it had been so long since I had been back. I heard a rabbit scamper through the snow and jet into the bushes just in front of me. The sky was a deep purple and provided enough light on the snow to see my old tracks back to the abandoned Explorer.

Aside from the two elk that I spooked, the trip back was uneventful. When I rounded the bend I saw that the Explorer was still there. Nobody had attempted to get around it and nobody attempted to even come down this road. I'm probably the only one foolish enough to even attempt these back roads mid-winter.

The sun was just coming up casting the sky with multiple shades of fiery red, orange, and yellow. The snow sunk beneath my feet as I tugged again and again on the frozen door before breaking it free. The dome light came on and I climbed in, casting clouds of steam from my breath. I looked up into the rearview mirror to see that some old man was in the back seat looking back at me. In a fright I spun around to see nobody there. I looked over the back seat to see if maybe he hopped over, an unlikely feat. With my heart pounding with fear I turned back around to see the same old man looking back at me through the rearview mirror. To my surprise it was only me looking back at myself. I hadn't recognized myself with my beard, eye brows, and hair covered in a white mist of snow and icicles.

I began to laugh at myself as I broke the icicles from my beard and eyebrows. For a second there I thought I might have seen Tilauth only with a beard. I fired up the SUV and made the slow crawl back. It was a little easier since I broke most of the way through the snow yesterday.

Chapter 37
Journeys Into The Past

I thought about going to the old camp where Tilauth had nursed me back to health after I took that major spill so many years ago, but decided against it. If Tilauth wanted for us to talk, he would reveal himself to me.

I was starting to feel very lonely and began to think that I might not ever see Tilauth again. Maybe he felt that our time is done or maybe he already knows that I know about him being my grandfather. Perhaps, this is what he meant by telling me not to tell anyone about him. I understand now why he was so reclusive, no one else could have seen him anyways and they would have thought me crazy for sure. This explains why I never saw him when I was around other people. It also explains his way of speedy travel. "In the world of spirit there is no time or place," Tilauth used to say. No time or place meant that one could be anywhere at anytime with a simple thought to pull them there.

I was reaching my wit's end. I traveled all over the States looking for Tilauth so I might be able to sit and talk with him again and tell him that I know, and now understand everything. But Tilauth seems to have disappeared into thin air once again.

I drove the Explorer back to the Spokane Airport and caught a flight back to Seattle. Exhausted from driving; I slept for almost the whole flight. After a bite to eat in Seattle, I drove north to catch the ferry in Anacortes. I caught the last boat heading out for the night and slept for most of the ride. All this traveling was beginning to wear on me.

The ferry docked and I rubbed my eyes and fired up my rig. I drove off the boat and headed straight for the camp Tilauth and I stayed at on the island. Something in me knew that Tilauth wasn't going to be there, but I was running out of options. I had to see him and he had to know that I was searching for him. I pressed on through the darkness, navigating through the winding roads. I slipped through the town of Eastsound and pushed on to the park. After parking the Jeep in the bushes I headed into the woods in complete darkness. I could hardly see anything and I had to travel predominately by my gut, since landmarks were no longer visible.

What would have normally taken me about a half and hour to walk ended up taking me two hours to walk. As I anticipated, Tilauth wasn't there at the camp. I walked down to the beach and sat on some driftwood. The waves lightly lapped up against the shore. I looked out over the ocean like I had a thousand times before. The water looked black like coffee under the night sky. I reminisced about the things Tilauth and I had done there in my mind. As I sat on the driftwood with a night breeze blowing in off the water when I remembered a lesson that Tilauth taught me about time travel.

One day I was exploring the beaches when a strange

feeling encompassed me. I was suddenly stopped in my tracks and couldn't walk any further. The hairs stood up on the back of my neck and I felt like I was being watched. I looked around carefully to see if my instincts were correct but I saw nothing. The trees loomed out over the beach in front of me, no boats, no one on the beach, and from what I could see there was no one in the forest. But I couldn't move forward or backward. My chest was tight and forced me to breathe slowly and I struggled to force the air in. It took everything in me to step back in the direction I came. I sprawled out one foot behind me and placed it in the old footprint I just made. I could hear an old bone whistle being played as I stepped back with the other foot. My head spun around in the direction of the whistle but saw nothing.

I took a few more steps backward before I was able to breathe freely and move without restriction. The sensation was bizarre and I had never experienced anything quite like it. I went back to camp and told Tilauth about what had happened to me. He seemed to know of the place that I was talking about and he asked me to go back there again with him.

As we walked Tilauth began to talk, "The place you walked into was something you were sensing from the past. As you begin to learn more and more and your awareness grows, you will become hypersensitive to these sorts of things."

"So what I sensed was something from the past?" I asked.

"Yes."

"So what was it that I was sensing?"

"That is what you are going to find out in a minute. You remember me telling you that the spirit world of place and time does not have the same rules as it does in the physical world?" he said as we approached the area.

"Yes."

"Well...I want you to go back in time and tell me what you saw when you get back."

We walked right up to the edge of the area where I knew that if I walked any further I would be encompassed by that same restricting feeling. Tilauth had me sit down and close my eyes. I listened to his words as he guided me back in time. We went back hundreds and hundreds of years.

I sat on the beach as I watched time go in reverse in my minds eye. I watched the earth change in a hyper-speed kind of way. The forests on the islands were cut down at one point then replaced by old growth. The air smelled fresh and reviving. Decades slipped past my minds eye in seconds and centuries went by in minutes.

Then it all came to a blistering halt. I looked out off the beach onto the water and saw hundreds of canoes filled with tribal peoples. There was a mist on the water so it was difficult to see them but I could feel them out there. They moved in quietly and stealthily towards the shore. I could tell that they were ready for war. Their hearts seemed to pierce through the darkness and run right through me.

I sat quietly as they moved in closer and closer without a sound. I could now see most of them clearly as they emerged from the marine fog. It was early morning and the sun had not yet risen but the sky was lighting up. Behind me I could feel a temporary camp had been set up and many people were still sleeping.

The canoes slid up on to the shore silently like sharp daggers. The warriors climbed out gracefully and crept up the beach and into the camp. It wasn't long before the silence was broken by a warriors cry as he made the first kill. The air quickly filled with a shower of cries as the war began. The defenders were caught off guard but many of them quickly maneuvered and fought back fiercely. The fight spread out through the camp and across the beach. What was a place of silence and peace suddenly became a loud clamor of war cries and wielding weapons slinging blood. Warriors of both sides fell to their death all around me. The beach was a sea of sweat, blood, and muscle as both sides fought for their loved ones. I watched the horrific massacre unnoticed by any of the warriors. The attacking side was fighting for their hunting grounds. The natives that had camped there were asked to leave these grounds because these were the prized hunting grounds of the natives that lived in the area. The encroaching natives continued to hunt there because their hunting grounds were depleted and they needed food for their families.

Previous weather for the past few years had taken its toll on the salmon and whales that had once populated the area in large quantities. Now tribes in the area began to span out and encroach on other tribe's hunting grounds in search of food. All tribes were hurting for food so they defended what little they had mercilessly.

The beach was becoming littered with dead bodies. The ground was blanketed so thick with the dead warriors that they were being stood on as they fought. The ocean was now a deep red from the rivers of blood that ran down the water.

After what seemed like hours the fighting finally stopped. All the hunters in the camp had been killed and nearly half of the attackers were dead. The fight left my stomach turned with anguish as I watched many of the men carry the wounded and dead back to the canoes. Tears streamed down my face as I felt the loss of both sides. Neither wanted to fight but neither felt they had any other choice.

I watched as an older man walked down the beach towards me. He wore a cedar blanket and had a ring pierced through the septum of his nose. Blood was splattered across his face and along his cedar blanket. Although he was only in his early forties his face was aged and he appeared to be in his seventies. He walked up slowly towards me and I realized that he was looking at me. Everyone paid no attention to me except for this man. His eyes were deep like Tilauth's, and he seemed to look through me the way Tilauth would look at me. He stopped about ten feet away from me as he studied me carefully. I no doubt must have appeared very strange to him. My white skin and modern clothes were unquestionably something he had probably never seen before. He looked at me in silence and I stared back. We looked into one another's eyes and understood each other without words. He knew that I was an entity of the future and came to observe, nothing more. And I knew that he was a shaman and he was marking the area as sacred to protect the spirits that had fallen in the battle on both sides. He knew that it would take long time for the area to heal itself from all that had happened. He was honoring the dead and helping the spirits transition from this world to the next. I was just a spirit that must have seemed really out of place to him.

He walked away from me without a word going about his business. Time sped up as I suddenly heard Tilauth's voice pull my awareness forward. Time spun by in split seconds, wielding me back to the present moment.

I looked up to see Tilauth sitting in front of me with his knowing glance. I wiped the tears from my face and regained my composure.

"This is why you have a difficulty walking through this area. There are many spirits that still linger here. The shaman you saw organized the energy in this area to protect it, so it may heal and the spirits could heal. The protection was also for you, so that you did not just walk into the area aimlessly and accidentally pick up some of that anger and violence of those past warriors. When there is someplace that has a history with significance like what had happened here long ago, there is a footprint that is laid down. This foot print carries energy and all those that walk into that footprint experience that energy. If that shaman hadn't placed an energetic barrier around this area, you would've walked straight into it and could have caught something that could make you very sick or even bring you to your death." I looked up at Tilauth and could see that his face was unmistakably serious.

This memory reminded me that I was by no means trapped to the confines of place and time. Tilauth lived in the past and I could go back in time to talk to him. Why I hadn't thought of that sooner, I have no idea. So without the restriction of space and time, I could be anywhere at anytime.

I closed my eyes and began to relax. With a goal in mind and my intentions set, time began to spin backwards. Floating high above the earth, I watched the land change from the mass developments of man to healthy forests, open prairies, and a large abundance of North American animals.

My body sank down to the earth to what is now known as Missouri near the Missouri River valley. It was a clear night and a half moon shined down lighting the area. The village was scattered with huts made with a simple frames, lined with thatched grasses or buffalo hides. Smoke streamed up from many of the huts filling the night sky with a very pleasant scent.

The village was quiet except for the faint murmur of voices inside some of the huts. I walked up slowly to the door of the nearest hut. I could only assume that it was Tilauth's home. I approached cautiously. Inside a small fire burned with a faint pop and crackle. Before I stepped into the light of the fire a dog near the door began to growl at me. I heard a voice inside silence the dog in a language I did not understand. I could only assume that it was Lakota, the language Tilauth could speak. I stepped into the doorway and the light of the fire. An old woman that silenced the dog was looking right at me but couldn't see me. The man sleeping next to her looked over his shoulder to see his wife staring at the doorway. He mumbled something in Lakota to her and changed his glance to me.

Tilauth smiled at me and said, "Come on in, Grandson." I smiled back at him feeling the relief of hearing his voice. "This is your grandmother, Taheschne." I smiled at her and she nodded back, still unsure as to my presence. Tilauth got up and went to the other side of the hut. He pulled out a small stick from the fire and placed it in another fire at the other end. Tilauth motioned for me to sit down on a ground chair made out of sticks and grass reeds woven together. Tilauth stoked up a second fire while I watched him silently. Taheschne rolled over and went back to sleep.

"So Grandson, you know who I am?"

"Yes."

"Are you surprised?" he asked.

"I would say so, yes," I said stating the obvious. He began to laugh quietly, not wanting to disturb Taheschne.

"Now you know why I couldn't have you going around telling everyone about me," he said, smiling.

"Yeah…I suppose that would've caused some eyebrows to raise when they found out I was talking to my great, great, great, great grandfather," I said and we both laughed quietly. "So why didn't you come when I called you?" I asked. He smiled and sat back in his chair that was almost identical to mine. "Since you seemed to know who I was I thought it would be best if you came to see me for a change. I taught you many skills and sometimes you forget to use them. I knew that you would figure it out."

I began to chuckle, "Well it took me awhile."

We both began to laugh like two old friends, but now we were grandfather and grandson. This however, didn't seem to change the way we were around each other. We still were mentor and student, although Tilauth looked at me more as a fellow peer than a student.

"So Taheschne is my great, great, great, great grandmother?" I asked?

"Yes she is."

"Why can't she see me?"

"Because she is like you, Grandson. She can hear you but has difficulty seeing the spirit world. She can see you but she has to focus real hard at it."

"I see," I said.

"So you came into the future to teach me?"

"Yes." Tilauth said simply.

"And this is where my ancestry comes from?"

"Yes."

"So are you going to stop teaching me now?"

"No. You can come back anytime to learn more and I will teach you." he said grinning.

"I'd like that," I said grinning back at him.

"I would too, Grandson."

"I feel like I've got a thousand questions for you but can't seem to think of any right now."

"That's ok, Grandson, you have forever to remember," he said with a smirk.

I talked to Tilauth for hours before returning to the present moment. That night I camped in our old shelter on the island, and felt the relief of not losing my friend, teacher and grandfather.

I now visit with Tilauth almost every night, where he continues to teach me and helps me with my walk in life. You will never be forgotten my friend, as every day I celebrate the death of my ordinary life.

Author's Note

As I've mentioned before, this story closely mirrors my personal life, not necessarily in the events, but the lessons learned. One of the major lessons and struggles I've faced in life was the conflict of religion. I was raised in a conservative, non-denominational, Christian, and let's not forget Godfearing home. With this in mind, anything that varied in the slightest from outside of this faith was considered untrue and the work of the devil. So when my life began to venture down a different path, I became very conflicted internally. In this story I've brought that inner conflict to the surface. By doing this, I've brought up some strong criticisms I've had regarding Christianity. By re-establishing my point of view regarding Christianity, I became very anti-Christian at first because of how difficult it was to unlearn what had been established in my life since day one. I began to blame many of the world's problems, from family problems to global problems, on Christianity. Whether or not Christianity, or any religion, for that matter, is the cause of the world's problems makes no difference in this story. Placing the blame is not the answer.

Nevertheless, my wounds from religion have long since healed. My point is, this book is meant for personal growth, not anti-religion. At no point do I condone or judge any person following there religion. It is not my intention to offend anyone's faith with this story but rather to enhance, strengthen, or encourage personal growth, regardless of their faith.

In my eyes, questioning one's faith is healthy, and if someone says something that offends your faith, perhaps it's time to question it. An unwavering faith cannot be offended. In the long run, I feel that it is extremely important to not deem a religion, faith, or belief system as better than any other. This idea of 'my God is better than your God' is at the heart of many of the worlds problems today. All faiths, or lack there of, are an individual's chosen path and should be respected without conveying judgment upon them.

The teachings put forth in this book were not completely taught to me from Tilauth. I've had many teachers, some short term, some long term, and some were not even human but rather a tree, a rock, a fish, an animal, a cloud, or a drop of water. I've used Tilauth as the primary teacher for the sake of simplifying it into a story.

Tilauth is not his real name, but rather a nickname that I've given him for this book; his real name is One Who Runs On Water. His name was given to him by some elders who saw him as a young man running across the hot radiating soil that created the illusion of water. Although he is just a spirit from the past, he is my closest friend, teacher, and of course my several 'greats' grandfather.

I dedicate this book to One Who Runs On Water and to the many teachers that have gone to extraordinary lengths to teach these old ways and keep them alive.

Acknowledgements

I of course would like to thank my many teachers for taking the time to teach these important things. Thanks to Thomas Dalton, Elder of the Tlingit Nation for sharing your stories and experiences, Stormy Paul of the Snohomish Nation, Quil Ceda area for your helpful wisdom and supportive traditional songs, Robert Loe of the Cherokee Nation for your stories, experiences, and practical sense of humor, Jeanette Wahl from the Snoqualmie Nation, Medicine Woman for your healing positive sense of being, Malcolm Ringwalt, PhD for your sensitivity, well thought out words, and your support, to the many instructors at Wilderness Awareness School for your passion for the Earth and your willingness to share it, to the many instructors and Tom Brown, Jr. at the Tracker School for your commitment to the vision and simple yet potent teachings, to my family for the generous support and love, to my wife's family for their support and encouragement, to the many teachers to numerous to mention for your wisdom and knowledge, to my Grandpa Mitchell whom I love and miss for your gentle spirit , to Iris Behr and John Muir for their support, to Jorgen Embreos for your wisdom and supportive friendship, to my cousin Breana Langan whom I miss dearly for your much needed incessant questioning, to Amie O'Grady for your time and extremely helpful tips in writing, to my many friends who offered support, encouragement, life lessons, and wisdom Sean Depp, Cindy Manning, Amy Ostenberg, Andrew Bermingham,

James Beaulieu, Meghan Fluharty, Jeni Hoffert, Arnoux Goran, Matthew Majores, James Mcardall, Pearl James, Stephen Schmidt, Megan Williams, Marc Nee, Carla Nee, and the many others, a big thanks to Chad and Sonja Lilly of InnerCircle Publishing for making this book a reality, and last but not least my wife, Anna Mitchell, for her support, friendship, love, and encouragement.

I highly recommend the following books to further your understanding with regards to the appropriate subjects.

Many of the ideas regarding our culture and religion today and its journey from the past were inspired by the thoughts of Daniel Quinn. To find out more I highly recommend reading his works such as "Ishmael," "The Story of B," "My Ishmael," "Beyond Civilization," "If They Give You Lined Paper, Write Sideways," "Tales of Adam," "The Holy," or "After Dachau."

Knowledge of Native American philosophies was obtained from but not limited to books and classes by Tom Brown, Jr., "God is Red," by Vine Deloria Jr., "Fools Crow, Wisdom and Power," a dialogue with Thomas E Mails and Teton Ceremonial Chief and Sioux Holy Man, Fools Crow, "Black Elk," by Wallace Black Elk and William S. Lyon, "Black Elks The Sacred Pipe," recorded and edited by Joseph Epes Brown, and "Lame Deer, Seeker of Visions, The Life of a Sioux Medicine Man," by John (Fire) Lame Deer and Richard Erdoes.

Some ideas with regards to religion today and our relationship with God were inspired by the "Conversations With God," series by Neal Donald Walsch and religious writer Thomas Merton.

Aware Talk Radio

Join Us - LIVE - 5 Nights A Week!!!
Or Listen To Past Archvies @:
www.innercirclepublishing.com

http://www.blogtalkradio.com/aware

Call In Number: *(646) 716-8138*

Aware Talk Radio incorporates all fields of science, from the normal to the paranormal, from the physical to the metaphysical. We seek to expand the awareness of humankind. Your Comments, Questions, and Guest Suggestions are welcome.

INNERCIRCLE PUBLISHING

Catalog of Original Titles

ISBN	Title
0-9720080-9-8	the sometimes girl by Lisa Zaran
0-9720080-5-5	A Metaphysical Interpretation of the Bible by Dr. Steven Hairfield
0-9720080-2-0	Return To Innocence by Dr. Steven Hairfield
0-9720080-3-9	Interview With An American Monk by Dr. Steven Hairfield
0-9720080-4-7	Interview II: Heath and Healing by Dr. Steven Hairfield
0-9723191-4-X	Poetry to Touch the Heart and Soul by Marla Wienandt
0-9755214-9-7	Touched by Spirit by Marla Wienandt
0-9723191-8-2	Stress Fractures by Andew Lewis
0-9723191-7-4	One Hundred Keys to the Kingdom by Prince Camp, Jr.
0-9723191-0-7	the voice by Rick LaFerla
0-9755214-0-3	On the Edge of Decency by Rick LaFerla
0-9723191-5-8	A Day in the Mind by Chad Lilly
0-9755214-6-2	uncommon sense by Chad Lilly
0-9755214-7-0	Peace Knights of the Soul by Dr. Jon Snodgrass
0-9755214-1-1	Petals of a Flower by Patricia McHenry
0-9755214-2-X	Poetry-Prose-Stories by J.L. Montgomery
0-9762924-0-8	The Weave that Binds Us by Martin Burke
0-9762924-2-4	Dare to Question by Jack Perrine
0-9762974-2-6	The Twelve Mastery Teachings of Christ by Lea Chapin
0-9762924-3-2	Alnombak by Ken Delnero
0-9762924-7-5	Life is a Song Worth Singing by Clarissa LeVonne Bolding
0-9762974-3-4	The Spirit Within by Susan Marie Ratcliffe
0-9720080-8-X	And the Angels Spoke by Rebecca J. Steiger
1-882918-00-2	From Ashes To Angel Light by Rebecca J. Steiger
0-9762974-6-9	The One Minute Miracle by Daniel Millstein
0-9762974-5-0	Unemployed: A Memoir by Reginald L. Goodwin
1-882918-03-7	Look and Remember by Marie taBonne
1-882918-02-9	Poetry of Comfort and Light by Marla Wienandt
1-882918-01-0	Life Happened Here by Marilyn Wendler
0-9728127-2-5	The Nature of the Self by Douglas H. Melloy
1-882918-04-5	Seven Stars: Mystical Poetry by Michaela Selfer
1-882918-05-3	Esoteric Dictionary by Christine A. Hale
1-882918-06-1	Uncovering the Divine Within - Kerri Kannan

Are You Aware?

www.innercirclepublishing.com

Printed in the United States
112617LV00004BE/11/P